Credits

Author

Christopher Caleb

Reviewers

Daniel Albu

JP Berrie

Simon Buckley

Mark Doherty

Richard England

Stuart McLeman

Brian Rinaldi

David Wagner

Acquisition Editor

Douglas Paterson

Lead Technical Editor

Dayan Hyames

Technical Editor

Kedar Bhat

Copy Editor

Neha Shetty

Project Coordinator

Alka Nayak

Proofreader

Mario Cecere

Indexer

Rekha Nair

Graphics

Valentina D'Silva

Manu Joseph

Production Coordinator

Arvindkumar Gupta

Cover Work

Arvindkumar Gupta

About the Author

Christopher Caleb has been developing rich interactive experiences with the Flash platform for almost a decade. He remembers a time when browsers didn't support images, and has witnessed technologies such as Flash help drive the web to where it is today. During that period he has been fortunate enough to have worked with a wide range of clients including the BBC, Activision, Samsung, and Aardman Animations on projects encompassing film, games, education, and children's entertainment.

He has a love for all things mobile and has been a proponent of Flash in this space since its emergence. He is also an active member of the Flash community, both through his personal blog and the various articles he contributes elsewhere. Whenever he finds a spare minute, Christopher likes to chip away at the many apps and experiments he has inspired to undertake.

Christopher is currently a lead Flash developer at WeeWorld—an avatar-based social network and virtual world for teens. He blogs at `www.yeahbutisitflash.com` and tweets as `@chriscaleb`.

Flash iOS Apps Cookbook

100 practical recipes for developing iOS apps with Flash
Professional and Adobe AIR

Christopher Caleb

PUBLISHING

BIRMINGHAM - MUMBAI

Flash iOS Apps Cookbook

Copyright © 2012 Packt Publishing

First published: February 2012

Production Reference: 2250112

Published by Packt Publishing Ltd.
Livery Place
35 Livery Street
Birmingham B3 2PB, UK.

ISBN 978-1-84969-138-3

www.packtpub.com

Cover Image by Charwak A (charwak86@gmail.com)

Acknowledgement

This book would not have been possible without the help and support of so many individuals.

First and foremost, I'd like to thank the people at Packt Publishing; in particular, Steven Wilding for providing me with this wonderful and unexpected opportunity; Maitreya Bhakal for his guidance and encouragement; and Kedar Bhat for his assistance and endless patience.

I'm extremely lucky to have had such talented technical reviewers (Daniel Albu, JP Berrie, Simon Buckley, Mark Doherty, Richard England, Stuart McLeman, Brian Rinaldi, and David Wagner) who, despite their workloads, managed to find the time to provide invaluable feedback. Dave and JP: I really owe you both for your perseverance over the last few weeks.

Various individuals at Adobe have also helped me along the way. Particularly, I'd like to thank Mark Doherty and Brian Rinaldi for their immense contribution and enthusiasm towards the project. I'd also like to extend thanks to Robert Christensen for always taking the time to answer my questions over the past twelve months.

A huge debt of gratitude is also owed to my brother Alan (alancaleb.com), Steve Koren (popjunk.co.uk), and Selina Wagner (blobina.com) whose creative talents grace the many code examples found within these pages. Also, a mention must go out to Matt McKenna (maketh.com) and Andrew Nicolson (drewnotweird.co.uk) for the part they both played.

I would also like to thank Graham MacDonald for affording me the time to write and, at the same time, earn a living; Helen and my little nephew Freddy (I love him even more than Flash) for making me smile; Gregory for providing the arm wrestling training that helped develop my typing stamina; and Amanda who makes every day better than the last. Special thanks must also be extended to Bobby Farmer who has always made time for me over the years and has been a constant source of encouragement.

Finally, to my father, mother, brother, and sister, I cannot thank you enough for your love and support, without which I am nothing.

About the Reviewers

Daniel Albu is a freelance Flash platform developer with more than ten years of experience in the production and deployment of rich media websites, games, and applications.

Daniel has unique expertise in production and integration of Flash and Flash platform-based technologies. Most recently, Daniel entered the mobile development field by using Adobe AIR to develop for the Android and iOS platforms.

Daniel also provides worldwide remote training and consultancy around Flash platform technologies for companies and individuals alike.

JP Berrie first encountered Macromedia Director 4 in 1995 while at university studying Multimedia Technology, and subsequently embarked upon a career as a Multimedia Developer, specializing in Director Lingo and latterly Flash ActionScript 3.0 programming.

He was appointed lead programmer for several BBC games titles, including Walking with Beasts, Bill & Ben the Flowerpot Men, and Rotten Ralph. Other titles include the Chicken Run game for Activision / Aardman Animations, and a title for interactive publishing giants Dorling Kindersley.

Since 2002, JP has freelanced for many clients including global brands such as AstraZeneca, BP, Diageo, Guinness, Kellogg's, Pepsi, Pfizer, and the Post Office.

Website: `www.jpberrie.com`.

Simon Buckley received his M.Sc in Physics from the University of Birmingham, England, in 2007 before moving into Computer Science to gain a M.Sc in Intelligent Systems Engineering at the same university in 2008.

After graduating, Simon spent some time as an enterprise Java developer before opting to go freelance. He is now a Flex Adobe Certified expert and his company, Techjump, specializes in developing workflow tools and Rich Internet Applications for desktop and mobile platforms. He loves working with new technologies, developing rich user experiences, and solving tough programming problems.

Mark Doherty is the Platform Evangelist for Mobile and Devices at Adobe, working to create a vibrant ecosystem around Flash Player and Adobe AIR for devices. He has spent ten years in the mobile and devices industry, including seven at Adobe, holding Engineering, Consulting, Business Development, and Marketing roles. Prior to this, Mark has worked with leading OEMs at Mobile Innovation, Nokia, Samsung, and Panasonic.

Richard England is an award winning freelance developer, who has worked with Flash technology for over 10 years, including building BAFTA-nominated educational games, interactive learning resources, and truly Rich Internet Applications.

An eternal student of all things digital, Richard is enthused by the ever-evolving mobile development landscape, creating applications for iOS both natively in Objective-C and with Adobe AIR.

Richard can be contacted through Twitter—@englandrp.

Stuart McLeman has been involved with web and mobile software development for ten years since his previous life in electronic engineering. From working on educational Flash content for the BBC through to his current role as lead iOS developer at WeeWorld, he has always been passionate about aesthetics and usability as well as good code. Although Objective-C is his new love, he still has fond memories of AS3. He can't wait to see how the mobile landscape will evolve so he can decide what to learn next!

Stuart can be contacted through his website: www.stuartmcleman.com where he promises to someday start a blog, or through Twitter—@stuartmcleman.

Brian Rinaldi is a content and community manager for the Adobe Developer Center team, where he oversees community strategy for developers with a focus on HTML5 and JavaScript. Brian has been a Flex, Flash, and ColdFusion developer for over a dozen years and has been always known for his contributions to the community as an open source developer, a speaker, and an author. Brian founded the ColdFusion user group in Boston as well as the RIA Unleashed conference. Brian blogs regularly at `http://remotesynthesis.com` and is an unreformed twitter addict—`@remotesynth`.

David Wagner has been creating mobile phone games and applications for over a decade—from the days when 96x64 pixel displays with four shades of green were a luxury, through to the present with multi-cored, GPU-accelerated devices of pure awesomeness. In between, he has played with assembler, made a career of embedded C programming, decided browsers were more fun with ActionScript, and then went back to the future with Objective-C. He is currently a senior engineer at HuzuTech, working on a cross-platform virtual world framework.

If you want to read his occasionally coherent ravings, visit `www.noiseandheat.com`, or you can follow his stream of sarcasm on Twitter—`@kaeladan`.

www.PacktPub.com

Support files, eBooks, discount offers, and more

You might want to visit www.PacktPub.com for support files and downloads related to your book.

Did you know that Packt offers eBook versions of every book published, with PDF and ePub files available? You can upgrade to the eBook version at www.PacktPub.com and as a print book customer, you are entitled to a discount on the eBook copy. Get in touch with us at service@packtpub.com for more details.

At www.PacktPub.com, you can also read a collection of free technical articles, sign up for a range of free newsletters, and receive exclusive discounts and offers on Packt books and eBooks.

http://PacktLib.PacktPub.com

Do you need instant solutions to your IT questions? PacktLib is Packt's online digital book library. Here, you can access, read, and search across Packt's entire library of books.

Why Subscribe?

- ► Fully searchable across every book published by Packt
- ► Copy and paste, print, and bookmark content
- ► On demand and accessible via web browser

Free Access for Packt account holders

If you have an account with Packt at www.PacktPub.com, you can use this to access PacktLib today and view nine entirely free books. Simply use your login credentials for immediate access.

Table of Contents

Preface

The iPhone is revolutionary. Every day, it seems, someone finds an innovative use for it and, in the App Store, the perfect outlet for their work. Its success has made apps cool and helped shift delivery of content away from the browser. Adobe has reacted to this change by repositioning the Flash platform, and providing the tools required for the creation and publication of native iOS applications directly from Flash Professional.

The **Flash iOS Apps Cookbook** is a culmination of my experience working with AIR for iOS since its beginnings. I have paid particular attention to the fundamentals, focusing on the groundwork that many newcomers find daunting. For those with a firm grasp of the basics, there is plenty to learn, from working with the device's many sensors, to maximizing the performance of graphics using hardware acceleration.

By the end of this book, you will have acquired the necessary skills to write and distribute your own native iOS applications using Flash. I hope that you will use what you have learned here to create beautiful applications that befit the talented and inspiring community you are about to become a part of.

What this book covers

Chapter 1, Getting Started with iOS App Development, leads you through the often intimidating process of becoming a registered iOS developer. By the end of the chapter you will have the necessary files required to publish native iOS apps from Flash Professional.

Chapter 2, Building iOS Apps Using Flash, covers everything required to configure Flash Professional and publish native iOS apps from it. You will also learn how to install apps on an iPhone for testing.

Chapter 3, Writing your First App, takes you through the steps necessary to build and test your very first iOS app using Flash Professional with a modest amount of ActionScript. Some best practices for development will also be explored.

Chapter 4, Porting Flash Projects to iOS, will get you started on the right foot when converting Flash projects from the desktop to iOS. You will learn how to work within mobile constraints and how to avoid common pitfalls that can often cripple an app's performance.

Chapter 5, Multi-touch and Gesture Support, will show you how to take full advantage of the touch-screen. You will learn how to detect multiple touch points and respond to swipe, pan, and pinch gestures with ActionScript.

Chapter 6, Graphics and Hardware Acceleration, provides invaluable recipes for an area that often causes frustration. We will cover powerful techniques for dramatically boosting your application's frame rate and learn the intricacies of Flash's rendering pipeline. With this knowledge, you will be able to push the graphics performance of your own creations to the limit!

Chapter 7, Working with Text and the Virtual Keyboard, will help you adjust to life without physical keys by exploring support for iOS's virtual keyboard and native text-input controls. Time will also be spent covering relevant features of Flash's own text engine.

Chapter 8, Screen Resolution and Orientation Changes, details how to render content on any iOS device regardless of its screen resolution or physical orientation. Support for the high resolution Retina display can also be found, along with instructions detailing how to set up a universal app that can target iPhone, iPad, and iPod touch.

Chapter 9, Geolocation and Accelerometer APIs, covers recipes that utilize both the device's GPS sensor and its accelerometer. Learn how to make location-aware apps, respond to changes in physical orientation and detect vibration.

Chapter 10, Camera and Microphone Support, will help you master two of the most popular sensors built into iOS devices. With the camera, you will learn how to shoot video, capture photos, and access the image library. This chapter will conclude by covering how to record and play back audio captured with the microphone.

Chapter 11, Rendering Web Pages, focuses on the presentation of web content—both directly within your app and by launching Safari. It also covers how to dynamically generate HTML, navigate the browsing history, and capture a snapshot of the current page.

Chapter 12, Working with Video and Audio, explores the many A/V options available when targeting iOS. In addition to utilizing Flash's popular FLV video format, this chapter will detail how to take advantage of hardware-accelerated H.264 video for best quality high-definition playback.

Chapter 13, Connectivity, Persistence, and URI Schemes, ties up some loose ends, beginning with Internet connectivity. Next, file system access is discussed—a topic touched upon by a number of recipes throughout the book. At the end of the chapter, space is given over to the use of URI schemes to launch various system apps including Mail, YouTube, App Store, and Maps.

Chapter 14, Using Native Extensions and ADT, details how to use the command line to take advantage of AIR for iOS features that aren't currently provided from Flash Professional directly. Specifically, you will learn how to use native extensions to access iOS-specific APIs missing from the AIR SDK. This chapter is not present in the book but is available as a free download at the following link: `http://www.packtpub.com/sites/default/files/downloads/1383_Chapter14.pdf`

Chapter 15, ActionScript Optimization, covers a range of invaluable optimizations that can be applied to your project's ActionScript. You will see how even the simplest of changes can improve your application's execution speed or improve its memory usage. This chapter is not present in the book but is available as a free download at the following link: `http://www.packtpub.com/sites/default/files/downloads/1383_Chapter15.pdf`

Appendix A, Flash Professional CS5.5 Specific Recipes, contains a list of the recipes throughout this book that require Flash Professional CS5.5 and AIR 2.6 or above. The appendix is not present in the book but is available as a free download at the following link: `http://www.packtpub.com/sites/default/files/downloads/1383_AppendixA.pdf`

Appendix B, ActionScript Optimization Measurements, provides the results from various optimizations detailed in *Chapter 15*. This appendix is not present in the book but is available as a free download at the following link: `http://www.packtpub.com/sites/default/files/downloads/1383_AppendixB.pdf`

What you need for this book

This book has been written for users of Adobe Flash Professional CS5 or CS5.5.

The majority of recipes covered are compatible with both CS5 and CS5.5. However, some are specific to CS5.5 and require the latest version of the Adobe AIR SDK.

You will also need an iPhone, iPad, or iPod touch. Flash Professional CS5.5 supports the development of applications for iOS 4 or above, whereas CS5 also provides support for older devices running iOS 3.

You can build native iOS apps using either Flash Professional for Mac OS X or Microsoft Windows.

Who this book is for

The material throughout this book is written for both beginners and seasoned developers with a working knowledge of ActionScript 3.0 and Flash Professional. If you ever want to leverage your existing Flash skills to write iOS apps, then this book will show you how, starting with the basics. Those users who are already up to speed can go directly to the more advanced topics that are on offer.

Conventions

In this book, you will find a number of styles of text that distinguish between different kinds of information. Here are some examples of these styles, and an explanation of their meaning.

The development of iOS apps using Flash Professional is commonly referred to as AIR for iOS. However, Flash Professional CS5 uses the term iPhone OS. This book will almost exclusively use the term AIR for iOS throughout.

Code words in text are shown as follows: "Keep the default location set to C:\OpenSSL-Win32."

A block of code is set as follows:

```
public function Main() {
   application = NativeApplication.nativeApplication;
   application.systemIdleMode = SystemIdleMode.KEEP_AWAKE;
   application.addEventListener(Event.ACTIVATE, activate);
   application.addEventListener(Event.DEACTIVATE, deactivate);
}
```

When we wish to draw your attention to a particular part of a code block, the relevant lines or items are set in bold:

```
public function Main() {
   application = NativeApplication.nativeApplication;
   application.systemIdleMode = SystemIdleMode.KEEP_AWAKE;
   application.addEventListener(Event.ACTIVATE, activate);
   application.addEventListener(Event.DEACTIVATE, deactivate);
}
```

Any command-line input or output is written as follows:

```
openssl genrsa -out mykey.key 2048
```

New terms and **important words** are shown in bold. Words that you see on the screen, in menus or dialog boxes for example, appear in the text like this: "Scroll down the page until you see the **Join the iOS Developer Program** link as shown in the following screenshot".

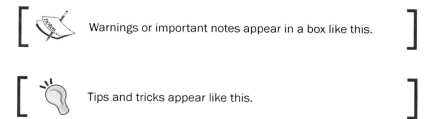

Warnings or important notes appear in a box like this.

Tips and tricks appear like this.

Reader feedback

Feedback from our readers is always welcome. Let us know what you think about this book—what you liked or may have disliked. Reader feedback is important for us to develop titles that you really get the most out of.

To send us general feedback, simply send an e-mail to feedback@packtpub.com, and mention the book title via the subject of your message.

If there is a topic that you have expertise in and you are interested in either writing or contributing to a book, see our author guide on www.packtpub.com/authors.

Customer support

Now that you are the proud owner of a Packt book, we have a number of things to help you to get the most from your purchase.

Downloading the example code

You can download the example code files for all Packt books you have purchased from your account at http://www.PacktPub.com. If you purchased this book elsewhere, you can visit http://www.PacktPub.com/support and register to have the files e-mailed directly to you.

Errata

Although we have taken every care to ensure the accuracy of our content, mistakes do happen. If you find a mistake in one of our books—maybe a mistake in the text or the code—we would be grateful if you would report this to us. By doing so, you can save other readers from frustration and help us improve subsequent versions of this book. If you find any errata, please report them by visiting `http://www.packtpub.com/support`, selecting your book, clicking on the **errata submission form** link, and entering the details of your errata. Once your errata are verified, your submission will be accepted and the errata will be uploaded on our website, or added to any list of existing errata, under the Errata section of that title. Any existing errata can be viewed by selecting your title from `http://www.packtpub.com/support`.

Piracy

Piracy of copyright material on the Internet is an ongoing problem across all media. At Packt, we take the protection of our copyright and licenses very seriously. If you come across any illegal copies of our works, in any form, on the Internet, please provide us with the location address or website name immediately so that we can pursue a remedy.

Please contact us at `copyright@packtpub.com` with a link to the suspected pirated material.

We appreciate your help in protecting our authors, and our ability to bring you valuable content.

Questions

You can contact us at `questions@packtpub.com` if you are having a problem with any aspect of the book, and we will do our best to address it.

1
Getting Started with iOS App Development

In this chapter, we will cover:

- ▶ Joining the iOS Developer Program
- ▶ Accessing the iOS Provisioning Portal
- ▶ Generating a Certificate Signing Request using Windows
- ▶ Generating a Certificate Signing Request using Mac OS X
- ▶ Obtaining your development certificate
- ▶ Creating a P12 certificate using Windows
- ▶ Creating a P12 certificate using Mac OS X
- ▶ Registering a device
- ▶ Creating an App ID
- ▶ Creating a development provisioning profile
- ▶ Installing a provisioning profile on your device

Introduction

When writing iOS applications, the creation and management of certain files is necessary in order to test on a real device. The exact files required depends on whether you are currently developing or preparing for distribution. We will focus primarily on development.

By the end of this chapter, you will have created a **P12 certificate** file and a **development provisioning profile**, both of which are required if you want to make full use of the recipes throughout this book. Along the way, you will learn the ins and outs of various tools including Apple's **iOS Provisioning Portal**, which you will come to use extensively during your time as an iOS developer.

Don't worry if it doesn't all make perfect sense at first. If you follow the steps detailed in each recipe, you will end up with the development files required to work through the rest of the book.

Joining the iOS Developer Program

Registering as an Apple developer and enrolling in one of the iOS Developer Programs are prerequisites for anyone wishing to write iOS apps.

Although you can enroll in a free program, if you want to install your applications on devices and distribute them in the **App Store**, you will need to pay a $99 annual fee to join the standard program.

Those developing with the iOS SDK can select the free program and test their apps using the iOS simulator, which is provided with Apple's official development tools. Unfortunately, native iOS apps built with **Flash Professional** do not run on the simulator. Therefore, if you want to fully test the examples provided in this book, you will need to install them on an iOS device.

 Within Flash Professional, you can use the **AIR Debug Launcher** (**ADL**) to test your applications on the desktop; however, no iOS device capabilities are supported thus restricting ADL's usefulness.

Let us take a look at the steps required to enroll.

Getting ready

Enrollment takes place on the Apple Developer website. If you aren't using Apple's **Safari** browser, then it is recommended that you download and install it, as problems are reported from time to time when trying to use certain areas of the site on other browsers.

Safari is the default web browser preinstalled on Mac OS X. Those using Windows, who don't already have Safari, can download it from `www.apple.com/safari/download`.

If you already have Safari installed, then make sure that you have the most recent version.

There are several paths you can take during the enrollment process and once you have completed it, it may not be possible to change some of your choices. Think carefully before submitting your enrollment details and purchasing your Developer Program. You may want to first read through this recipe in its entirety to ensure that you are fully aware of all the options available to you.

How to do it...

1. Visit the Apple developer website at `http://developer.apple.com`. Scroll down the page until you see the **Join the iOS Developer Program** link as shown in the following screenshot:

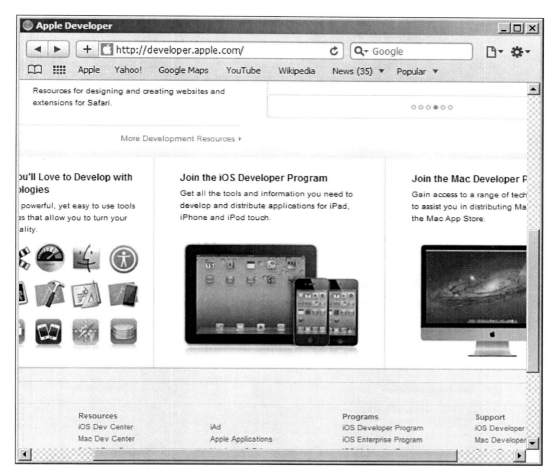

Be aware that Apple regularly makes alterations to its various developer websites. Therefore, the location of items shown within this chapter's screenshots may differ slightly by the time you read this. The links described throughout the chapter may be subject to change too.

2. Click on the link. You will be taken to the **iOS Developer Program** page where you will find an **Enroll Now** button at the top of the page.

3. Click on the **Enroll Now** button to move to the **Enroll in the Apple Developer Programs** page. The three main steps required for enrollment are listed on this page. They are:

   ❑ Register as an Apple Developer

   ❑ Select Your Programs

   ❑ Complete Your Purchase

4. At the bottom of the page is a **Continue** button, which will begin the process of taking you through each of these steps. Go ahead and click on it.

 Next to the **Continue** button you will find text outlining the technical requirements for enrollment. This refers to developers using Apple's iOS SDK and does not apply to those using Flash Professional. Ignore it.

Register as an Apple developer

1. From the **Are you new or a registered Apple developer?** page, you will be able to register as a new Apple developer. Within the **New Apple Developer** column, click on the **I need to create a new account and Apple ID for an Apple Developer Program** radio button as shown in the following screenshot:

If you currently have an Apple ID, then click on the second radio button within the column. If you are an existing Apple developer, then you should select the appropriate radio button from the **Existing Apple Developer** column instead.

2. Click on the **Continue** button to move to the **Are you Enrolling as an Individual or Company?** page.

   Two options are provided. Enroll as an individual or enroll on behalf of a company.

 To enroll as a company, you will need to provide Apple with business documents and have the legal authority to bind your company to the legal agreements presented to you during enrollment.

3. Depending on your needs, click on either the **Individual** or the **Company** button at the bottom of the page.

4. Now complete your personal profile by performing the following tasks:

   ❑ Specify a desired Apple ID and password.

   ❑ Set up some security information that can be used to verify your identity.

   ❑ Submit your personal information.

 When submitting your contact information, the name you specify will appear as the "seller" for any apps you distribute on the App Store.

Do not attempt to add an alias or organization name within the name fields. This will most likely result in failure of your Apple Developer registration or suspension of your account when the error is eventually noticed by Apple.

If you want to have a company name to appear as the "seller", then enroll as a company and provide Apple with the relevant legal documentation to verify your identity.

If you are registering as an individual, then enter your first and last name into the **Company/Organization** field.

5. Read the information provided on the displayed page carefully and once you have completed the form, click on the **Continue** button which will take you to the **Complete your professional profile** page.

6. For the **Which Apple platforms do you develop with?** field, check on the **iOS** checkbox. This will reveal a list of additional fields that must be populated.

7. When you come to the **Please select the primary category for your application(s) field**, ensure that you click on the **Commercial Applications** radio button.

By selecting to develop commercial applications, you will have to provide your banking details before you can distribute your apps; however, you won't be asked for this information as part of the enrollment process. If you plan only to distribute free apps, then you can select the **Free Applications** radio button and no banking details will be required. This option will suffice for the examples within this book; however, if you plan to sell apps at some point, then stick with the **Commercial Applications** option.

8. Once you have provided answers for all the fields in the form, click on the **Continue** button at the bottom of the page.

9. Carefully read the **Registered Apple Developer Agreement** that is displayed. Acknowledge that you have read it by checking on the checkbox and then clicking on the **I Agree** button at the bottom of the page.

10. A verification code will be sent to your e-mail address. Retrieve the code and enter it into the text field provided on the **Enter the verification code sent to your email** page. Click on **Continue**.

A second e-mail will be sent confirming that you are now a registered Apple developer.

The e-mail will also contain the Apple ID you chose. Keep this e-mail safe as you will need your Apple ID (along with your password) to access certain resources on the Apple Developer website.

Select your program

Within your web browser you will be taken to the **Enter your billing information for identity verification** page.

1. Enter your first and last name exactly as they appear on your credit card. Also provide your credit card billing address.

2. Click on the **Continue** button at the bottom of the page.

At this point your credit card details will be used for identity verification. You will not be asked for your credit card number and won't be charged.

3. The **Select Your Program** page will appear. As shown in the following screenshot, check on the **iOS Developer Program** checkbox and click on **Continue** at the bottom of the page:

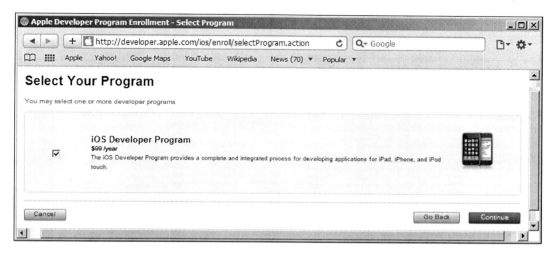

4. The next page will let you review your enrollment information. Verify that you have selected the **iOS Developer Program** and that your personal details and billing information are correct. If any of the information is incorrect, click on the **Go Back** button at the bottom of the page and make any necessary alterations.

5. Click on **Continue** to submit your enrollment information to Apple.

6. The **Program License Agreement** page will appear. Acknowledge that you have read it by checking on the checkbox, then click on the **I Agree** button at the bottom of the page.

Complete your purchase

1. A purchase page will appear. Click on **Add to cart** to proceed to your country's online store in order to purchase your program.

2. A new browser window will open and you will be taken to the Apple Store. Confirm that your iOS Developer Program is in your basket and click on the **Checkout Now** button on the right side of the page to purchase the item.

3. An activation e-mail will be sent to you within 24 hours. When you receive it, follow the instructions to activate your iOS Developer Program.

How it works...

Registering as an Apple developer and activating your Developer Program enables you to access the iOS Provisioning Portal through Apple's **iOS Dev Center** website. The iOS Provisioning Portal takes you through the necessary steps to test and distribute your apps on iOS devices, and will be used throughout this chapter.

You will use the Apple ID and password that you set up to log into the iOS Dev Center at http://developer.apple.com/devcenter/ios.

There's more...

The following additional pieces of information are worth considering.

Working with multiple team members

If you opt to enroll as a company, then you can add additional team members to your account who can access iOS Developer Program resources. This will allow, for example, other team members to generate and download the developer files required to build and deploy apps to an iOS device.

If you enroll as an individual, then you will be the sole developer who has access to the program resources. It will be your responsibility to generate all required developer files and manage the list of test devices.

iOS SDK, tools, and documentation

The iOS Dev Center contains a wealth of resources. While the documentation and tools available are aimed at developers using the iOS SDK, you will find some that will be of use when building your own apps with Flash Professional.

An important document to start with is the **iOS Human Interface Guidelines** at `http://developer.apple.com/library/ios/#documentation/UserExperience/ Conceptual/MobileHIG`. It describes the guidelines and principles that help you create apps that feel as though they were designed specifically for iOS.

Also, if you are planning to release your apps on the App Store, then read the **App Store Review Guidelines** at `http://developer.apple.com/appstore/guidelines.html`.

If you are developing on Mac OS X you may also want to download the developer toolset. While this book will not cover Apple's developer tools, spend some time exploring the **Instruments** application, which comes as part of the bundle, and provides powerful profiling and debugging features that can help you fine tune your apps.

A good place to start is the Introduction to Instruments User Guide at `http://developer. apple.com/library/ios/#documentation/DeveloperTools/Conceptual/ InstrumentsUserGuide/Introduction`.

Accessing the iOS Provisioning Portal

The iOS Provisioning Portal is an online tool designed to take you through the steps required to test your apps on iOS devices and prepare them for distribution on the App Store.

This is where you will create and download the developer files that are required to build your apps with Flash Professional.

Let us go through the steps required to access it.

Getting ready

You will need an Apple ID to enroll on the iOS Developer Program.

If you haven't already done so, follow the steps detailed in the *Joining the iOS Developer Program* recipe.

How to do it...

1. Visit the iOS Dev Center website at `http://developer.apple.com/devcenter/ios`. Click on the **Log in** button at the top of the page.

2. On the **Sign in with your Apple ID** page, enter your Apple ID and password into the text fields. Click on the **Sign in** button.

3. If successful, you will be taken back to the iOS Dev Center home page where you will now have access to the main areas of your Developer Program including the iOS Provisioning Portal. Links to these can be found near the top-right of the home page underneath the **iOS Developer Program** heading.

4. Click on the **iOS Provisioning Portal** link to access the portal's home page, which is shown in the following screenshot:

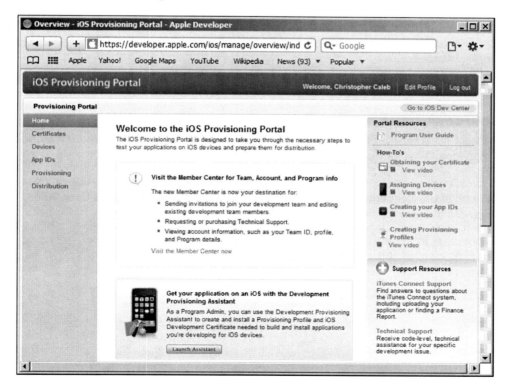

How it works...

The Provisioning Portal provides you with the resources to develop and distribute your iOS apps.

For the examples in this book, you only need to concern yourself with development. The following are the four main steps required to do this:

- ▶ Obtain a development certificate
- ▶ Register iOS devices for testing
- ▶ Create unique IDs for your apps
- ▶ Create and download development provisioning profiles

These steps can be performed from the links on the left-hand side of the Provisioning Portal page and are broken down and covered throughout the remainder of this chapter.

Alternatively, Apple has provided the **Development Provisioning Assistant**, which can be used to guide you through the process. However, the Provisioning Assistant is not covered in this book.

There's more...

You are encouraged to spend time exploring the Provisioning Portal as it is integral to the iOS development process.

The following information may also be of some use.

Resources

On the right-hand side of the portal's home page is the **Resources** section where you can find links to guides, "how to" videos, documentation, and user forums.

The "how to" videos are ideal if you need further clarification regarding the provisioning steps. At the head of the **Resources** section you will also find a link to the **Program User Guide**, which covers the provisioning process in detail.

Remember that all content on the site will be aimed at Mac OS X owners. If you are using Windows, then some of the content may not be applicable.

Adding team members

If you enrolled on behalf of a company, then you will also be able to add other team members to your account.

As the original enrollee, you have access to all iOS Provisioning Portal capabilities and can assign roles for any members you invite. The role you assign to an individual determines the privileges they get and dictates the tasks they can undertake.

Team management is handled within the **Member Center**, which you can access from the Provisioning Portal's home page. Simply click on the **Visit the Member Center now** link on the center of the portal's home page.

Those who have signed-up as an individual will not be able to add team members but will have access to all Provisioning Portal capabilities.

For a comprehensive guide to team administration, take a look at the **Program User Guide** within the **Resources** section.

Distribution

The steps required for preparing your apps for App Store submission and distribution are not covered within this book. However, once you are comfortable with the provisioning process for application development, you will find that distribution isn't too dissimilar.

Comprehensive documentation regarding distribution is available from the **Program User Guide** in the Provisioning Portal's **Resources** section.

Technical support

As a member of the iOS Developer Program, you are entitled to support from the **Apple Developer Technical Support** team, where you can receive direct one-to-one help from a qualified Apple engineer.

Included with your Developer Program membership is free technical support for two incidents during your membership period.

However, you should be aware that this support is primarily for developers using the iOS SDK. Apple engineers will not be able to help with questions regarding Flash Professional.

Generating a Certificate Signing Request using Windows

A **Development Certificate** is used to identify a developer for the purpose of installing and testing apps on iOS devices. Without one you can't publish native iOS apps from Flash Professional. You obtain a development certificate from Apple's iOS Provisioning Portal but to do that you must first generate a **Certificate Signing Request (CSR)** file.

The process for generating a CSR differs depending on your choice of operating system.

The steps for Microsoft Windows are covered here. If you are using Mac OS X, then refer to the *Generating a Certificate Signing Request using Mac OS X* recipe.

Getting ready

1. CSR files are generated using **OpenSSL,** which can be downloaded and installed from `www.slproweb.com/products/Win32OpenSSL.html`. You will actually need to install two files from the site.

2. First scroll down to the **Download Win32 OpenSSL** section and download the **Visual C++ 2008 Redistributables** installer. Simply run the executable and follow the wizard through the installation process.

3. Next, download and run the **Win32 OpenSSL v1.0.0e Light** installer. The wizard will ask you to select where OpenSSL should be installed. Keep the default location set to `C:\OpenSSL-Win32`. Additionally, when prompted, instruct the installer to copy OpenSSL's DLLs to **The Windows system directory**.

How to do it...

1. Open a command prompt window using administrator privileges.

> How you run a command session with administrator privileges depends on your choice of operating system.
>
> If you are a Windows 7 or Vista user, then click on the **Start** button and type cmd into the search box. However, rather than simply pressing *Enter,* you should press *Ctrl + Shift + Enter.* A dialog will appear asking if you want to allow the program to make changes to your computer. Click on the **Yes** button.
>
> If you are using Windows XP, then ensure you are logged on with an administrator account. Click on the Windows **Start** button and then select **Run**. From the Run dialog box, type cmd and press *Enter.*

2. From the command prompt move to OpenSSL's `bin` folder by entering the following command:

    ```
    cd C:\OpenSSL-Win32\bin
    ```

3. Now create a private key by entering:

    ```
    set RANDFILE=.rnd
    ```

    followed by:

    ```
    openssl genrsa -out mykey.key 2048
    ```

4. The file, `mykey.key`, will be output to OpenSSL's `bin` folder.

> OpenSSL may still output a file after reporting an error on the command line. If you find an error, check your syntax and run the command again as it's unlikely your file will be usable.

5. Using your private key you can now create the CSR file. To do this, a command with the following format is required:

```
openssl req -new -key mykey.key -out CertificateSigningRequest.
certSigningRequest  -subj "/emailAddress=yourAddress@example.com,
CN=John Doe, C=US"
```

You will need to make some changes when typing the preceding command into the command line. Replace the e-mail address and certificate name with the same e-mail address and name you enrolled within the iOS Developer Program. Also, if you live outside the United States, you will need to edit the country code.

> A list of country codes that can be used when creating a CSR can be found on the DigiCert website at `www.digicert.com/ssl-certificate-country-codes.htm`.

A CSR file named, `CertificateSigningRequest.certSigningRequest` will be created and output to the `bin` folder.

How it works...

You now have a CSR file that contains your personal information (your name, e-mail address, and country) and will be used to request a development certificate from Apple.

When the CSR file was created, OpenSSL also created a public and private key. The public key is included within the CSR file while the private key is used to sign the request.

Don't delete your CSR file or the private key as they will both be required later in this chapter.

See also

▶   *Obtaining your development certificate*

Generating a Certificate Signing Request using Mac OS X

A **development certificate** is used to identify a developer for the purpose of installing and testing apps on iOS devices. Without one you can't publish native iOS apps from Flash Professional. You obtain a development certificate from Apple's iOS Provisioning Portal but to do that you must first generate a **Certificate Signing Request** (**CSR**) file.

The process for generating a CSR differs depending on your choice of operating system.

The steps for Mac OS X are covered here. If you are using Microsoft Windows then refer to the *Generating a Certificate Signing Request using Windows* recipe.

How to do it...

Follow the steps to generate a CSR:

1. Launch the **Keychain Access** application from the `Applications/Utilities` folder.
2. Once opened, select **Preferences** from the **Keychain Access** (*Cmd + ,*) menu.
3. From the **Preferences** dialog box, click on the **Certificates** tab and ensure that both **Online Certificate Status Protocol (OCSP)** and **Certificate Revocation List (CRL)** are set to **Off**. Close the dialog box.
4. On the Keychain Access menu select **Certificate Assistant | Request a Certificate from a Certificate Authority**.
5. The **Certificate Assistant** dialog box will appear where you can enter your personal information. In the text fields provided, enter the e-mail address and name you enrolled within the iOS Developer Program. Leave the **CA Email Address** field blank and click on the **Save to disk** radio button. Now click on **Continue**.
6. When asked, select to save the certificate to your desktop.

A CSR file named `CertificateSigningRequest.certSigningRequest` will be created and saved on disk.

How it works...

You now have a CSR file that contains your personal information (your name and e-mail address) and will be used to request a development certificate from Apple.

When the CSR file was created, the Keychain Access application also created a public and private key. The public key is included within the CSR file while the private key is used to sign the request. Using Keychain Access you can see both keys listed within the **Keys** category.

Don't delete your CSR file or the private key as they both will be required later in this chapter.

▶ *Obtaining your development certificate*

Obtaining your development certificate

Now that you have a Certificate Signing Request (CSR), you can use it to obtain a development certificate from Apple. This is done by uploading your CSR file to the iOS Provisioning Portal and waiting for approval.

Getting ready

If you haven't already done so, generate a CSR file. Depending on your choice of operating system, see either the *Generating a Certificate Signing Request using Windows* recipe or the *Generating a Certificate Signing Request using Mac OS X* recipe for more details.

How to do it...

1. Log into the iOS Dev Center at `http://developer.apple.com/devcenter/ios` and make your way to the Provisioning Portal.

2. Click on the **Certificates** link on the left-hand side of the portal's home page to move to the certificates section. As shown in the following screenshot, ensure that the **Development** tab is selected:

3. Now, click on the **Request Certificate** button on the far-right of the screen, which will take you to the **Create iOS Development Certificate** page.

4. At the bottom of the page is a **Browse** button. Scroll down a little further and to the far-right you will also see a **Submit** button.

5. First, click on **Browse** and navigate to the CSR file on your hard drive.

If you created your CSR file using OpenSSL on Windows, then you can find it at `C:\OpenSSL-Win32\bin\CertificateSigningRequest.certSigningRequest`.

If you are a Mac OS X, user then you should have previously saved `CertificateSigningRequest.certSigningRequest` on your desktop.

6. Once you have selected your CSR file, click on **Submit**.

7. You will be taken back to the **Certificates** section where a certificate will now be listed. Its status will initially be set to **Pending Issuance** and an e-mail will be sent to you from Apple with the subject heading **Certificate Request Requires Your Approval**.

This e-mail is intended for those working in a team environment. If you are registered as an individual then you don't need to take any further action. Simply refresh the page in your browser and the certificate's status will automatically change to **Issued**.

You may need to refresh your web page a few times before the certificate's status eventually updates.

8. Click on the **Download** button underneath the **Action** column and save the development certificate to your hard drive.

9. Where you save the certificate depends on your choice of operating system. If you are on Windows, then save it to OpenSSL's `bin` folder at `C:\OpenSSL-Win32\bin\developer_identity.cer`. If you are using Mac OS X, then simply save the `developer_identity.cer` file to your desktop for the time being.

How it works...

A development certificate is restricted to app development only and is valid for a limited period. Take a look at the **Expiration Date** column from the Provisioning Portal's **Certificates** section to see when your digital certificate will expire. Typically certificates are valid for a year.

Once a certificate expires, you will need to revoke it and request a new one from the Provisioning Portal.

You are now one step closer to being able to compile iOS apps directly from Flash Professional. However, before Flash can digitally sign any of the iOS apps you create, your development certificate will have to be converted to a P12 certificate file, which we will cover in the next recipe.

There's more...

Let us cover some additional detail, some of which is particularly important for those who enrolled on behalf of a company and are working in a team.

Approving Certificate Signing Requests

All team members can make iOS development certificate requests. As the original enrollee, it will be your responsibility to approve or reject those requests.

When a team member requests a development certificate, you will receive an e-mail with the subject heading **Certificate Request Requires Approval**. This is identical to the e-mail sent to those registered as an individual; however, when working in a team environment, you will need to take action by clicking on the link provided within the e-mail.

The link will open in your default web browser and take you to the Provisioning Portal where you can log in and view any certificate request awaiting approval. On the **Certificates** page, simply find the certificate request that is waiting for approval and click on either **Accept** or **Reject** from the **Actions** column.

For additional details, refer to the **Program User Guide**, which can be found within the Provisioning Portal's **Resources** section.

Team roles

As stated, the original enrollee has the authority and responsibility to either approve or reject development certificate requests. The original enrollee has access to all Provisioning Portal capabilities and is designated as the Team Agent.

The **Team Agent** can invite others and assign them the role of either a Team Admin or a Team Member.

Team Admins can themselves invite new Team Admins and Team Members. In addition, they can approve or reject certificate signing requests.

A **Team Member** has the lowest privileges and must have any certificate signing requests approved by either the Team Agent or Team Admin.

Importantly, all three types of members can test apps on iOS devices.

From now on, the original enrollee within a team environment will be referred to as the Team Agent throughout this book.

For a thorough explanation of working within a team environment including a full list of member responsibilities, refer to the **Program User Guide** within the Provisioning Portal's **Resources** section.

Distribution certificates

In order to distribute your app on the App Store, you will need to request a distribution certificate. Although the steps aren't covered in this book, they are similar to those carried out to obtain and work with a development certificate.

For further information, refer to the **Distribution** section of the **Program User Guide**, which can be found within the Provisioning Portal's **Resources** section.

Creating a P12 certificate using Windows

Now that you have downloaded your development certificate from the Provisioning Portal, the final step is to convert it to a P12 certificate file.

Flash Professional will use this P12 file to digitally sign any iOS apps you create.

The process for generating a P12 certificate file differs depending on your choice of operating system.

The steps for Microsoft Windows are covered in this recipe. If you are using Mac OS X, then refer to the *Creating a P12 certificate using Mac OS X* recipe.

Getting ready

You will need the development certificate that you created and downloaded from the iOS Provisioning Portal. If you haven't already done this, then follow the steps outlined in the *Obtaining your development certificate* recipe.

How to do it...

As was the case when creating a CSR, you will need to use OpenSSL to convert your development certificate into a P12 file by executing the following steps:

1. Open a command session in Windows as the administrator.
2. Move to OpenSSL's `bin` folder by entering the following command into the command prompt:

   ```
   cd C:\OpenSSL-Win32\bin
   ```

3. The first step is to convert your development certificate file into a PEM certificate file by entering the following command line statement:

    ```
    openssl x509 -in developer_identity.cer -inform DER -out
    developer_identity.pem -outform PEM
    ```

    For this to work you will need to save the `developer_identity.cer` file, that you downloaded from the Provisioning Portal to OpenSSL's `bin` folder.

4. Now using the PEM file and your private key, generate a valid P12 file by entering:

    ```
    set RANDFILE=.rnd
    ```

    followed by:

    ```
    openssl pkcs12 -export -inkey mykey.key -in developer_identity.pem
    -out ios_dev.p12
    ```

5. During this process, OpenSSL will ask you to specify an export password. Flash Professional will prompt you for this password while compiling your `.swf` files into native iOS apps, so choose something you aren't likely to forget. Enter your password and confirm it when OpenSSL asks you to verify it.

 When entering the password it may look like the command line isn't responding to your keystrokes. Don't worry, your keys are being registered but for security reasons aren't being echoed to the screen.

6. If successful, an `ios_dev.p12` file will be created in the `bin` folder. It is important that you keep this file safe as you will need it to publish any of the examples in this book.

7. Using Windows Explorer, navigate to your `Documents` folder and create the following folder structure within it: `packt\flash-ios-cookbook\developer-files\`. This is where we will keep our P12 certificate file from now on.

 The location of your `Documents` folder depends on the version of Windows you are running. For Windows Vista and Windows 7, it can be found at: `C:\Users\<username>\Documents\`. If you are using Windows XP, then it is at: `C:\Documents and Settings\<username>\My Documents\`.

8. Copy `ios_dev.p12` from `C:\OpenSSL-Win32\bin\` to the `developer-files` folder you just created.

How it works...

When publishing iOS apps from Flash Professional, you will be prompted for your P12 certificate file and password. Both are used to digitally sign your app allowing it to be deployed and tested on an iOS device.

The P12 certificate is the first of the two files that will be used by Flash Professional every time you make an iOS build.

Testing without a device

If you decide to test from the AIR Debug Launcher (ADL) rather than deploying to an iOS device, then a P12 certificate file isn't required.

There's more...

Finally, a few additional words regarding certificates.

Certificate expiration

When your developer certificate eventually expires, you will need to request a new one from the Provisioning Portal before converting it to a P12 file. Any apps that were published using the old certificate will no longer run on your iOS device and will need to be republished using a new valid P12 file.

If you accidentally delete your existing P12 file, then you can simply recreate it from the steps outlined in this recipe. There is no need to request a new development certificate from the Provisioning Portal.

Creating a P12 certificate using Mac OS X

Now that you have downloaded your development certificate from the Provisioning Portal, the final step is to convert it to a P12 certificate file.

Flash Professional will use this P12 file to digitally sign any iOS apps you create.

The process for generating a P12 certificate file differs depending on your choice of operating system.

The steps for Mac OS X are covered here. If you are using Microsoft Windows, then refer to the *Creating a P12 certificate using Windows* recipe.

Getting ready

You will need the development certificate that you created and downloaded from the iOS Provisioning Portal. If you haven't already done this, then follow the steps outlined in the *Obtaining your development certificate* recipe.

How to do it...

Execute the following steps:

1. Launch the **Keychain Access** application from the `Applications/Utilities` folder.

2. Select **File | Import Items** (*Shift + Cmd + I*) from the drop-down menu. From the file browser, select your certificate from `Desktop/developer_identity.cer`.

3. Your certificate will be installed in the Keychain Access application. You can confirm this by clicking on the **Certificates** category where you will see your **iPhone Developer** certificate listed.

4. Now, select the **Keys** category and find the private key associated with your certificate. Both your public and private keys will be listed and named using the name you entered when creating your CSR. This is shown in the following screenshot:

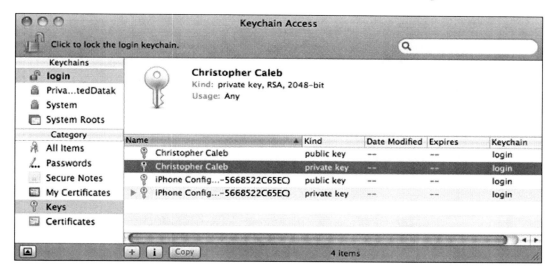

5. Context-click on the private key and select **Export**. A dialog box will appear asking you to specify where to save the P12 file when it is created. Choose the desktop and click on **Save**.

 Take care to context-click the private key and not the public key. You can check by looking for **private key** listed in the **Kind** field next to each key.

6. Keychain Access will ask you to specify an export password. Flash Professional will prompt you for this password while compiling your `.swf` files into native iOS apps, so choose something you aren't likely to forget. Enter your password and confirm it by re-entering it into the **Verify** field and then click on **OK**.

> You may also be prompted by Keychain Access to enter your Mac's login password. If so, do this and click on **Allow** to grant Keychain Access permission to export the key.

If successful, a P12 certificate file will be created and saved to your desktop.

It is important you keep this file safe as you will need it to publish any of the examples in this book.

7. Using Finder, navigate to your `Documents` folder and create the following folder structure within it: `packt/flash-ios-cookbook/developer-files/`.

8. Copy your P12 file to this new location. We will keep it here from now on.

How it works...

When publishing iOS apps from Flash Professional, you will be prompted for your P12 certificate file and password. Both are used to digitally sign your app allowing it to be deployed and tested on an iOS device.

The P12 certificate is the first of two files that will be used by Flash Professional every time you make an iOS build.

> **Testing without a device**
>
> If you decide to test from the AIR Debug Launcher (ADL) rather than deploying to an iOS device, then a P12 certificate file isn't required.

There's more...

Finally, a few additional words regarding certificate expiration.

Certificate expiration

When your developer certificate eventually expires you will need to request a new one from the Provisioning Portal before converting it to a P12 file. Any apps that were published using the old certificate will no longer run on your iOS device and will need to be republished using a new valid P12 file.

If you accidentally delete your existing P12 file, then you can simply recreate it from the steps outlined in this recipe. There is no need to request a new development certificate from the Provisioning Portal.

Registering a device

Any devices that you want to use for testing will have to be registered. Every iOS device has a **Unique Device Identifier** (**UDID**) that needs to be entered into the Provisioning Portal as part of the registration process.

We will learn in this recipe how to locate a device's UDID and add it to the Provisioning Portal.

Getting ready

A device's UDID can be obtained using iTunes.

iTunes typically comes installed on Mac OS X. Those using Windows, who don't already have iTunes, can download it from `www.apple.com/itunes/download`.

If you already have iTunes installed, then make sure that you have the latest version.

How to do it...

Follow the steps to register your device:

1. Launch iTunes and connect your iOS device through USB. After a brief moment the device will appear within the **DEVICES** section in iTunes.
2. Click on the device's name to display a summary.

3. Here, you will find its 11-character serial number listed near the top of the screen. Click on the serial number to reveal the device's 40-character UDID, as you can see in the following screenshot. The UDID will replace the serial number that was shown in the following screenshot:

4. Take a copy of the UDID by selecting **Edit | Copy** (*Ctrl + C or Cmd + C*) from iTunes' drop-down menu.

5. Log into the iOS Dev Center at http://developer.apple.com/devcenter/ios and make your way to the Provisioning Portal.

6. Move to the **Devices** section by clicking on the link on the left-hand side of the Portal's home page. Ensure that the **Manage** tab is selected. From this page, you will be able to manage the devices you would like to test with your apps.

7. Click on the **Add Devices** button near the top-right corner of the page. You will be shown an **Add Devices** page where you can enter your device's UDID and also assign a name to it for identification purposes.

Testing with multiple devices

If you are planning to test with several devices, then try to assign meaningful names to each to help distinguish them from one another. This will be of particular importance when working for organizations with large development teams.

8. Add your device's UDID and enter a name for it. Once you are done, click on the **Submit** button near the bottom-right corner of the page. The page will refresh and as shown in the following screenshot, you will see your newly registered device listed on the screen:

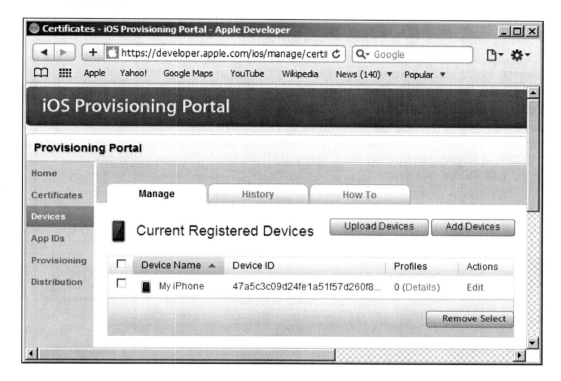

9. If you have additional iOS devices that you would like to use for testing then go ahead and add them now.

How it works...

Fundamentally, the provisioning process is there to allow you to test an app that you have written on a device that you own.

Registering devices on the Provisioning Portal is another step towards achieving that. If device registration wasn't required, then you could theoretically circumvent the App Store's distribution model by simply installing apps on an arbitrary number of devices.

Apple's restrictions are in place to not only guard its distribution model but to also protect your own development apps from falling into the wrong hands and being run on unauthorized devices.

There's more...

Registering devices is a fairly trivial process. However, there are a few other options and scenarios you should be aware of.

Adding devices in a team environment

When working in a team environment, only a Team Agent or Team Admin can add devices. Team Members do not have the required privileges to do this.

Editing device names

If you are unhappy with the identifier you assigned to a device, you can change it at a later date. Within the Provisioning Portal, simply move to the **Devices** section and find the device in the **Current Registered Devices** list. On the right-hand side within the **Actions** column, click on the **Edit** link for that device.

Device limit

You can only add a maximum of 100 devices per year to your Developer Program. Any devices you add and then later remove will still count towards that total, so think carefully when managing your list.

If at the end of the year you renew your iOS Developer Program, you will be able to reset your devices list before adding any additional devices. However, once you begin adding devices again, any device you choose to remove will once again count against your device limit.

UDID Sender

There is an app available from the App Store called **UDID Sender** that you may find useful. UDID Sender will extract your device's UDID and automatically populate it in an e-mail for you to send.

This can be particularly useful for large organizations where the Team Agent or Team Admin can expect a large number of device registration requests from Team Members.

To save the Team Admin from having to individually retrieve each device and discover its UDID from iTunes, they can simply rely on a Team Member e-mailing the device's ID directly to them.

UDID Sender can be downloaded from iTunes or the App Store and is free.

Creating an App ID

Every app you write must be assigned an **App ID**, which is a unique identifier used by iOS.

There are two types of App IDs: **Explicit App IDs** and **Wildcard App IDs**. To ease development, you can use a wildcard rather than an explicit App ID. This removes the need to generate an ID for every single app and will be particularly useful when it comes to working through and testing the examples within this book.

Let us create a wildcard App ID that can be used across multiple apps.

How to do it...

Execute the the following steps:

1. Log into the iOS Dev Center at `http://developer.apple.com/devcenter/ios` and make your way to the Provisioning Portal.

2. Move to the **App IDs** section by clicking on the link on the left-hand side of the Portal's home page. Ensure that the **Manage** tab is selected. From this page, you can add new App IDs and view any that you previously created.

3. On the far-right side of the page, across from the **App IDs** heading is the **New App ID** button. Click on it to be taken to the **Create App ID** page.

4. A common name should be assigned to every new App ID. This is used throughout the Provisioning Portal to identify that App ID. Enter **General Development** into the text field directly below the **Description** heading.

5. Now you can create the App ID. Enter * into the **Bundle Identifier** text field. Your **Create App ID** page should resemble the following screenshot:

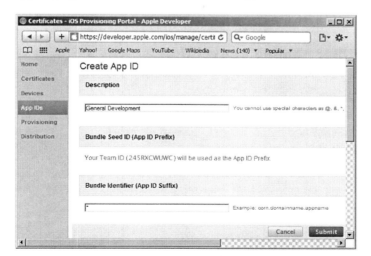

6. Click on the **Submit** button at the bottom-right of the page. You will be taken back to the **App IDs** page where you will see your newly created App ID listed in a table.

How it works...

An App ID is a unique string used to identify an app (or multiple apps) from a developer or team.

It consists of two parts: a **Bundle Seed ID** and a **Bundle Identifier**. The Bundle Seed ID is a universally unique 10-character prefix generated by Apple. The Bundle Identifier is a unique suffix determined by yourself, which can include the wildcard symbol "*".

When compiling an iOS app from Flash Professional, you will need to choose an App ID you want associated with your app and provide it to Flash. Although you will be asked to submit the App ID as part of the publishing process, you actually only provide Flash with the Bundle Identifier portion of the App ID.

If your Bundle Identifier contains the wildcard character, then you will need to substitute the wildcard with an arbitrary string that will uniquely represent your app. If a wildcard has not been used, then you will have to specify the Bundle Identifier exactly as it was entered into the Provisioning Portal.

The benefit of a wildcard is that it allows you to create a single App ID that can be used with any application you develop. This will be particularly useful when working through this book as it removes the need to revisit the Provisioning Portal to create a unique App ID for each recipe.

There's more...

The App ID you just created by following this recipe's steps is all that is required for working through the examples provided within this book. However, you may find the following additional details useful for your own personal projects.

Bundle Identifier naming convention

Although we used a single asterisk to represent the Bundle Identifier, Apple's recommended practice is to use a reverse-domain name style.

You should be familiar with this naming convention as it is commonly used for naming packages in ActionScript and helps prevent namespace collisions; a domain name can only be owned by an individual or organization.

Take, for example, the domain name `yeahbutisitflash.com`. Rather than using a single asterisk, an App ID can be created that will work across multiple apps by using the following Bundle Identifier: `com.yeahbutisitflash.*`.

To use this App ID to publish multiple apps from Flash Professional, provide Flash with the full Bundle Identifier but replace the asterisk with a unique string of your choice for each of your apps.

For example, if you are working on two individual test apps, then you could specify to Flash that the first app's ID is `com.yeahbutisitflash.test1` whereas the other's could be set to `com.yeahbutisitflash.test2`.

Both apps are still using the `com.yeahbutisitflash.*` ID registered in the Provisioning Portal, but the wildcard has been replaced in each with a unique string that distinguishes the apps from one another.

App distribution

An app that is ready for distribution on the App Store cannot have a wildcard specified within its Bundle Identifier.

When you are ready to submit your app to the App Store, you will need to create a new App ID from the Provisioning Portal and publish your app from Flash Professional using the new ID.

For example, you may have been using the Bundle Identifier `com.yeahbutisitflash.*` during the development of a camera app, but for distribution you will have to create a new App ID that has the wildcard removed and is guaranteed to be unique to that app. The following Bundle Identifier would suffice: `com.yeahbutisitflash.camera`.

It is worth noting that during development you don't have to use the wildcard within your Bundle Identifiers either, but it is useful as it allows you to quickly deploy multiple test apps to your device. If you are using an App ID that doesn't contain a wildcard, then you will be unable to deploy separate apps to your device that uses that App ID, forcing you to register a new App ID within the Provisioning Portal for each app.

Editing App IDs

The Provisioning Portal does not allow you to delete or edit any of the App IDs that you have created. Take care while naming your App IDs and assigning their Bundle Identifiers as these details cannot be changed at a later date. There is no limit to the number of App IDs you can register, so if you do make a mistake you can create and add a new one later.

Creating a development provisioning profile

Once you have a development certificate and at least one registered iOS device and an App ID, you are ready to create a provisioning profile. A **development provisioning profile** is a file that ties an app (or group of apps) to one or more authorized developers and a set of devices. Before you can test an app on a device, you must first install a provisioning profile onto it. A device can have multiple provisioning profiles installed.

Provisioning profiles are created from the iOS Provisioning Portal.

This recipe will take you through the steps required to create a provisioning profile that will allow you to test this book's examples on a device.

Getting ready

In order to complete this recipe, you will need to create a development certificate, register an iOS device, and have an App ID. If you haven't already done this, then complete the following recipes first:

- *Obtaining your development certificate*
- *Registering a device*
- *Creating an App ID*

How to do it...

Follow the steps to create a development provisioning profile:

1. Log into the iOS Dev Center at `http://developer.apple.com/devcenter/ios` and move to the Provisioning Portal.

2. Click on the **Provisioning** link on the left-hand side of the Portal's home page. You will be taken to the provisioning page and the **Development** tab will be selected.

3. Click on the **New Profile** button found at the far-right of the **Development Provisioning Profiles** heading. You will be taken to the **Create iOS Development Provisioning Profile** page.

4. From this page you will generate a provisioning profile by performing the following steps:
   - Assigning a name to the provisioning profile.
   - Associating a development certificate with it.
   - Selecting an App ID.
   - Selecting one or more iOS devices that can be used for testing.

5. First, enter **Flash iOS Cookbook** into the **Profile Name** text field. From the **Certificates** field, check on the checkbox next to your development certificate. From the **App ID** drop-down box, select the **General Development** App ID you created a while ago. Finally, check on the checkbox next to the device you would like to test this book's examples with. If you have registered more than one device, then you can select them all.

6. Click on the **Submit** button at the bottom-right of the page.

7. You will be taken back to the **Development Provisioning Profiles** page where your provisioning profile will be listed with a status of **Pending** assigned to it. Refreshing the page in your browser will change the provisioning profile's status to **Active**.

You may need to refresh your web page a few times before the status eventually updates.

8. Now click on the **Download** button underneath the **Actions** column. Save the `Flash_iOS_Cookbook.mobileprovision` file to the same location as your P12 certificate file. For the exact path, refer to either the *Creating a P12 certificate using Windows* recipe or the *Creating a P12 certificate using Mac OS X* recipe.

How it works...

Your development provisioning profile has been associated with the `General Development` App ID from the *Creating an App ID* recipe. Being a wildcard App ID, this provisioning profile can be used to run and test any of this book's examples on an authorized device.

The provisioning profile needs to be installed on authorized devices and is also required by Flash Professional. In order to compile a native iOS app, you need to provide Flash with not only your P12 certificate file, but also the provisioning profile associated with the app you are attempting to compile.

 Testing without a device

If you are testing from the ADL rather than deploying to an iOS device, a provisioning profile isn't required.

There's more...

Before we move to the final recipe, you may find the following additional information useful.

Profile expiration

A development provisioning profile is restricted to app development and is valid for only three months. If your provisioning profile expires during development, then you will need to create a new one from the Provisioning Portal. Remember to install the new profile on any authorized devices and to rebuild your app from Flash using your new profile.

Editing provisioning profiles

Unlike App IDs, a provisioning profile can be removed from the Provisioning Portal. From the list of provisioning profiles, simply check on the checkbox next to each one you would like to delete. And click on the **Remove Selected** button at the bottom of the list of profiles.

You can also edit an existing provisioning profile. On the right-hand side within the **Actions** column, click on the profile's **Edit** link. You can either modify the original details you associated with the profile or even make a duplicate copy of a profile before making changes to it.

Additional provisioning profile types

There are in fact three types of provisioning profile that can be created. This book will focus on the use of the development provisioning profile but the provisioning process also covers two methods of distribution—Ad Hoc and App Store.

An **Ad Hoc Distribution Provisioning Profile** is used to share an app with up to 100 other iOS users for testing. An App Store **Distribution Provisioning Profile** on the other hand is used to build and submit an app to the App Store.

When creating either an Ad Hoc or App Store distribution provisioning profile, you will need to request and use a distribution certificate rather than the development certificate required by a development provisioning profile.

For more details, refer to the **Distribution** section of the **Program User Guide**, which can be found within the Provisioning Portal's **Resources** section.

Working with multiple team members

If you are working in a team environment, you must be either the Team Agent or a Team Admin to create a provisioning profile. When creating a provisioning profile, check on the checkbox next to the certificate of each team member who is to be granted permission to build and test the app(s) associated with the provisioning profile's App ID.

Installing a provisioning profile on your device

Now that you have a provisioning profile you need to install it onto a device. This will allow any apps that are associated with the provisioning profile to be tested on that device.

In this recipe, we will use iTunes to copy a provisioning profile to a connected device.

Getting ready

If you haven't already created a provisioning profile then refer to the *Creating a development provisioning profile* recipe before proceeding.

How to do it...

Execute the following steps:

1. Launch iTunes and connect your iOS device through USB.
2. After a brief moment, the device will appear within the **DEVICES** section in iTunes.
3. Select **File | Add File to Library** (*Ctrl + O | Cmd + O*) from iTunes' drop-down menu.

On Mac OS X, the drop-down menu option is listed as **Add to Library**, which allows you to add both files and folders. On Windows, this is split into two separate options: **Add File to Library** and **Add Folder to Library**.

4. Navigate to your Documents folder and select your provisioning profile at: packt\flash-ios-cookbook\developer-files\Flash_iOS_Cookbook. mobileprovision. The provisioning profile will be added to iTunes.

5. In the **DEVICES** section in iTunes, click on your device's name. You will be shown the device's summary information.

6. Click on the **Sync** button at the bottom-right corner of iTunes to copy the provisioning profile to your device.

How it works...

A provisioning profile will only install on a device that is tied to that profile.

On your iOS device, you can confirm that the provisioning profile has been added by selecting **Settings | General | Profiles**. You should be able to see the profile listed along with its expiry date. If no provisioning profiles are installed on your device, then the Profiles option will not be made available.

When installing apps for testing, the app will be checked against the device's list of provisioning profiles first. It will only be copied onto the device if a provisioning profile associated with that app is found.

There's more...

Once you are comfortable adding provisioning profiles to your devices, you may want to consider the following information.

Removing provisioning profiles

You can remove provisioning profiles from your device through **Settings | General | Profiles**. Typically, you will want to do this when the profile expires. However, after removing a profile you may find that it re-appears on your device the next time it is synchronized with iTunes on your computer.

A copy of every provisioning profile you install is kept on your computer as well as your device. If you remove a profile from your device, then make sure you also remove the local copy from your computer.

Here is where provisioning profiles are stored:

- ▶ Windows 7 and Vista: `C:\Users\<username>\AppData\Roaming\Apple Computer\MobileDevice\Provisioning Profiles\`

- ▶ Widows XP: `C:\Documents and Settings\<username>\AppData\Roaming\Apple Computer\MobileDevice\Provisioning Profiles\`

- ▶ Mac OS X: `<username>/Library/MobileDevice/Provisioning Profiles/`

Simply delete the profiles using either Windows Explorer or Finder depending on your operating system.

iPhone Configuration Utility

As an alternative to iTunes, you may want to download and install the iPhone Configuration Utility from Apple.

It allows you to easily manage provisioning profiles and capture console log information from a connected device. You can check to see when a provisioning profile is about to expire and also discover which App ID is associated with each installed app.

The iPhone Configuration Utility is available for both Mac OS X and Windows and can be downloaded from `www.apple.com/support/iphone/enterprise`.

2
Building iOS Apps Using Flash

In this chapter, we will cover:

- ▶ Installing the AIR SDK
- ▶ Creating an AIR for iOS document
- ▶ Adding content to the stage
- ▶ AIR for iOS general settings
- ▶ AIR for iOS deployment settings
- ▶ Compiling from Flash Professional
- ▶ Installing your app with iTunes

Introduction

Now that you are registered on the iOS Developer Program and have obtained the necessary files from the iOS Provisioning Portal, we can turn our attention towards building native iOS apps from Flash Professional.

This chapter will cover the fundamental tasks required to set up and compile iOS applications. While we will primarily focus on configuration, we will lay the groundwork for a basic app, which we will complete in the following chapter.

But first, let us spend some time introducing the toolchain.

Upon the release of Flash Professional CS5, Adobe included the **Packager For iPhone (PFI)**—a command line tool that was also integrated into the Flash IDE and allowed ActionScript 3.0 projects to be compiled into native iOS apps.

Initial support provided access to the majority of the Adobe AIR 2.0 and Flash Player 10.1 APIs, and also targeted both ARMv6 and ARMv7 iOS devices.

For those unfamiliar with **Adobe AIR**, it extends Flash beyond the browser sandbox, giving developers the power to directly access features of desktop computers and mobile devices that are off limits to the Flash Player.

With the release of **Flash Professional CS5.5** and introduction of AIR 2.6, the APIs made available for iOS development were extended. Adobe also made significant performance improvements; in particular to the rendering engine. However, support for iOS 3 and older ARMv6 devices has been dropped, meaning you can no longer target the original iPhone, iPhone 3G, or the first-generation and second-generation iPod touches if you are using CS5.5.

The PFI command line tool was also removed and replaced by the **AIR Development Tool** (**ADT**). This made sense as ADT is the tool that AIR developers have traditionally used to package AIR apps for delivery on desktop and more recently Android handsets.

Adobe quickly followed up AIR 2.6 with 2.7. Although it didn't provide any new APIs for iOS development, rendering performance was improved yet again and a new build option was added which dramatically improved compile times.

The most recent major version of the **AIR SDK** is 3.0, which brings a raft of exciting new features, performance enhancements, and bug fixes. Perhaps, the most significant additions are the eagerly anticipated hardware-accelerated 3D APIs and the ability to write custom ActionScript libraries implemented with native code.

The majority of the recipes covered in this book are compatible with both Flash Professional CS5 and CS5.5. The newer features provided by AIR 2.6 and above, however, are specific to CS5.5 and will be clearly marked.

Development of iOS apps using Flash is more commonly referred to as **AIR for iOS**, which is the term used throughout this book.

Installing the AIR SDK

Before we begin, it is important that you take the time to ensure your installation of Flash Professional is up-to-date and that the latest version of the AIR SDK is installed.

Getting ready

You will need either Flash Professional CS5 or CS5.5 in order to compile native iOS apps.

A 30-day trial of Flash Professional CS5.5 can be downloaded from the Adobe site at www.adobe.com/downloads.

How to do it...

We will split this recipe into two parts. First, we will install any updates required by Flash Professional. Secondly, we will download and install the most recent version of the AIR runtime and SDK.

Updating Flash Professional

Occasionally, Adobe makes updates to Flash Professional available. These updates tend to include bug fixes or additional features that for one reason or another weren't available upon release.

Visit www.adobe.com/support/flash/downloads.html and check for updates for your version of Flash.

If you are using Flash Professional CS5, then you should specifically download the following two updates for your operating system of choice:

- Flash Professional CS5 Update 11.0.2
- Flash Professional CS5 Update for iOS

 It is important that the 11.0.2 update is installed before you apply the iOS update. Also, if you currently have Flash Professional CS5 open, then close it before attempting either.

The update for iOS has to be applied manually by copying various files to your installation of Flash Professional CS5. Documentation is provided with the update and you should read it carefully before attempting it.

A video detailing the update process for Flash Professional CS5 is also available and can be found at www.gotoandlearn.com/play.php?id=133.

Overlaying the AIR SDK

It is advisable that you install the latest version of the AIR runtime on your development computer. You can download and install it from http://get.adobe.com/air.

In addition, if you are using Flash Professional CS5.5, you will also need the latest version of the AIR SDK. By default, CS5.5 provides support for AIR 2.6, however, it can be updated to use the most recent version. This is a necessary step if you wish to work through all recipes covered in this book.

To achieve this you must download and manually overlay the latest AIR SDK onto your Flash Professional CS5.5 installation. A download link to the SDK and step-by-step instructions can be found at www.yeahbutisitflash.com/?p=2949. Follow these instructions carefully before moving on.

Unfortunately, if you are using Flash Professional CS5, you will be restricted to the AIR 2.0 SDK as it is not possible to overlay a more recent AIR SDK onto it. Don't worry though; you will still be able to tackle a majority of this book's recipes. For the recipes you can't attempt, consider upgrading to Flash Professional CS5.5 or downloading a 30-day trial from the Adobe site.

The official Adobe AIR website can be found at www.adobe.com/products/air.html.

How it works...

It is important that you are working with the most up-to-date version of Flash Professional and the AIR SDK. With each new release, AIR for iOS goes from strength to strength, both in terms of API coverage and performance.

Creating an AIR for iOS document

When you create a new FLA, there are several document types you can select from.

Each document type configures the publish settings, stage size, and frame rate to best suit the content you intend to create. Your choice of document will depend on whether you want to target the Flash Player and its APIs or take advantage of the additional capabilities of AIR.

This recipe will take you through the necessary steps to create a new FLA that targets AIR for iOS. We will use this FLA as the starting point for a simple app that we will create throughout the course of this and the next chapter.

Getting ready

Make sure that your version of Flash Professional has all available updates applied to it and that you are using the latest AIR SDK. If you haven't already done this, then perform the steps outlined in the *Installing the AIR SDK* recipe before proceeding.

How to do it...

Follow the steps to create your FLA:

1. Launch Flash Professional and select **File** | **New** (*Ctrl + N* | *Cmd + N*) from the drop-down menu.

2. The **New Document** dialog box will appear. Ensure that the **General** tab is selected and click on one of the following document types depending on the version of Flash Professional that you are using:

   ❑ CS5: **iPhone OS**

   ❑ CS5.5: **AIR for iOS**

Both **iPhone OS** and **AIR for iOS** refer to the exact same thing. From now on, this book will use the term AIR for iOS. If you are using Flash CS5, then simply select iPhone OS when creating a new document.

 In CS5.5, you will see various properties of your selected document type on the right-hand side of the **New Document** panel. Notice that the stage size changes to 320x480 pixels when you select **AIR for iOS**. This is the standard screen size of the iPhone 3GS when held in portrait orientation.

3. Click on the **OK** button at the bottom-right of the dialog box as shown in the following screenshot:

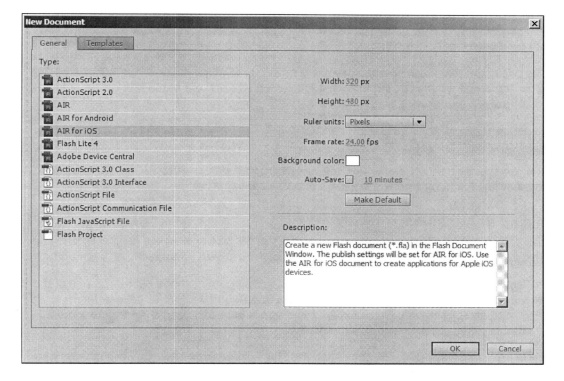

Your AIR for iOS document will be created.

This FLA will be used as the starting point for the simple app that we will create during the course of this and the next chapter.

Depending on your choice of operating system, use either Windows Explorer or Finder to navigate to `packt\flash-ios-cookbook\` within your `Documents` folder. Create a new sub-folder and name it as `my-first-app`.

4. Select **File | Save As** (*Ctrl + Shift + S | Shift + Cmd + S*) from the drop-down menu and save your FLA to the `my-first-app` folder as `bubbles.fla`.

How it works...

You should carry out the simple steps, which we just saw, every time you are starting a new AIR for iOS project.

The document that Flash creates for you will be set up to utilize ActionScript 3.0 and the AIR APIs. The **stage** will also be set to a valid iOS screen size and the frame rate will be defaulted to 24 fps.

There's more...

You can change many of the default settings associated with an AIR for iOS document. You may find the following among them to be of particular importance.

Stage dimensions

The default AIR for iOS document type assumes you will be targeting the original iPhone and iPod touch devices and that your app will use a portrait screen orientation.

In Flash CS5.5, you will see your document's default properties on the right-hand side of the **New Document** panel. Simply change the **Width** and **Height** fields to target a different screen resolution and orientation. For example, if your app is to be locked to a landscape screen orientation, then set the stage size to 480x320.

If you are using Flash CS5, you can adjust the stage dimensions after you have created your document. You can do this from the **Properties** panel.

The available iOS screen resolutions (portrait orientation) are:

▸ 320x480—iPhone 3GS, third-generation iPod touch

▸ 640x960—iPhone 4, iPhone 4S, fourth-generation iPod touch

▸ 768x1024—iPad, iPad 2

The 640x960 screen resolution is not supported when working with Flash CS5.

For the majority of its recipes, this book will stick to the default resolution of 320x480, which is supported by all iOS devices. Retina and iPad display resolutions, however, are covered in *Chapter 8*.

Frame rate

A default frame rate of 24 fps is used for all new documents. Although you can increase this value, be aware that higher frame rates can be difficult to achieve on older generation devices due to CPU and GPU constraints. Given the performance difference between various generations of iOS devices, you should consider your frame rate carefully, especially if you want to target as many devices as possible.

See also

▸ *AIR for iOS general settings*

▸ *Supporting multiple resolutions, Chapter 8*

Adding content to the stage

One of the many advantages of building iOS apps with Flash is the ability to use the authoring tools that you are already familiar with. You can still perform much of your layout visually by dragging content from the **library** onto the stage allowing rapid development.

Let us do just that to build a simple scene.

Getting ready

Accompanying this book are various graphical resource files that you should use when working through certain recipes. This will save you considerable time and effort and also ensure that your end result matches that of the recipe you are following.

If you haven't already done so, download the code bundle from this book's companion website.

You can find the resources used by this chapter within chapter2\resources\. Additionally, you will find completed code examples for each of this chapter's recipes.

Make sure you are working from the bubbles.fla file you created in the preceding recipe. Each of the following recipes in this chapter will build on top of the previous, adding more to bubbles.fla as you progress.

How to do it...

We will start by copying library symbols into your FLA.

1. Select **File | Open** (*Ctrl + O* | *Cmd + O*) and browse to chapter2\resources\resources.fla. Click on **Open** to load the FLA.

2. Copy all the library symbols from resources.fla, and paste them into the library of bubbles.fla.

   Your library will now consist of a collection of bitmaps and the following five movie clips: **Background, Bubble Huge, Bubble Large, Bubble Medium**, and **Bubble Small**. From the library, double-click into each movie-clip symbol and take a closer look at the contents of each. You will see that each clip consists of a single bitmap image.

3. Drag the Background movie clip symbol from the library onto the stage. From the **Properties** panel, expand the **POSITION AND SIZE** section and position the movie clip at (0,0). If you are using Flash Professional CS5, then you should also expand the **DISPLAY** section and check on the **Cache as bitmap** checkbox. There is no need to set this option if you are using CS5.5 as it could actually degrade the performance of this app if you do.

4. Now, drag three instances of Bubble Small from the library to the stage. If you are using Flash CS5, then from the **Properties** panel check the **Cache as bitmap** checkbox for each instance.

5. Using the **Properties** panel, name the instances bubble1, bubble2, and bubble3. Also, set the position of each to (206, 421), (162, 160), and (122, 53) respectively. The following screenshot shows the first of the bubble instances being positioned on the stage:

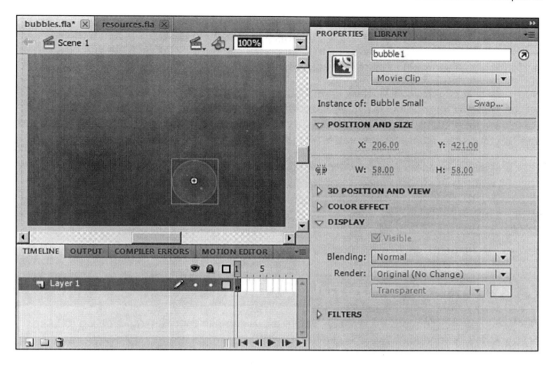

6. Drag three instances of `Bubble Medium` to the stage. For Flash CS5, check the **Cache as bitmap** checkbox for each instance.

7. Name the instances `bubble4`, `bubble5`, and `bubble6`. Set the position of each to (162, 290), (318, 274), and (203, 119) respectively.

8. Only two instances of `Bubble Large` are required. Again, check the **Cache as bitmap** checkbox from the **Properties** panel if you are using CS5.

9. Assign instance names of `bubble7` and `bubble8` and set their positions to (74, 329) and (297, 12).

10. Finally, position **Bubble Huge** on the stage and if you are using CS5, ensure you check the **Cache as bitmap** checkbox. Give it an instance name of `bubble9` and position it partially off stage at (440, 303).

11. Save your FLA.

How it works...

What we just covered should feel familiar even to those with only a basic understanding of Flash. You simply dragged various movie-clip instances onto the stage to create a scene that you will be able to display on an iOS device.

You may not be familiar with the **Cache as Bitmap** render option. This will be explained in more detail in *Chapter 6*; but for the time being, it is enough to know that when working with Flash Professional CS5, choosing this option will significantly improve the graphics performance of your app in certain situations.

Note also that all graphical content in this recipe was provided in PNG format rather than vector. This was intentional as iOS devices can render bitmaps to the screen faster than Flash's vector content. Where appropriate, try to use bitmaps, although this doesn't mean you should completely ignore Flash's vector renderer as it is one of Flash's many strengths.

Now that you have some visual content, we can start to configure Flash's additional iOS specific settings in order to build and deploy your content to a device.

See also

▶ *Using Cache as Bitmap, Chapter 6*

AIR for iOS general settings

Flash requires a little more information before it can compile your FLA into a native iOS app. First, you will need to specify some general iOS settings, which we will now cover.

Getting ready

We will continue to work from `bubbles.fla`.

How to do it...

When working from an AIR for iOS document, an additional settings panel is made available from Flash Professional. From it, you will be able to apply some iOS specifics that will be used by Flash when outputting a native iOS app.

Select **File | AIR for iOS Settings** to open the panel. Ensure that the **General** tab is selected.

 If you are using Flash Professional CS5, select **File | iPhone OS Settings** instead. Remember, CS5 uses the term **iPhone OS** whereas CS5.5 refers to it as **AIR for iOS**.

Within the **AIR for iOS Settings** panel, options can be set for the following fields:

Option	Description
Output file	The file name for your native iOS app
App name	The name of your app
Version	A version number for your app
Aspect ratio	The app's default screen orientation
Full screen	Whether to use the full screen or show the status bar along the top
Auto orientation	Whether the screen orientation is to automatically rotate with the device
Rendering	Sets the rendering mode used by your app
Device	The iOS devices you are targeting
Resolution	Standard or Retina screen resolution support
Included files	Additional resources to be bundled with your app

Let us set some of these options:

▶ The **Output file** and **App name** fields will default to the name of your FLA. For this chapter's example app, ensure that the **Output file** is set to **bubbles.ipa** and that the **App name** is set to **Bubbles**.

▶ Set a value of **0.1** within the **Version** field.

▶ The bubbles app has been designed for a portrait screen orientation and will consume the entirety of your device's screen display. Therefore, ensure that the **Aspect ratio** field is defaulted to **Portrait** and also check on the **Full screen** checkbox.

▶ Leave the **Auto orientation** option unchecked.

▶ Select **GPU** from the **Rendering** field's drop-down box.

▶ Ensure that the **Device** field is set to **iPhone** and that the **Resolution** field is set to **Standard**. The **Resolution** field is not available on Flash CS5.

Now click on the **OK** button on the bottom of the panel and save your FLA.

How it works...

Let us examine some of the choices made earlier in a little more detail.

The output `.ipa` file is produced by Flash when you publish your FLA and contains your native app. This is the file that you will install on your device and is often referred to as an IPA.

The app name is the name that is shown beneath your app's icon on your device's home screen. Consider the app's name carefully. Names that are over 13-characters in length will be truncated due to screen space limits.

The version number is compiled into each app you build and consists of a major and minor value. When installing new versions of your app onto a device, you need to remember to increase the version number. If you don't, then the app won't actually be installed over the existing version.

Although your stage dimensions may already imply it, you still need to explicitly state the aspect ratio of your app by setting the **Aspect Ratio** field to either **Portrait** or **Landscape**.

The render mode specifies whether your application should be rendered with the device's **Graphics Processing Unit** (**GPU**) or using the CPU. In certain situations, GPU rendering will increase the rendering performance of your app. See *Chapter 6* for more information regarding GPU acceleration.

Selecting the **Device** field tells Flash which family of device you are targeting and dictates how your IPA will run on certain devices. You can select from **iPhone**, **iPad**, or **iPhone and iPad**.

Selecting **iPhone** restricts your screen size to that of the iPhone's. Your IPA will still run on the iPad but the app won't attempt to take advantage of the iPad's screen resolution. Instead, the iPad will run the app using the iPhone's standard 320x480 resolution and scale up the image to fit the iPad's screen. Selecting **iPad** takes advantage of the iPad's resolution and restricts your app to that device. If you have written an app that can take advantage of both the iPhone and iPad's screen resolutions, then you should select **iPhone and iPad**.

It should also be noted that the iPod touch is treated as an iPhone. Therefore, selecting either **iPhone** or **iPhone and iPad** from the **Device** field will allow your `.ipa` file to be installed on an iPod touch too.

AIR 2.6 and above provides the ability to utilize the **Retina display** introduced on iPhone 4 and the fourth-generation iPod touch. This will provide you with access to a 640x960 screen resolution. If you do want to take advantage of the Retina display and you also want to support the standard resolution of 320x480, then you will need to write a single app that handles both. The App Store does not allow you to upload two separate versions; one for each resolution. Retina display support is not available on Flash Professional CS5.

This book will, for the most part, concentrate on the standard resolution as it will ensure that the examples will work across all iOS devices. Both the iPad and Retina display devices will scale up content that targets the standard 320x480 resolution. However, for more details regarding Retina and iPad resolutions, see *Chapter 8*.

There's more...

The following are a few more options you should consider.

Adding the status bar

You can add the default iOS status bar to your application by deselecting the **Full screen** checkbox.

The status bar consumes 20 vertical pixels (40 pixels on Retina display screens) and sits along the top of the screen. Flash will attempt to scale down your app to fit the remaining screen height, leaving borders on either side of the screen.

There are several ways to prevent this from happening. The simplest is to reduce the stage height to accommodate the remaining vertical space.

Alternatively, leave the stage's dimensions unaltered and use ActionScript to prevent it from being scaled. By doing so, you will need to sacrifice some pixel real estate from either the top or bottom of your stage.

In the following example, the status bar will overlay and obscure the content at the top of your stage:

```
stage.scaleMode = StageScaleMode.NO_SCALE;
stage.align = StageAlign.BOTTOM_LEFT;
```

Whereas the following piece of code positions the stage directly below the status bar, cropping content off the bottom of the stage:

```
stage.scaleMode = StageScaleMode.NO_SCALE;
stage.align = StageAlign.TOP_LEFT;
```

In either case, you will also need to import the `flash.display.StageScaleMode` and `flash.display.StageAlign` classes.

 The status bar also consumes 20 vertical pixels on iPad.

Including files

At the bottom of the AIR for iOS Settings panel is the **Included files** list, which contains resources that are to be bundled with your `.ipa` file or used during compilation.

By default, two files appear in this list: the `.swf` file that represents your app, and an XML file known as the application descriptor file. The application descriptor file contains properties for your entire application including those set within the AIR for iOS Settings panel.

Additional files can be bundled with your IPA by adding them to the list. We will see how to do this and why it is useful at various points throughout the book.

See also

▶ *Including an application launch image, Chapter 3*

▶ *Editing the application descriptor file, Chapter 3*

AIR for iOS deployment settings

We are almost ready to publish a native iOS app from Flash. Now it is actually time to use the development files that you created during *Chapter 1, Getting Started with iOS App Development*. As part of the deployment process, Flash Professional requires both your P12 certificate file and your development provisioning profile. Without these files it will be unable to compile your FLA into a native iOS app.

Let us go through the steps required to configure the iOS deployment settings.

Getting ready

Before attempting this recipe, you will need to create a P12 certificate file and a development provisioning profile. If you haven't already done this, then complete the following recipes first:

▶ *Creating a P12 certificate using Windows, Chapter 1*

▶ *Creating a P12 certificate using Mac OS X, Chapter 1*

▶ *Creating a development provisioning profile, Chapter 1*

You should also have set your general iOS settings within Flash Professional, which was covered in the *AIR for iOS general settings* recipe.

How to do it...

You will be working within the AIR for iOS Settings panel again.

1. Open the **AIR for iOS Settings** panel by selecting **File | AIR for iOS Settings** from Flash Professional's drop-down menu.
2. Click on the **Deployment** tab in the settings panel.

   From here you will be able to set the following:

   ❑ The P12 certificate file required to digitally sign your app

   ❑ The provisioning profile associated with your app

   ❑ The App ID

   ❑ The deployment type to be used

3. Let us start by specifying the P12 certificate file. Click on the **Browse** button to the far right of the **Certificate** field. From the file browser, navigate to `packt\flash-ios-cookbook\developer-files\` within your `Documents` folder. Select the `.p12` file and click on **Open**.

4. In the **Password** field directly below, enter the password you associated with your P12 certificate. This is the export password you set up during the *Creating a P12 certificate using Windows* recipe or the *Creating a P12 certificate using Mac OS X* recipe from *Chapter 1*.

5. Also, check on the **Remember password for this session** checkbox directly underneath the **Password** field.

 The **Remember password for this session** option will prevent Flash from asking you for the password every time you publish your FLA. However, you will be asked for the password again each time you re-launch Flash as it is only stored on a per-session basis.

6. Now that Flash Professional knows what certificate to use, you can specify the **Provisioning profile** that your app is to be tied to.

   Click on the **Browse** button to the far right of the **Provisioning profile** field and select the `.mobileprovision` file from the `developer-files` folder.

7. The **App ID** field directly below expects a unique identifier for your app. Enter **bubbles** for this application's ID.

8. The final step is to make a selection for the deployment type.

   The **Quick publishing for device testing** option should be selected by default. If it isn't, then select it.

9. Click on **OK** and save your FLA.

How it works...

Your FLA is now ready to be compiled into a native iOS app. In fact, you can actually publish the app directly from the **AIR for iOS Settings** panel, but we will hold off publishing until the next recipe.

There's more...

Before proceeding, it is worth spending some time understanding the role of the App ID and the deployment type setting.

Specifying an App ID

You may remember creating and associating an App ID with the provisioning profile you created during the *Creating a development provisioning profile* recipe from *Chapter 1*.

An App ID consists of two parts: a bundle seed ID and a bundle identifier. Flash Professional expects you to provide it with only the bundle identifier.

If your bundle identifier contains the wildcard symbol * , then you need to substitute the symbol with an arbitrary string that will uniquely represent your app. Wildcard App IDs allow you to use the same provisioning profile to publish multiple apps.

The App ID associated with your provisioning profile is solely the wildcard symbol, meaning that the identifier you enter into the **App ID** field within Flash Professional is an arbitrary string entirely of your choice.

It makes sense in such cases to assign an App ID that is related to the name of your app, making `bubbles` an appropriate ID for this chapter's example app.

Deployment types

Within Flash Professional, there are four different deployment types that you can choose from:

- ▸ Quick publishing for device testing
- ▸ Quick publishing for device debugging
- ▸ Deployment—Ad hoc
- ▸ Deployment—Apple App Store

Of these, you only need to select from the first two when developing.

From Flash Professional, the **Quick publishing for device testing** option is the quickest path for deploying and running an app on a device. However, if you want to debug your app directly from a device, then you will need to select **Quick publishing for device debugging**, which will allow you to use Flash Professional's remote debugger to see `trace()` statements and pause your application at breakpoints.

The remaining deployment types are for building apps that are being prepared for beta testing or App Store submission, and will require you to have a distribution certificate.

For more details regarding distribution, refer to the **Distribution** section of the **Program User Guide**, which can be found within the iOS Provisioning Portal's **Resources** section.

See also

- ▸ *Obtaining your development certificate, Chapter 1*
- ▸ *Creating an App ID, Chapter 1*
- ▸ *Creating a development provisioning profile, Chapter 1*

Compiling from Flash Professional

With the iOS settings successfully configured, you can go ahead and compile your FLA into a native app.

Getting ready

If you haven't already configured the iOS settings for your app, then perform the following two recipes before proceeding:

- *AIR for iOS general settings*
- *AIR for iOS deployment settings*

How to do it...

Compiling your FLA into a native iOS app from Flash Professional can take several minutes depending on your computer's hardware specification. It is, therefore, advisable to publish your FLA using the **AIR Debug Launcher** (**ADL**) first. This will let you quickly find and correct any compiler errors before attempting to build a native iOS version.

Let us use ADL to quickly publish `bubbles.fla`.

1. From Flash Professional's drop-down menu, select **Control | Test Movie | in AIR Debug Launcher (Mobile)**.

2. If successful, a `.swf` file will be published and run within ADL. You should see the scene that you created in the *Adding content to the stage* recipe earlier in this chapter.

> At the moment, your SWF will only show a static scene consisting of various sized bubbles sitting against a background. The `bubbles.fla` file will become more dynamic as we add more functionality throughout the course of this and the next chapter.

If there are any compiler errors, then correct them and re-publish. You can make subsequent publication attempts by pressing *Ctrl + Enter* (*Cmd + Enter* on Mac) rather than using the drop-down menu each time.

Once you are satisfied that you have eliminated all compiler errors, you can publish your FLA for deployment on an iOS device.

3. To do this, simply select **File | Publish** (*Alt + Shift + F12 | Shift + Cmd + F12*) from Flash's drop-down menu and compilation will begin.

If the **AIR for iOS Settings** panel appears, then it is likely that Flash requires your certificate's password again. This will happen if you forget to check the **Remember password for this session** checkbox or if you have re-launched Flash after closing it.

In either case, enter the password, check on the checkbox, and then click on the **Publish** button at the bottom of the panel.

If successful, a file named `bubbles.ipa` will be output to the same folder as your FLA.

How it works...

The `.ipa` file is the native iOS version of your app and is what you install onto your device for testing.

In order to perform cross compilation of your app's `.swf` file into an `.ipa` file, Flash Professional CS5 makes a call to the **Packager for iPhone (PFI)** while CS5.5 makes a call to the **AIR Development Tool (ADT)**.

Compile times can be lengthy, particularly for large projects.

Although there is no real substitute for actual on-device testing, you might want to test small incremental changes to your app from ADL. This will save considerable time, although, be aware that not all iOS features are supported on the desktop and will have to be tested on a device instead.

In addition, Adobe introduced a new build target in AIR 2.7 called **Interpreter Mode**, which reduces compilation time from minutes to a few seconds. This feature is aimed at advanced developers as it requires the use of the command line.

There's more...

You may be curious as to why compiling an `.ipa` file takes considerably longer than publishing a `.swf` file using ADL. The following section may help your understanding.

The LLVM compiler infrastructure

Rather than being interpreted at runtime, a compiler was written to convert `.swf` files into native iOS applications.

This was achieved by using the widely used open source, **Low Level Virtual Machine (LLVM)** compiler infrastructure. Adobe created a new compiler frontend for LLVM allowing it to understand ActionScript 3.0. LLVM's existing ARM backend was then used to output native ARM machine code, which is understood by the CPUs used in iOS devices. This is more commonly known as **ahead-of-time compilation**.

Although your application is written in Flash, the final result is a completely native iOS application.

However, the ahead-of-time compilation process is quite involved and takes significantly longer than simply publishing a .swf file from Flash.

You can find out more about LLVM at http://llvm.org.

Installing your app with iTunes

Once you have compiled your FLA into an .ipa file, it can be installed onto your device for testing. There are various applications available that you can use to do this, one of which is iTunes.

Let us see how this is done.

Getting ready

You must already have installed on your device the same provisioning profile you used when compiling your IPA from Flash Professional.

If you haven't yet done this, then first perform the steps detailed in the _Installing a provisioning profile on your device_ recipe from _Chapter 1_.

How to do it...

1. Launch iTunes and connect your iOS device through a USB.

2. Select **File | Add File to Library** (_Ctrl + O | Cmd + O_) from iTunes' drop-down menu.

> On Mac OS X, the drop-down menu option is listed as **Add to Library**.

3. From the file browser, navigate to and select the .ipa file you want to install. For this recipe, simply locate the bubbles.ipa file you created earlier. You should find it in your Documents folder at packt\flash-ios-cookbook\my-first-app\ bubbles.ipa.

4. The .ipa file will install on iTunes. Confirm this by checking your iTunes library for an app named **Bubbles**. You can see your installed apps by clicking on the **Apps** category underneath the **LIBRARY** section in iTunes.

5. The final step is to move the app from your computer's iTunes library to your device.

   Underneath the **DEVICES** section in iTunes, click on your device's name. By default you will be shown the device's summary information. Above the summary information is a row of tabs. Click on the **Apps** tab.

6. From here, you can synchronize your device's library with that of your computer. On the left-hand side, you will find a list of the apps stored on your computer and on the right is the list of apps installed on your device. Scroll down the list on the left until you find the **Bubbles** app. If it isn't already selected, check on the checkbox next to it.

7. Now to copy the app to your device, click on the **Apply** button near the bottom-right corner of iTunes.

From the **Apps** tab, ensure that the **Sync Apps** checkbox is selected. If not then you will first have to manually synchronize your device before the latest version of your app can be copied to your device.

8. Find the **Bubbles** app on your device and launch it by tapping its icon.

On older iOS devices such as first-generation and second-generation iPhones and iPod touches, you may find the performance of some apps particularly sluggish when you first launch them. This tends to be caused by your device updating its library in the background after being synced with your computer.

If you are experiencing problems, then you may want to wait until this update process has completed before launching your app. You can check to see if your device's library is being updated by selecting the **Music** app from the home screen. If the library is currently being updated, you will be informed and prevented from selecting from your music library.

How it works...

Copying your app using iTunes is a fairly trivial process but for the procedure to succeed, everything needs to be correct with the development files you created and obtained from the iOS Provisioning Portal.

If there are problems, then your app may fail to copy to the iTunes library on your computer or fail to install on your device. If you experience either of these problems, then it may be for one or more of the following reasons:

► Your provisioning profile has not been copied to the iTunes library.

► Your provisioning profile has not been copied to your device.

► The provisioning profile has expired.

► The device hasn't been registered with the provisioning profile.

- ▸ The IPA was compiled using a different provisioning profile than what is on your device.

- ▸ The App ID you specified within Flash does not match your provisioning profile's bundle identifier pattern.

- ▸ Your development computer's firewall may interfere with installation of your app. If all else fails, deactivate the firewall and retry installing the app to your device.

Unfortunately, the errors you receive from iTunes when an app fails to install can be obscure. If you do experience problems and you are still finding your feet with iOS development, then it might be better to delete your development files and go back through the provisioning process again.

There's more...

We have deployed our first app to our device. When you go to install and test subsequent versions of your app, you should consider the configurations mentioned in the following section.

Updating version numbers

Each time you make a new build that you would like to test on your device; you will also need to update your app's version number from Flash's AIR for iOS Settings panel.

If you forget to do this, then iTunes will not copy the latest version of the app to your device when syncing; iTunes will only replace an existing app with one that has a higher version number.

However, updating the version number every time you make a build is easy to overlook. For more rapid development, you might instead want to delete the existing version of the app from your device before installing the latest version.

To remove an app directly from your device, simply hold your finger on the icon for a few seconds, then tap the cross that appears at its top-right corner.

iPhone Configuration Utility

As an alternative to iTunes, you may want to consider downloading and installing the iPhone Configuration Utility from Apple.

It allows you to install and remove applications from your device, and also lets you see what version of the app is actually installed—something iTunes doesn't currently do.

The iPhone Configuration Utility is available for both Mac OS X and Windows and can be downloaded from `www.apple.com/support/iphone/enterprise`.

TestFlight

For team environments, take a look at **TestFlight**. It is a free over-the-air platform used to distribute apps to team members during development and testing. The service allows iOS developers to create a team, invite team members, add team members' devices, and distribute their latest builds to them.

Each new build is made available to testers through an e-mail with a link to install it. Clicking on the link will download and install the build to the device wirelessly. There is no need for team members to physically connect their device to a computer in order to install a build.

You can sign up for TestFlight at `https://testflightapp.com`.

3
Writing your First App

In this chapter, we will cover:

- ▶ Creating a basic document class
- ▶ Preventing screen idle
- ▶ Handling multitasking
- ▶ Exiting gracefully from an app
- ▶ Linking classes to movie-clip symbols
- ▶ Using an update loop
- ▶ Including an application launch image
- ▶ Including icons
- ▶ Editing the application descriptor file
- ▶ Remote debugging

Introduction

You should now be comfortable compiling and deploying native iOS apps from Flash Professional. In this chapter, we will continue where we left off, building on top of our FLA to create our first iOS app.

Although there are differences compared to targeting desktop computers, the process for writing iOS applications in Flash will feel familiar to any Flash developer. Along the way, a few best practices will be covered and you will have a first-hand experience of just how easy it is to write a simple application using some basic ActionScript. We will also apply the finishing touches to the app by adding a default launch image and icon artwork.

Creating a basic document class

Although you can write ActionScript 3.0 code directly onto the timeline, it isn't a recommended practice. Instead you really should apply a more object-oriented approach and develop your own custom classes. This is of particular importance on large-scale projects.

Most ActionScript developers should already be comfortable creating classes but we will cover the steps here for the avoidance of doubt. Specifically, this recipe will have you create a basic document class that can be applied to the example app you started in the previous chapter.

Getting ready

We will be working from the latest version of `bubbles.fla` from *Chapter 2*. Alternatively, you can open `chapter3\recipe1\bubbles.fla` from the book's accompanying code bundle.

How to do it...

Follow the steps to create a document class:

1. First ensure that no instances on your stage are currently selected. Then, from the **PUBLISH** section within the **Properties** panel, click on the pencil icon next to the **Class** field.

   The **Create ActionScript 3.0 Class** dialog box will appear.

2. Within the dialog box you may be asked which application should be used to create the ActionScript 3.0 class. If prompted, select the **Flash Professional** radio button.

3. Enter **Main** into the **Class name** field and click on **OK**.

   A skeleton class named `Main` will be created and shown within a new tab in the Flash IDE.

4. Save the class by selecting **File | Save As** (*Ctrl + Shift + S | Shift + Cmd + S*) from Flash's drop-down menu. When prompted, name the file `Main.as` and save it within the same folder as `bubbles.fla`.

5. Move back to `bubbles.fla` by clicking on its tab.

 Every class you create or open will be shown as a tab along with any currently open FLA files. You can find these tabs directly below Flash Professional's drop-down menus.

You now have a document class associated with your FLA.

6. Ensure that there are no compiler errors by testing your FLA using ADL. You can do this by selecting **Control | Test Movie | in AIR Debug Launcher (Mobile)** from Flash's drop-down menu. Alternatively, if you have previously tested from ADL (Mobile), then simply press *Ctrl + Enter (Cmd + Enter* on Mac).

How it works...

The document class provides your application with a main entry point. Any code you add to the class' constructor will be executed when your app is launched, giving you an ideal location to perform initialization.

Here is how the constructor currently looks:

```
public function Main() {
  //constructor code
}
```

As you can see, the constructor is empty but that will change during the remainder of this chapter.

There's more...

The following are a few more points regarding class creation.

Naming the document class

The name of the document class is not significant. You can choose any valid name for the class; however, in this book, we will stick with the convention of naming the document class `Main` for each new app.

Using packages

Given the simplicity of this chapter's example, it will suffice to add all the code to the same folder as `bubbles.fla`. Of course, for more complex projects you are likely to package your classes into individual sub-folders preventing namespace collisions with classes written by third parties.

Editing with Flash Builder

Some developers find Flash Professional's code management and editing features too limited. Adobe has addressed this by integrating Flash Professional with Flash Builder.

Flash Builder is a powerful coding environment that offers features over and above those provided by Flash Professional. It is now possible to edit and compile your AIR for iOS projects from Flash Builder.

When you create classes within Flash Professional, you will be given the option to select whether to edit that class directly from within Flash Professional, or to open and use Flash Builder for your code editing.

This book won't cover Flash Builder but you can purchase it or download a trial version from the Adobe site at `www.adobe.com/downloads`.

While you can use other third-party IDEs, such as Flash Develop and FDT, to edit your ActionScript, they can't be launched directly from Flash Professional.

Creating other ActionScript 3.0 classes

Other custom ActionScript 3.0 classes can be created from Flash Professional. However, these class files are created from Flash Professional's drop-down menu.

Simply select **File | New** (*Ctrl + N | Cmd + N*) to open the **New Document** panel. From here, you can select the **ActionScript 3.0 Class** type and provide a name for the class.

See also

▸   *Linking classes to movie-clip symbols*

Preventing screen idle

To conserve battery life, mobile devices lock the screen a short period after they are last touched. However, this can be inconvenient for applications where the user might not be expected to interact with the screen that often.

For applications where this is the case, screen locking can be disabled.

Getting ready

We will be adding code to the skeleton document class created in the previous recipe. If you haven't already done this, then complete the *Creating a basic document class* recipe before proceeding. Alternatively, using the book's accompanying code bundle, open `chapter3\recipe2\bubbles.fla` in Flash Professional and work from there.

How to do it...

Let us write some ActionScript to disable screen locking:

1.   Open the FLA's document class by selecting **File | Open** (*Ctrl + O | Cmd + O*) from Flash Professional's drop-down menu. From the file browser select **Main.as**.

2. Add the following two import statements to your class:

```
import flash.display.MovieClip;
import flash.desktop.NativeApplication;
import flash.desktop.SystemIdleMode;
```

Both these classes are required in order to prevent your device from locking while the screen is idle.

3. Create a member variable that will be used to store a `NativeApplication` object:

```
public class Main extends MovieClip {
  private var application:NativeApplication;
```

4. Within the constructor, obtain a `NativeApplication` reference and store it within your `application` member variable:

```
public function Main() {
  application = NativeApplication.nativeApplication;
}
```

5. Using the `application` variable, force the device's screen to stay awake:

```
public function Main() {
  application = NativeApplication.nativeApplication;
  application.systemIdleMode = SystemIdleMode.KEEP_AWAKE;
}
```

6. Save your class file.

7. Move to your FLA by clicking on its tab and open the AIR for iOS Settings panel by selecting **File | AIR for iOS Settings** from the drop-down menu.

8. From the settings panel, ensure the **General** tab is selected and update the **Version** field to **0.2**.

9. Click on **OK** and save your FLA.

10. Now, check your FLA for any compile-time errors by testing your movie using ADL.

    Once you are satisfied that there are no errors, publish your app for iOS by selecting **File | Publish** (_Alt + Shift + F12 | Shift + Cmd + F12_) and deploy the resultant `.ipa` file to your device using iTunes.

11. Launch the app. You should notice that the screen doesn't dim or lock during the application's lifetime.

 You will need to increment the app's version number every time you wish to deploy a new build to your device. If you don't see any changes after launching your app, then it is likely to be a version issue.

For testing purposes, set the auto-lock time on your iOS device to the minimum duration. You can do this by selecting **Settings | General | Auto-Lock** on your iOS device. This will reduce the time you need to wait before confirming that the auto-lock has been disabled within your app.

How it works...

The `NativeApplication` class provides the `systemIdleMode` property that can be set to allow or prevent your device's screen from locking. From `NativeApplication`, you can also obtain application information, access application-wide functions, and capture application-level events.

In the code example, we set `systemIdleMode` to `SystemIdleMode.KEEP_AWAKE`, ensuring that the screen doesn't lock during the application's lifetime. Auto-locking can just as easily be re-enabled with `SystemIdleMode.NORMAL`.

To prevent excessive battery usage, it is advisable to use `SystemIdleMode.KEEP_AWAKE` sparingly. You may want to consider only disabling auto-lock within your application at points where it is absolutely necessary.

Also, you may have noticed that an instance of `NativeApplication` wasn't explicitly created within your code. `NativeApplication` is a singleton object that is automatically created when your application is launched. Only one instance of it can exist, and is accessed using the class' static `nativeApplication` property.

Handling multitasking

Multitasking is supported in iOS 4 or above. When the user exits from an app by pressing the device's home button, the app is moved into the background rather than being fully closed. This can also occur for a variety of other reasons, such as the user accepting an incoming call or the app itself launching another application.

When the user, or some other application, launches the app again, it can simply continue where it left off rather than being completely re-loaded. This also significantly reduces the start-up time when you return to the app.

Events are dispatched when your application is moved to the background, or resumed by the operating system. This recipe will explain how to listen for and capture these events.

Getting ready

We will expand the Bubbles app, providing our document class with methods that can handle the app being moved to the background and resumed.

This recipe follows on from the work done in the *Preventing screen idle* recipe.

The AIR 2.0 SDK does not provide support for iOS multitasking. If you are using Flash Professional CS5, then skip this recipe and move to the *Exiting gracefully from an app* recipe.

How to do it...

Make the following changes to your document class:

1. Open `Main.as` within Flash Professional CS5.5.

2. You will require the use of the `Event` class. Add it to your list of import statements:

```
import flash.display.MovieClip;
import flash.desktop.NativeApplication;
import flash.desktop.SystemIdleMode;
import flash.events.Event;
```

3. Within the constructor, listen for `NativeApplication` dispatching `Event.ACTIVATE` and `Event.DEACTIVATE`:

```
public function Main() {
   application = NativeApplication.nativeApplication;
   application.systemIdleMode = SystemIdleMode.KEEP_AWAKE;
   application.addEventListener(Event.ACTIVATE, activate);
   application.addEventListener(Event.DEACTIVATE, deactivate);
}
```

4. Add a handler for each event:

```
private function deactivate(e:Event):void {
   application.systemIdleMode = SystemIdleMode.NORMAL;
}

private function activate(e:Event):void {
   application.systemIdleMode = SystemIdleMode.KEEP_AWAKE;
}
```

5. Move back to your constructor and remove the following highlighted line:

```
public function Main() {
   application = NativeApplication.nativeApplication;
   application.systemIdleMode = SystemIdleMode.KEEP_AWAKE;
   application.addEventListener(Event.ACTIVATE, activate);
   application.addEventListener(Event.DEACTIVATE, deactivate);
}
```

   This line is no longer required as it is now performed by the `activate()` method.

6. Save your class file and check for any compile-time errors by testing `bubbles.fla` using ADL (*Ctrl + Enter | Cmd + Enter*).

How it works...

Whenever your app is about to be moved to the background, the `NativeApplication` class dispatches `Event.DEACTIVATE`. Alternatively, `Event.ACTIVATE` is fired when iOS resumes your app or when it is launched. You can listen for and respond to these events in order to initialize your app, prepare it for being moved to the background, or re-activated again.

In this recipe's example, we have simply taken the opportunity to disable auto-lock when your app is launched or resumed, and enable auto-lock when your app is suspended.

There's more...

You may find the following additional information regarding iOS multitasking of interest.

Background processing

The majority of background apps on iOS actually get suspended. They are still in system memory but are effectively paused. This saves CPU resources and increases the device's battery life.

Certain types of apps, however, can continue to run in the background rather than being suspended. These apps are given limited CPU resources to perform a few specific tasks, such as playing audio or accessing location-based information.

In either case, AIR's `NativeApplication` class will dispatch `Event.DEACTIVATE`.

App closing

Do not assume your background app will remain in memory.

A user or the operating system itself may decide to close your application. If your app is closed by a user, then you may be given an opportunity to save its state and perform any final clean-up code.

Exiting gracefully from an app

Pressing the home button on iOS 3 devices closes the current app and removes it from memory. Performing the same action on a device running iOS 4 or above places the app in a suspended or background state rather than closing it. However, a user can close and remove these apps from memory using the fast app switcher. Additionally, when system memory is low, iOS itself may decide to close suspended or background apps.

If the user decides to close your app then, just before it exits, you will be given an opportunity to perform any house keeping, such as saving state or freeing memory.

Getting ready

We will add some more code to the current version of your Bubbles app, allowing it to gracefully exit. Alternatively, from the book's accompanying code bundle, open `chapter3\recipe4\bubbles.fla` and work from there.

How to do it...

Let us listen for and handle the Bubbles app being closed:

1. Open `Main.as` within Flash Professional.

2. We will make use of the `Event` class. Ensure that it is added to your class' list of import statements:

```
import flash.display.MovieClip;
import flash.desktop.NativeApplication;
import flash.desktop.SystemIdleMode;
import flash.events.Event;
```

3. Within the constructor, listen for `Event.EXITING` being dispatched by the `NativeApplication` object:

```
application.addEventListener(Event.EXITING, exiting);
```

4. Add an event handler that will perform any required clean-up before your app exits:

```
private function exiting(e:Event):void {
    application.removeEventListener(Event.EXITING, exiting);
    application.systemIdleMode = SystemIdleMode.NORMAL;
}
```

5. If you are using Flash Professional CS5.5 and have completed the previous recipe—*Handling multitasking*—then add the following lines to your `exiting()` event handler:

```
private function exiting(e:Event):void {
    application.removeEventListener(Event.ACTIVATE, activate);
    application.removeEventListener(Event.DEACTIVATE,
        deactivate);
    application.removeEventListener(Event.EXITING, exiting);
    application.systemIdleMode = SystemIdleMode.NORMAL;
}
```

6. Save your class file and check for any compile-time errors.

How it works...

Whenever your app is about to exit, the `NativeApplication` class dispatches the `EXITING` event. By responding to this event you can perform any necessary clean-up, such as saving state or freeing memory.

You may also notice within the `exiting()` method that we have taken the opportunity to re-enable auto-lock. Although iOS should actually enable auto-lock for you when your app exits, it is good practice to explicitly do this within your code.

It is also good practice to perform other forms of clean-up such as removing event listeners, which we have also done. It is important that event listeners are removed from objects as failing to do so is a common source of memory leaks. This applies throughout the lifetime of your application and not just when exiting.

There's more...

Finally a little more detail regarding the exit sequence.

The app switcher

On iOS 4 or above, you must explicitly kill an app using the fast app switcher. To access the app switcher, double-press on the home button. To kill an app, tap and hold its icon until the minus symbol appears at the icon's corner. Tap the minus symbol and the app will be removed from the background. This will force `Event.EXITING` to be dispatched from the app as it is being closed.

Cleaning up

Along with saving the application's state, you should also perform any necessary clean-up in response to `Event.EXITING`. It is important that your app cleans up itself by completely freeing memory. You should dispose of any objects, remove any remaining event listeners you added, stop any timers and timeline animations that are still running, stop all sound from playing, cancel any network requests, and finally close any sockets, file streams, or database connections.

Script execution time

Ensure that the code within your event handler executes as quickly as possible. If it takes more than a handful of seconds, then iOS may terminate your application prematurely. This could be particularly harmful, if it happens while you are still saving state information to the device.

To limit the chances of a timeout happening, minimize the amount of data you save during the exit process. You should also ensure you save data before performing any other clean-up tasks. This will increase the chances of your app's state being preserved when performing lengthy exit and clean-up operations.

Linking classes to movie-clip symbols

It is possible to add additional behavior to a movie-clip symbol by creating and linking a custom class to it. Typically the class will listen for, and respond to events dispatched by the movie clip. Of those available, Event.ENTER_FRAME is the most widely used, providing a means to programmatically update the movie-clip's appearance on every frame redrawn.

We will write a custom class that makes each of the bubbles from the latest version of our example app float upwards.

How to do it...

Let us write the custom class and link it to each of the bubbles:

1. Within Flash Professional select **File | New** (*Ctrl + N | Cmd + N*). From the **New Document** panel, create an **ActionScript 3.0 Class** and name it **Bubble**. A skeleton class will be created.

2. Add the following code to the class:

```
package {

    import flash.display.Sprite;
    import flash.events.Event;

    public class Bubble extends Sprite {

        private var _speed:Number = 1;

        public function Bubble() {
            addEventListener(Event.ENTER_FRAME, enterFrame);
        }

        public function set speed(s:Number):void {
            _speed = s;
        }

        private function enterFrame(e:Event):void {
            y -= _speed;
            if(y < -(height / 2))
            {
                y = stage.stageHeight + (height / 2) +
                    (height * Math.random());
                x = -(width / 2) +
                    ((stage.stageWidth + width) * Math.random());
            }
        }
    }
}
```

3. Save the class as `Bubble.as` in the same folder as `Main.as`. Move back to your FLA by clicking on its tab.

4. Now you can link your `Bubble` class to each of the bubble movie-clip symbols within your library. Let us start with **Bubble Huge**.

   Move to the **LIBRARY**, right-click on **Bubble Huge**, and select **Properties**.

5. Check the **Export for ActionScript** checkbox from the **Advanced** section within the **Symbol Properties** dialog box. The **Class** field will contain the name of your symbol but with the spaces removed. Within the **Base Class** field, replace the existing text with **Bubble** as shown in the following screenshot:

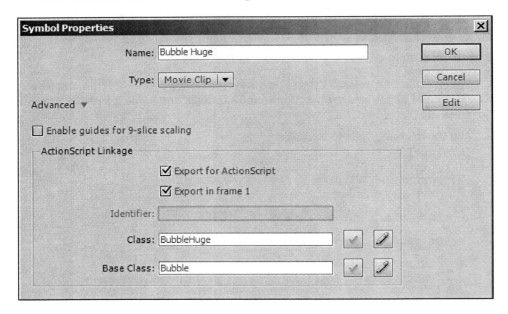

6. Click on the **OK** button near the top-right of the panel.

7. Depending on your preference settings within Flash Professional, a warning panel may appear containing the following text:

   A definition for this class could not be found in the classpath, so one will be automatically generated in the SWF file upon export.

   This is expected. Although you have written code that represents the symbol's base class, you will rely on Flash to generate the code for the symbol's actual class. Click on the **OK** button.

8. Repeat this process linking the `Bubble` class to the following movie-clip symbols: **Bubble Large**, **Bubble Medium**, and **Bubble Small**.

9. Save your FLA and test using ADL. The bubbles that were previously stationary within your app will now drift up the screen.

How it works...

The class' structure is fairly conventional. At its heart is an event handler that gets called every time `Event.ENTER_FRAME` is dispatched by the movie clip. Inside the handler is the logic that controls and updates the clip.

In our case, the class' `enterFrame()` handler is used to update the bubble's position on every frame redraw. If the bubble moves off the top of the screen, then it is randomly repositioned at the bottom, where it can start floating upwards again.

A private member variable named `_speed` has been used to define the number of pixels that the bubble is moved each time `Event.ENTER_FRAME` is dispatched. And although it hasn't yet been used, a public setter was also added to the class allowing the bubble's vertical speed to be changed using the `speed` property.

Although it won't be noticeable in your demo, excessive usage of the `ENTER_FRAME` event can actually degrade the performance of your iOS apps. We will address this in the next recipe and also tidy up the movement of the bubbles within the demo. At present, the sense of depth is lost due to the fact that the bubbles all travel at the same speed.

There's more...

You may have noticed that your `Bubble` class actually extends `Sprite` rather than `MovieClip`. The following is the reason.

Extending sprite

Although the bubbles within the library are actually movie clips, the `Bubble` class inherits from `flash.display.Sprite` rather than `flash.display.MovieClip`.

It is perfectly acceptable to extend `MovieClip`, but considering that the bubble library symbols only use a single frame from their timeline, it is actually unnecessary. You are only required to extend `MovieClip` if you intend to navigate the clip's timeline; otherwise the functionality provided by `Sprite` will do and has less overhead.

Using an update loop

Listening for events can be expensive. For a handler to receive an event, Flash must create an object in memory that represents that event. Repeatedly allocating memory can hurt the performance of your app, and this is especially true if you are listening for `Event.ENTER_FRAME` from a large number of display objects.

Let us see how to minimize the impact of handling multiple `ENTER_FRAME` events by making some adjustments to the architecture of your example app. We will also add some additional code to individually control the speed of each bubble, making the app a little more polished.

How to do it...

You will be required to make code changes to both `Main.as` and `Bubble.as`:

1. First start by opening `Bubble.as`.

2. Within the constructor, remove the highlighted line of code that listens for `Event.ENTER_FRAME`:

```
public function Bubble() {
    addEventListener(Event.ENTER_FRAME, enterFrame);
}
```

3. Change the `enterFrame()` method's signature by renaming it to `update()` and removing its `Event` parameter. Also make it publicly accessible:

```
public function update():void {
    y -= _speed;
    if(y < -(height / 2))
    {
        y = stage.stageHeight + (height / 2) +
            (height * Math.random());
        x = -(width / 2) +
            ((stage.stageWidth + width) * Math.random());
    }
}
```

4. Remove the `Event` class import statement as it is no longer required:

```
import flash.events.Event;
```

5. Save the class and move to `Main.as`.

6. Add the following two member variables to `Main.as`:

```
private var bubbles:Array;
private var speeds:Array;
```

7. Within the class' constructor, populate both the `bubbles` and `speeds` arrays. The `bubbles` array will contain references to each of the bubble instances sitting on your FLA's stage. The `speeds` array will contain a vertical speed to be used for each bubble instance:

```
bubbles = [bubble1, bubble2, bubble3, bubble4, bubble5,
            bubble6, bubble7, bubble8, bubble9];
speeds = [1.3, 1.5, 1.8, 2, 2.2, 2.4, 4.5, 5, 8];
```

8. Now staying within the constructor, add some code to walk through the `bubbles` array, setting the vertical speed of each bubble using a value from the `speeds` array:

```
for(var i:uint = 0; i < bubbles.length; i++)
{
    bubbles[i].speed = speeds[i];
}
```

In the preceding code snippet, note the use of the `speed` property that was added to the `Bubble` class in the preceding recipe, _Linking classes to movie-clip symbols_.

9. Listen for the `ENTER_FRAME` event by placing the following statement at the end of the constructor:

```
addEventListener(Event.ENTER_FRAME, update);
```

10. At the end of the `exiting()` handler, add a line of code to remove the `Event.ENTER_FRAME` listener:

```
removeEventListener(Event.ENTER_FRAME, update);
```

11. Finally, add to the class an event handler for `Event.ENTER_FRAME`, which calls each bubble instance's `update()` method:

```
private function update(e:Event):void {
    for each(var b:Bubble in bubbles)
    {
        b.update();
    }
}
```

12. Save the class.

13. Test `bubbles.fla` using ADL.

When publishing, you may receive a list of compiler errors similar to the following:

1120: Access of undefined property bubble1.

Typically this occurs when Flash has not been instructed to automatically declare member variables within your class for each display object instance on the stage.

You can rectify this from the **Advanced ActionScript 3.0 Settings** panel by checking on the **Automatically declare stage instances** checkbox.

The bubbles will now move in a much more convincing manner, with those closest travelling faster than those at a distance. More importantly, the application's architecture has been changed, removing the need to listen for and handle multiple ENTER_FRAME events per frame.

14. Update your app's version number to **0.3** from the **AIR for iOS Settings** panel and publish it.

15. Deploy the resultant .ipa file to your device and test it.

How it works...

Rather than having every bubble instance listen for and handle its own ENTER_FRAME event, we now have only one listener that makes update() calls to each of the bubbles.

Essentially the update() method within the document class acts as a main loop for the application. Every object that needs to be updated has its own update() method that is called from the document class' main loop.

The following is the main update loop again:

```
private function update(e:Event):void {
  for each(var b:Bubble in bubbles)
  {
    b.update();
  }
}
```

The `bubbles` array was used in this example as a convenient mechanism to reference each bubble instance that required updating. You can see it being used in the main loop.

The advantages of using a centralized update loop within your application cannot be over emphasized. The performance benefits may not be obvious in this chapter's example app, but for more complex projects, this technique will help when trying to achieve consistent and high frame rates, especially on older devices.

Including an application launch image

Every iOS app can have a static launch image bundled with it. This will be shown to the user while the app loads.

Let us add a launch image to our example app.

How to do it...

We will continue from the *Using an update loop* recipe. If you haven't completed it, then you can work from `chapter3\recipe7\bubbles.fla` from the book's accompanying code bundle.

1. Using Windows Explorer or Finder, copy `chapter3\resources\Default.png` to the same folder as your FLA.

2. Revisit the AIR for iOS Settings panel by selecting **File | AIR for iOS Settings** from Flash's drop-down menu.

3. If it isn't already selected, click on the panel's **General** tab.

4. At the bottom of the panel is the **Included files** list. Click on the **+** symbol above the list and select **Default.png** from your FLA's root folder. Click on **OK** to select the file. You should now see **Default.png** in the **Included files** list.

5. Change the app's **Version** field to **0.4**.

6. Now click on **OK** to close the **AIR for iOS Settings** panel.

7. Save the FLA.

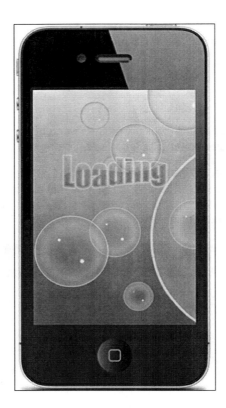

Publish and deploy the latest version of the app to your iOS device. As shown in the preceding screenshot, you should see the launch image while the app loads.

How it works...

The `Default.png` file is a 24-bit 320x480 PNG image that matches the initial visual state of the Bubbles app. Additionally, text has been superimposed onto the image to inform the user that the app is loading. Once the app's binary has been completely loaded, iOS will remove it from view and run the application. The switch between the launch image and the first frame of your app will be seamless.

It is important that your file is named `Default.png`, with an uppercase D, as iOS will look for this exact filename when loading your app. If your image cannot be found or one wasn't included, then a black screen will be shown while the app loads.

You should also ensure that `Default.png` is copied to the same folder as your FLA.

There's more...

Adding a launch image to your app isn't difficult but there are additional options to consider when supporting multiple iOS devices, screen resolutions, and orientations.

Landscape orientation

For iPhone and iPod touch applications that have been designed for landscape, you still embed a 320x480 PNG, but ensure that the image is provided in that orientation.

Supporting the Retina display

For iOS devices with Retina display screens, you can bundle with your IPA an additional launch image that takes advantage of the higher resolution. Simply create a 640x960 PNG file and name it `Default@2x.png`. When loading on a device that supports the Retina display, `Default@2x.png` will be used as the launch image rather than `Default.png`.

iPad launch images

Unlike the iPhone and iPod touch, an iOS app running on iPad can select from multiple launch images depending on its orientation. This is done by bundling a series of PNGs with the app, each with an orientation modifier string in the filename.

For example, if the user is holding the device in a portrait orientation when the app is launched, iOS will look for a PNG named `Default-Portrait.png`. When held in landscape, iOS will attempt to display `Default-Landscape.png`. The dimensions for `Default-Portrait.png` should be 768x1024, while `Default-Landscape.png` should be 1024x768.

It is even possible to specify an upside-down portrait version of the launch image by including a PNG named `Default-PortraitUpsideDown.png`. This will take precedence over `Default-Portrait.png` if both exist.

Similarly, additional control when the device is being held in a landscape orientation can be obtained by bundling images named `Default-LandscapeLeft.png` and `Default-LandscapeRight.png`. Both will take precedence over `Default-Landscape.png` if it too exists.

If no PNGs with an orientation modifier are found, then `Default.png` will be used.

Universal apps

It is possible to embed a range of launch images that cover the various screen resolutions and aspect ratios across all iOS device types. As an example, consider a universal app that can take advantage of the iPhone's standard and Retina screen resolutions, as well as both portrait and landscape orientations on iPad. Embedding images named `Default.png`, `Default@2x.png`, `Default-Portrait.png`, and `Default-Landscape.png` would cover this.

Using the status bar

If you plan to include the status bar in your app, then there is no need to reduce the size of your launch image. The status bar consumes 20 vertical pixels (40 pixels on Retina display screens) and will simply be placed over the top of your image while your app loads. The status bar also consumes 20 vertical pixels on iPad.

Bundling other files

In this recipe, we bundled a launch image with our app by adding it to the AIR for iOS Settings panel's **Included files** list. From this panel, you can also include other files or folders that will be bundled with your app and can even be loaded at runtime using ActionScript. Like the launch image, other files and folders to be added must exist within your FLA's root folder.

See also

> ▶ *Targeting a device, Chapter 8*

Including icons

Our app looks almost complete. The most obvious omission is the icon artwork, which we will now add.

How to do it...

Icons are added from the AIR for iOS Settings panel.

1. Move to the **AIR for iOS Settings** panel and click on the **Icons** tab.

    From here you can bundle various icons with your app. The icon types are listed at the top of the panel.

2. From the list, click on **icon 29x29**. The field directly below the icon list will be relabeled **29x29**. To the right of this field is a browse icon. Click on it as shown in the following screenshot. Browse to and select `chapter3\resources\icon29.png`.

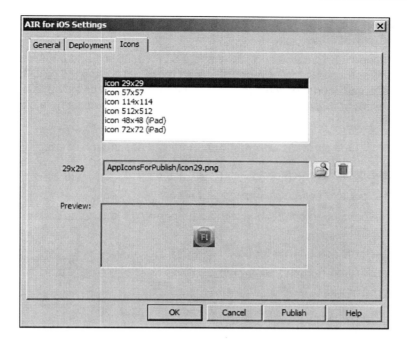

3. A dialog box will appear containing the following message:

   The icon must be copied to a folder relative to the root content folder so that it can be published. Do you want to proceed?

   Click on **OK** and a sub-folder named `AppIconsForPublish` will be created in the same location as your FLA. The icon you selected will be copied to this new location.

4. Now select **icon 57x57** from the list and browse to `chapter3\resources\ icon57.png`. Again you will be asked if you would like the icon copied to a folder relative to the root content folder. Click on the **OK** button.

5. Work your way through the remaining icons on the list, adding the appropriate PNG from the `resources` folder.

6. Once you have added the icons, click on the panel's **General** tab and update the **Version** field to **0.5**.

7. Click on **OK** to exit the **AIR for iOS Settings** panel.

Publish and deploy the latest version of the app to your device. Your app should now be represented by an icon in iTunes and on the device.

How it works...

All icon artwork should be created and saved as 24-bit PNGs. Don't add a reflective shine, rounded corners, or drop shadow to your artwork as these will be applied by iOS. Also, considering the largest icon that you add is 512x512 pixels, it makes sense to design your original icon artwork at this size at least; you don't want to have to scale up a smaller version for this.

You can actually include six icons with your app. Here is a description of each:

- 29x29—Spotlight search results icon for iPhone 3GS
- 48x48—Spotlight search results icon for iPad
- 57x57—Spotlight search results icon for iPhone 4/4S and home screen icon for iPhone 3GS
- 72x72—Home screen icon for iPad
- 114x114—Home screen icon for iPhone 4/4S
- 512x512—iTunes icon

 Flash Professional CS5 does not support the Retina display resolution and, therefore, does not permit the inclusion of a 114x114 icon for the iPhone 4/4S home screen. The 57x57 icon will be used instead.

The iPhone 3GS icons will also work on a third-generation iPod touch, and the iPhone 4/4S icons will work on a fourth-generation iPod touch.

Although the Bubbles app only utilizes the standard resolution of 320x480, this doesn't prevent you from bundling alternative icons for higher resolution screens such as the iPhone 4/4S and iPad.

Also, the iTunes icon is for development purposes only. When submitting your final app to the App Store, you submit the 512x512 icon separately as a JPEG file. It isn't included in the final `.ipa` file. While you should ensure that the iTunes icon is recognizable as your application icon, it is perfectly acceptable to make it richer and more detailed in appearance. Additionally, visual effects, such as the reflective shine, are not added to this icon.

As for the design of your icon artwork, Apple's **iOS Human Interface Guidelines** stresses the importance of strong visual design in order to create an instantly recognizable icon. It is important that your icon somehow conveys your application's purpose. Also avoid using text and remember that your icon will be viewed at various sizes. It is advisable that you use a vector format when designing as this will allow the icon to scale without loss of fidelity before outputting each of the required bitmap versions.

Editing the application descriptor file

Included with your FLA is the application descriptor file. It is an XML file that contains settings used when publishing AIR applications. This file also contains properties that describe your iOS application including those set within the AIR for iOS Settings panel. The application descriptor file can be edited to make changes that can't be directly set from within Flash Professional's various setting panels.

Let us alter the application descriptor file to remove the reflective shine that iOS applies to the Bubbles app's icons.

Getting ready

For this recipe, work from your current version of the Bubbles app, or alternatively use the FLA provided with the accompanying code bundle at `chapter3\recipe9\bubbles.fla`.

Flash Professional writes to the application descriptor file when you make changes from the AIR for iOS Settings panel. If you have the AIR for iOS Settings panel open, then close it before attempting to edit the application descriptor file from an external text editor.

How to do it...

You can also open and edit the application descriptor file from within Flash, which is what we will do:

1. Select **File | Open** (*Ctrl + O | Cmd + O*) and select **bubbles-app.xml**.

2. Scroll down the XML file until you find the following XML fragment:

```
<iPhone>
  <InfoAdditions>
    <![CDATA[<key>UIDeviceFamily</key>
          <array><string>1</string></array>]]>
  </InfoAdditions>
```

3. The CDATA node is where you can add additional iOS settings information. Go ahead and add the following key-value pair to the XML:

```
<iPhone>
  <InfoAdditions>
    <![CDATA[<key>UIDeviceFamily</key>
          <array><string>1</string></array>
          <key>UIPrerenderedIcon</key><true/>]]>
  </InfoAdditions>
```

4. Save the file.

5. Move to your FLA and from the **AIR for iOS Settings** panel, update its **Version** field to **0.6**.

Publish the FLA and deploy the new `.ipa` file to your device. Your app's home screen icon should no longer have a reflective shine applied to it.

How it works...

The application descriptor file is named using the name of your output SWF and takes the following format: `<swf_name>-app.xml`. By default, the output SWF name is identical to your FLA's name.

All iOS specific settings can be found within the XML file's `<iPhone>` node. Within the `<iPhone>` node is the `<infoAdditions>` node where you can set any custom iOS settings by adding key-value pairs. These key-value pairs should be placed within a CDATA tag.

During the recipe, you added the following key-value pair in order to disable the icon's reflective shine:

```
<key>UIPrerenderedIcon</key><true/>
```

You can just as easily re-enable the shine by changing the value to `<false/>` or simply removing the key-value pair completely. Before proceeding, change the value back and re-compile your app. Unless you have a very good reason, you really should keep the default reflective shine enabled.

Although you apply these iOS specific settings to the application descriptor file, it is specific to AIR applications and isn't understood by iOS. Instead, when you publish your FLA, Flash generates and includes with your IPA a configuration file that can be understood by iOS. This is known as the **Information Property List** file, which by convention is named `Info.plist`, and contains many properties used to describe your app, including any custom properties you set.

You can find more information regarding the Information Property List and the properties that can be set by visiting Apple's iOS Developer Library at `http://developer.apple.com/library/ios/#documentation/general/Reference/InfoPlistKeyReference/Articles/AboutInformationPropertyListFiles.html`.

There's more...

Although we have only used the application descriptor file to remove the icon's reflective shine, there are many more configuration options. Another option that is commonly used, and has been touched upon already within this and the previous chapter, is the status bar and its appearance.

Status bar style

On iPhone and iPod touch, the appearance of the status bar can be changed; the status bar cannot be changed on iPad and is always black. Although you can specify whether or not the status bar should be shown within your app, Flash does not provide any options for controlling the appearance. If you decide to use the status bar, you can add the `UIStatusBarStyle` key to the application descriptor file in order to set one of the following three styles supported by iOS:

- `UIStatusBarStyleDefault`—The default gray status bar
- `UIStatusBarStyleBlackOpaque`—Opaque black status bar
- `UIStatusBarStyleTranslucent`—Black status bar with 50% transparency

To opt for the opaque black status bar, add the following key-value pair to the application descriptor file:

```
<key>UIStatusBarStyle</key>
<string>UIStatusBarStyleBlackOpaque</string>
```

Try both `UIStatusBarStyleBlackOpaque` and `UIStatusBarStyleTranslucent`. Your options are a little limited but they can come in handy for certain apps where the default status bar doesn't visually sit with the design. If you want to use the default status bar, then there is no need to explicitly add a key-value pair to the application descriptor file.

See also

- *Specifying a persistent Wi-Fi connection, Chapter 13*
- *Declaring device capabilities, Chapter 13*

Remote debugging

Debugging is a critical aspect of the development process. Flash Professional allows you to send debug information from the device directly to the Flash IDE for inspection.

With the example Bubbles app now complete, we will finish off this chapter by learning how to deploy a debug build and receive trace data from it using Flash Professional's remote debugger.

Getting ready

We will be adding a line of ActionScript to the document class of the Bubbles app that you created throughout the course of this and the previous chapter. Alternatively, from the book's accompanying code bundle, open `chapter3\recipe10\bubbles.fla` within Flash Professional and work from there.

How to do it...

The debug process is split into two main steps:

- Creating a debug build
- Connecting to the Remote Debugger

Let us begin by creating a debug build that contains a single trace statement.

Creating a debug build

Follow these steps:

1. If you haven't already done so, open the document class by selecting **File | Open** (*Ctrl + O | Cmd + O*) from Flash Professional's drop-down menu. From the file browser, select `Main.as`.

2. Add a simple `trace()` statement at the beginning of the class' constructor:

   ```
   public function Main() {
       trace("Inside the constructor.");
   ```

3. Save your changes and move back to your FLA by clicking on its tab.

4. Open the AIR for iOS Settings panel by selecting **File | AIR for iOS Settings** from the drop-down menu.

5. From the settings panel, ensure the **General** tab is selected and update the **Version** field to **0.7**. Now move to the **Deployment** tab and select **Quick publishing for device debugging** from the **iOS deployment type** section.

6. Click on **OK** and save your FLA.

7. Now publish your FLA for iOS by selecting **File | Publish** (*Alt + Shift + F12 | Shift + Cmd + F12*) and install the IPA on your device.

Connecting to the Remote Debugger

Before launching the app, you will need to carry out the following actions in order to receive debug information from it:

1. Connect your device to your Wi-Fi network.

2. Obtain your development computer's IP address.

3. Begin a Remote Debug session from the Flash IDE.

Let us walk through these steps in detail:

1. Remote debugging takes place over Wi-Fi. Verify that your device is connected to the same network as your development computer by selecting **Settings | Wi-Fi** from the device's home screen. If it is not, then select the correct network from the **Choose a Network** section. This is shown in the screenshot on the following page.

2. You will also need to know the IP address of the computer you are running Flash Professional from. If you are using Microsoft Windows, then open a command prompt window and enter the following:

    ```
    ipconfig
    ```

    Network configuration details will be output to the command window. Your computer's IP address consists of four numbers separated by periods and can be found by looking for **IPv4 Address** among the output. The following is an example:

    ```
    IPv4 Address. . . . . . . . . . . : 192.168.0.4
    ```

    For those using Mac OS X, choose **System Preferences** from the Apple menu. In the **System Preferences** window, click on the **Network** icon from the **Internet & Wireless** section. Your IP address will be shown within the **Network** window, underneath the **Status** heading.

    We are now ready to perform remote debugging.

3. First activate Flash's remote debugger by selecting **Debug | Begin Remote Debug Session | ActionScript 3.0** from the drop-down menu. This will switch the IDE to its **DEBUG** workspace with the following message being sent to the **OUTPUT** window:

    ```
    Waiting for Player to connect...
    ```

    Essentially the Flash IDE is now ready to receive debug information from your debug app and will wait for up to two minutes for the app to connect to it.

 If it is not already available from the debug workspace, then open the **OUTPUT** window by selecting **Window | Output** (*F2*) from Flash's drop-down menu.

4. Now, move back to your device's home screen and launch the app.

5. The app will attempt to automatically connect to the Flash IDE. However, if it fails, a **Flash Debugger** dialog box will appear, similar to the preceding screenshot, asking you to enter the IP address of the computer it should connect to. If prompted, enter your development computer's IP address and tap on **OK** to connect.

6. Upon a successful connection, the name of the app's .swf file will be sent to the Flash IDE's **OUTPUT** window followed by any trace statements that are executed. For this recipe, the following will be output:

    ```
    [SWF] bubbles.swf - 327469 bytes after decompression
    Inside the constructor.
    ```

    As you can see, the message from your constructor's trace() statement has been sent to the output window.

7. Now, terminate the debug session by selecting **Debug | End Debug Session** (*Alt + F12*) from Flash Professional's drop-down menu. The Flash IDE will move back to the workspace you were using previously.

How it works...

Remote debugging is invaluable for identifying and fixing bugs and should be familiar to experienced Flash developers. Using the `trace()` statement, you can send information from your app to the Flash IDE's **OUTPUT** window.

When debugging, remember to select the **Quick publishing for device debugging** deployment type from the **AIR for iOS Settings** panel. It is also important that both your test device and development computer are connected to the same network. Although your device may be connected to your computer through its USB cable, remote debugging only works over Wi-Fi for AIR for iOS applications.

This recipe focused on the `trace()` statement, but remote debugging for iOS supports additional features including breakpoint control, stepping through code, and the monitoring of variables. These advanced debugging features are unfortunately out of the scope of this book. However, a comprehensive introduction to the ActionScript 3.0 debugger is available from the Adobe Flash Developer Center at `www.adobe.com/devnet/flash/articles/as3_debugger.html`.

There's more...

With any luck, your app will successfully connect to the remote debug session. However, if you are experiencing problems connecting then read on.

Remote connection attempts

A debug build of your app will attempt to connect, by default, to your development computer's IP address. If the connection attempt fails, then you will be asked to manually enter the correct IP address. Unfortunately, apps published using older versions of AIR can wait for up to one minute before giving up and prompting for an IP address, which is hardly ideal when rapidly deploying and testing new debug builds.

During this time, the screen will remain blank and your iOS device may eventually auto-lock if left untouched. If locked, you may miss the app's prompt for the correct IP address, which will lead to your debug session timing out.

To prevent this from happening, consider increasing the auto-lock time on your iOS device by selecting **Settings | General | Auto-Lock** from the home screen.

Those using Flash Professional CS5.5 and the latest version of AIR are unlikely to experience such lengthy timeout periods.

4
Porting Flash Projects to iOS

In this chapter, we will cover:

- ► Handling user interaction
- ► Saving application state
- ► Flattening the display list
- ► Converting vectors to bitmaps
- ► Resizing bitmaps
- ► Masking content
- ► Working with external SWFs

Introduction

Apple prohibits the installation of third-party plugins on iOS, preventing Safari or any other browser from running Flash content. Unfortunately, this prevents those using iOS devices from accessing the thousands of popular web-based Flash games and applications that are out there.

Until recently, the growing popularity of iOS had left Flash developers, who were wishing to deliver their existing content to Apple's platform, in a difficult position. The only realistic solution was to completely rewrite their projects for iOS using Objective-C, while continuing to maintain the existing ActionScript codebase for web users on other platforms.

However, one of the primary advantages of AIR for iOS is that developers can re-publish their existing Flash-enabled content as native iOS apps while leaving much of the project's codebase untouched. Adobe's multi-platform goal for the Flash Platform has meant that Flash developers can target iOS while using the same development environment that they are comfortable with.

This chapter will take you through recipes that will aid you when porting existing Flash projects to the iOS platform. These should get you started on the right foot and help you grow in confidence as you continue to work with AIR for iOS. And remember, what you will learn here isn't just applicable when porting existing content; you should also apply the same techniques and principles to any new applications you plan to create.

Of course, this chapter alone won't guarantee that your Flash projects can be successfully ported, but the recipes selected should give you a flavor of what is required if you are to succeed. The limitations of mobile platforms can make development daunting. However, as your knowledge of AIR for iOS grows, so will your ability to identify areas within your applications that can be optimized to fit those constraints.

Handling user interaction

Mouse interaction allows a level of accuracy that is impossible to achieve with a finger. Take for example a simple button within a menu screen. With a mouse, the user will be able to make a selection with almost pixel-perfect precision. A finger, however, obscures parts of the screen, including the item being selected, and also makes contact with a larger area.

If your existing Flash applications are designed primarily for mouse interaction, then you will need to redesign your user interface to accommodate touch. The most beneficial changes you can make are to increase the size of your buttons and create larger hit targets around them.

Getting ready

An FLA has been provided as a starting point for this recipe.

If you haven't already done so, download this book's code bundle from its companion website.

Open `chapter4\recipe1\recipe.fla` into Flash Professional.

Within its library are bitmaps that you will use to create a button. Also, its AIR for iOS settings have already been applied, saving you the time and effort when you eventually need to build and deploy the recipe to a device.

Going forward, a starting FLA will be provided for all recipes, with the majority of AIR for iOS settings for each being pre-configured.

How to do it...

We will split this recipe into two parts. First we will create a movie clip representing the button, before writing and linking a custom class to it.

Creating the button movie clip

Let us start by creating the movie clip:

1. Select **Insert | New Symbol** (*Ctrl + F8 | Cmd + F8*). From the **Create New Symbol** panel, enter `Start Button` into the **Name** field and select **Movie Clip** from the **Type** field's drop-down box. Click on the **OK** button.

    An empty movie-clip symbol will be created within the library and you will be moved to its timeline.

2. Drag the **button-normal.png** bitmap from the library to the stage. From the **Properties** panel, expand the **POSITION AND SIZE** section and position the bitmap at (0, 0).

3. Click on frame 2 of the timeline and select **Insert | Timeline | Blank Keyframe**. Also drag **button-select.png** from the library to the stage and position it at (0,0).

4. Create a new layer on the timeline by selecting **Insert | Timeline | Layer** from Flash Professional's drop-down menu. The layer will be named **Layer 2** by default and will sit on top of **Layer 1**.

5. From the **Tools** panel, select the **Rectangle Tool** (**R**). On **Layer 2**, draw a rectangle that has a width of 290 pixels and a height of 77 pixels. Position it at (-28,-14). The rectangle should span across both frames of the timeline and represents the button's hit region.

6. Finally, select the rectangle by double-clicking on it, then from the **Properties** panel set the alpha for both the rectangle's fill and stroke to **0%**, making it invisible.

You should now have a button movie clip that has a timeline identical to the following screenshot:

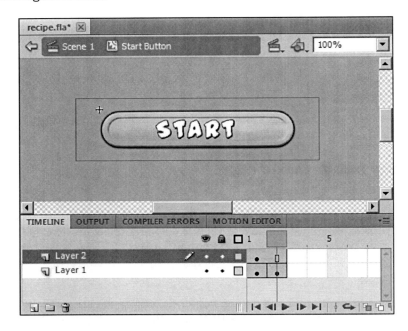

7. Move out of the **Start Button** movie-clip symbol and back to your FLA's root timeline.

8. Save the FLA.

Linking a class to the button

With the button's visual taken care of, it is time to add some interactivity using ActionScript:

1. Select **File | New** and create a new **ActionScript 3.0 Class**. Name the class as `Button`.

2. Add the following code to the class:

```
package {
  import flash.display.MovieClip;
  import flash.events.MouseEvent;

  public class Button extends MovieClip {

    public function Button() {
      addEventListener(MouseEvent.ROLL_OVER, touched);
      addEventListener(MouseEvent.ROLL_OUT, released);
      gotoAndStop(1);
    }
```

```
        private function touched(e:MouseEvent):void {
          gotoAndStop(2);
        }

        private function released(e:MouseEvent):void {
          gotoAndStop(1);
        }
      }
    }
```

3. Save the class as `Button.as` to the same location as your FLA.

4. Move back to your FLA. Now you can link the class to your button.

5. Within the **Library**, right-click on the **Start Button** movie-clip symbol and select **Properties**. Check on the **Export for ActionScript** checkbox. Enter `StartButton` into the **Class** field and `Button` into the **Base Class** field. Click on the **OK** button. Flash will inform you that a definition for the `StartButton` class will be generated. Click on the **OK** button.

6. Now, drag an instance of the **Start Button** movie-clip symbol from the **Library** onto the stage. Position it at (43,217).

7. Test your FLA using ADL (*Ctrl + Enter | Cmd + Enter*) to ensure that there are no compiler errors.

8. Finally publish your app for iOS.

The FLA will be compiled and a file named `c4-r1.ipa` will be created. Deploy the file to your device and test it.

> The remaining recipes within this book will follow a convention for the naming of their IPA file. The IPA's name will contain the chapter number that the recipe belongs to, followed by the recipe's position within the chapter.
>
> For example, this recipe belongs to Chapter 4 (c4) and is the chapter's first recipe (r1). Therefore, the IPA file generated by this recipe's FLA will be named `c4-r1.ipa`. To ensure you can easily find your installed apps on your device, each app's name will reflect that of the IPA. You will find the preceding recipe's example app listed on your home screen as `c4 r1`.

How it works...

With some simple timeline work and a small amount of ActionScript, you have constructed a two-state button that is suitable for use on an iOS device.

Being large in size and having a generous rectangular hit target makes the button an easy target. Even those who operate their device with one hand and make selections with their thumb should have no problems.

The `Button.as` class simply manages the timeline movement between the button's two states. When not being pressed, the first frame of the timeline is shown. When the user's finger touches the button, the second frame of its timeline is shown. Its state is also updated in response to the user's finger rolling onto or out of the button.

A strong user experience is vital to the success of your app. When porting your existing Flash projects to iOS, spend the necessary time adapting your buttons and other UI elements to the platform.

There's more...

The following are a few more points of interest regarding user interaction.

Re-using the button class

You can re-use the class provided with this recipe, linking it to any button within the library of your own projects. The class simply updates your button's visual state but you can easily add an event listener to any of your button instances in order to respond to a successful user selection.

As a quick example, name the button instance on your stage as `startButton`. Now, create a document class for your FLA. Name the class `Main` and add the following code to it:

```
package {
  import flash.display.MovieClip;
  import flash.events.MouseEvent;

  public class Main extends MovieClip {
    public function Main() {
      startButton.addEventListener(MouseEvent.MOUSE_UP,
        buttonPressed);
    }

    private function buttonPressed(e:MouseEvent):void {
      startButton.visible = false;
    }
  }
}
```

The code above simply listens for the `startButton` instance dispatching a `MouseEvent.MOUSE_UP` event. When it does, the `buttonPressed()` handler is called, which hides the button from view. Of course, for your own applications you will add your own functionality to the handler.

Handling keyboard controls

As well as mouse interaction, many Flash-enabled projects designed for the web expect the presence of a physical keyboard to control the application in some way or form. While iOS devices do support a virtual keyboard, it is only present when a text field is being edited. Your application should not rely on keyboard events as a control mechanism. You may need to redesign how users interact with the app before porting it to iOS.

See also

▸ *Linking classes to movie-clip symbols, Chapter 3*

▸ *Creating a basic document class, Chapter 3*

Saving application state

When writing applications for iOS, you should anticipate that the app may at any point be closed. This can happen for a number of reasons such as the user deliberately exiting from the app, an incoming call being received, or iOS closing the app due to memory constraints.

When an app is closed unexpectedly, the user will expect it to resume from its previous state when they eventually return to it. For any Flash projects you are porting to iOS, it is important you add functionality to save the app's state at convenient points throughout its lifetime.

This recipe will take you through the steps required to maintain the state of an application. We will use Flash's `SharedObject` class to save data locally to your device.

Getting ready

From the book's accompanying code bundle, open `chapter4\recipe2\recipe.fla` into Flash Professional.

On the stage, you will find a dynamic text field, and a movie clip that represents a button. A minimal document class has been written that increments a counter every time the button is pressed and shows its value within the text field.

The movie clip's library symbol is linked to a class named `Button`, which was introduced in the previous recipe, Handling user interaction.

Test the application using ADL (*Ctrl + Enter | Cmd + Enter*). Increment the counter a few times by clicking on the button and then close the window. If you test the application again, then you will notice that the counter has reset to zero—the application does not yet remember its state.

The document class, `Main.as`, can be found in the same location as the FLA. Open it and familiarize yourself with the code.

A `MOUSE_UP` event listener has been added to the button on the stage. Its handler function simply increments a `counter` member variable and then writes the value to the dynamic text field.

Let us update the document class to allow it to manage your application's state.

How to do it...

You will require the use of the `SharedObject` class for this recipe.

1. Within `Main.as` add an import statement for it:

   ```
   import flash.net.SharedObject;
   ```

2. Declare a member variable that will be used to store a reference to the shared object:

   ```
   private var so:SharedObject;
   ```

3. Now, add a private method that either initializes the shared object or retrieves any data already stored by it:

   ```
   private function initSharedObject():void {
     so = SharedObject.getLocal("savedData");
     if(so.data.counter == null)
     {
       so.data.counter = counter;
     }
     else
     {
       counter = so.data.counter;
     }
   }
   ```

4. Make a call to `initSharedObject()` within the constructor:

   ```
   public function Main() {
     initSharedObject();
     counterField.text = String(counter);
     btn.addEventListener(MouseEvent.MOUSE_UP, buttonPressed);
   }
   ```

5. Add a private method that saves the value of the `counter` member variable to the shared object:

   ```
   private function saveSharedObject():void {
     so.data.counter = counter;
     so.flush();
   }
   ```

6. Within the `buttonPressed()` event handler, make a call to the `saveSharedObject()` method:

```
private function buttonPressed(e:MouseEvent):void {
  ++counter;
  counterField.text = String(counter);
  saveSharedObject();
}
```

7. Save your class file.

8. Test your FLA using ADL. When you close the window and re-test the FLA, you will see that the counter's value has been successfully restored.

9. Publish your app for iOS and deploy it to your device. Increment the counter and then close the app. If your device is using iOS 4.0 or above, then you will also need to forcibly kill the app from iOS's app switcher. When you re-launch it, the counter's value will be restored.

 To access the fast app switcher, double-press on the home button. To kill an app, tap and hold its icon until the minus symbol appears at the icon's corner. Tap the minus symbol and the app will be removed from the background. The app switcher is available on devices running iOS 4 or above.

How it works...

A local shared object is a data file that is stored locally on your device. The `SharedObject` class provides an API that can be used to easily save and retrieve data from the file.

Before you can use a shared object, you must obtain a `SharedObject` instance by making a call to the static `getLocal()` method. If the shared object doesn't already exist, then one is created. When you call `getLocal()`, you must pass it a string that is used to name the data file that is written to the device's file system. This was done within the recipe's `initSharedObject()` method:

```
so = SharedObject.getLocal("savedData");
```

Once you have a reference to a `SharedObject` you can add or retrieve attributes through its `data` property. Each attribute represents data you would like to save and can be an object of any ActionScript type including `Array`, `ByteArray`, and `XML`. You can even save an instance of a custom class by first registering it using the `flash.net.registerClassAlias()` package-level function.

We stored the `counter` member variable's value by creating an attribute named `counter` and setting it to the value of the member variable. This was done within our `initSharedObject()` method to initialize the persistent data, and again within `saveSharedObject()` to store the counter's latest value. The following line of code is used to implement this:

```
so.data.counter = counter;
```

It is also useful to know if your shared object contains data or has just been created. You can determine this by simply checking for the existence of one of your known attributes. This was done within `initSharedObject()` where we checked to see if the `counter` attribute was `null`. If it was, then we set it to the `counter` member variable's current default value; otherwise we used the stored value to actually set the `counter` member variable. The following is the code again as a reminder:

```
so = SharedObject.getLocal("savedData");
if(so.data.counter == null)
{
   so.data.counter = counter;
}
else
{
   counter = so.data.counter;
}
```

Setting attributes within the data object doesn't actually save them. You must explicitly do this by making a call to the `flush()` method, which was done within our `saveSharedObject()` method.

Making calls to `flush()` can be expensive as data must be written to the file system. For this recipe's example code, it is acceptable to repeatedly make calls to `flush()` when the application's state changes. However, for real-world apps, you should attempt to save data as often as possible but without degrading the performance of your app. Try to find convenient moments to save, for example, between levels or during periods of user inactivity.

For more information regarding the `SharedObject` class, perform a search for `flash.net.SharedObject` within Adobe Community Help.

See also

▸ *Handling multitasking, Chapter 3*

▸ *Exiting gracefully from an app, Chapter 3*

Flattening the display list

Flash's drawing tools and rendering engine makes it convenient to create a deeply nested display list. When examining artwork created in Flash, it is fairly common to have to drill down into the top-level clip for several levels and navigate through a complex hierarchical structure until you find your target display object.

Unfortunately, while a desktop computer will be able to easily render complex scenes, the same content running on an iOS device may degrade performance. Deeply nested display lists also cause long event chains that can further hurt the performance. A touch event, for example, must traverse the display list in order to determine the display objects that are to receive the event.

When porting to iOS, rendering is often the biggest performance bottleneck. Consider flattening your display list in order to keep your application's frame rate as high as possible.

We will see how this is done by completely flattening an example nested display list.

Getting ready

From the book's accompanying code bundle, open `chapter4\recipe3\recipe.fla` into Flash Professional.

The FLA's scene should look familiar. It is the same content that was used in *Chapter 2* and *3*'s example Bubbles application, except the assets in this FLA have been arranged in a hierarchical structure.

At the top level is a single container movie clip named `bubbles` that holds all the bubble clips. Within `bubbles` are four additional container clips named `small`, `medium`, `large`, and `huge`. These containers are used to store collections of bubbles by size. For example, all the small bubbles are held inside the `small` container.

The following diagram shows the full hierarchy:

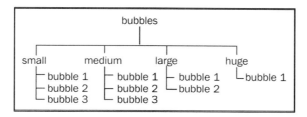

Explore the display list within Flash Professional. It isn't too dissimilar to how scenes are constructed in most Flash-based websites and games.

Let us now flatten this display list by breaking apart movie clips.

How to do it...

Ensure you are on the root timeline and walk through the following steps:

1. Using the **Selection Tool (V)**, click on the `bubbles` movie clip that is sitting on the stage.

2. Select **Modify | Break Apart** (*Ctrl + B | Cmd + B*).

   The `small`, `medium`, `large`, and `huge` movie clips will now be ungrouped from `bubbles`, which will now have been removed from the display list.

3. Select the `small` movie clip container by clicking on any of the small bubbles sitting on the stage. Now select **Modify | Break Apart** (*Ctrl + B | Cmd + B*) to break apart the `small` movie clip container, ungrouping the **Bubble Small** instances that are held within it.

4. Repeat the previous step to break apart the `medium`, `large`, and `huge` container clips.

5. You will now need to rename each of the bubble instances to ensure they all have unique names. This wasn't a problem when the clips were grouped within containers but now that they all sit on the same level their names need to be unique. Starting with the small bubbles and working your way to the largest, name the movie clip instances `bubble1` to `bubble9`.

6. Finally, remove symbols from the library that are no longer required. To do this, move to the **Library** panel and click on **Select Unused Items** from the panel menu. Right-click on one of the highlighted symbols in the library and select **Delete**. All the highlighted symbols will be removed.

 The library's panel menu is represented by a small icon on the top-right corner of the panel. Clicking it reveals a drop-down list of options.

7. Save your FLA.

How it works...

Breaking apart movie-clip instances is an ideal way to flatten the display list. Of course, you can reduce the display list's depth rather than completely flatten it. How far you want to take it really depends on the performance you are after and the complexity of the scene you wish to render.

Instance naming, however, can become a little trickier. A hierarchical structure allows several clips with the same name to co-exist. For example, both the `small` and `medium` movie clips from this recipe's example contained a clip named `bubble1`. Although both clips shared the same name, they belonged to different parent clips, avoiding a naming conflict. However, once flattened, we were left with several clips sitting on the stage that shared the same name.

If you decide to flatten your display list, then consider carefully the impact this will have on your code. Any target path references will have to be updated and you will need to spend time renaming display object instances to avoid potential naming conflicts. Flattening the display list will also affect the relative x and y position of display objects. However, if the application you are porting requires a consistent and high frame rate, then it may be your only choice, especially when targeting older devices.

Converting vectors to bitmaps

Most Flash projects take full advantage of Flash's vector rendering engine and timeline animation system. Rendering vector content, however, can be computationally expensive, particularly with complex vector shapes that contain a large number of control points, gradients, and alpha transparency.

Although even a modest desktop computer can easily render the vector graphics found in most Flash projects; mobile devices are optimized for bitmap graphics meaning compromises need to be made sometimes. Drawing bitmaps is typically less expensive than vectors.

Where performance is critical, consider converting complex vector artwork into bitmaps. If your project already contains existing vector content, then you can use Flash Professional to produce bitmaps from each library symbol. You can then replace your vector content with the bitmap renditions.

Let us see how this is done.

Getting ready

An FLA has been provided as a starting point for this recipe.

From Flash Professional, open `chapter4\recipe4\recipe.fla` from the book's accompanying code bundle.

You will be working with assets from the previous chapter's example Bubbles application. Although the application previously used bitmaps, the bubble assets within this FLA's library are now represented by vectors.

Inside the **Library** panel, you will find a movie-clip symbol named **Bubble Vector**. This is a master clip that is used and resized within the four bubble types—**Bubble Small**, **Bubble Medium**, **Bubble Large**, and **Bubble Huge**.

We will now use Flash Professional to convert the vector representation of each bubble into a bitmap.

How to do it...

Let us start by converting **Bubble Small** to a bitmap:

1. From the **Library** panel, double-click on **Bubble Small**. This will move you to that symbol's timeline.

2. Select **File | Export | Export Image** from Flash Professional's drop-down menu.

   A file-browser window will appear.

3. Using the browser window, navigate to your FLA's root folder. Within the **Save as type** field, select **PNG** and enter **bubble-small.png** into the **File name** field. Click on the **Save** button.

   An **Export PNG** dialog box will appear providing export options for the PNG that Flash is about to create as shown in the following screenshot:

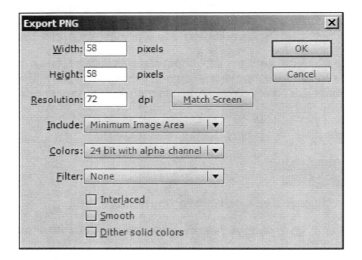

4. For the **Include** field, select **Minimum Image Area** from the drop-down box. Ensure that the **Colors** field is set to **24 bit with alpha channel** and that the **Filter** field is set to **None**. In addition, ensure that the **Smooth** checkbox is unchecked.

5. Click on **OK** to export the PNG.

6. Now, double-click on **Bubble Medium** from the **Library** panel. Again, select **File | Export | Export Image** and enter a file name of **bubble-medium.png**. From the **Export PNG** panel, use the same settings as before.

7. Repeat the process for **Bubble Large** and **Bubble Huge**, exporting them as **bubble-large.png** and **bubble-huge.png** respectively.

How it works...

You now have four bitmap images—one for each bubble—that you can import into your FLA and replace the vector versions with.

The **Graphics Processing Units** (**GPU**) found on mobile devices, such as the iPhone, are optimized for rendering bitmaps; for many situations you should see a significant performance increase if you opt to use bitmaps instead of vectors.

Your bitmap images will also look consistent whether you use CPU or GPU rendering modes, and with the exception of smoothing will remain relatively unaffected by the stage's render quality. This is in stark contrast to vectors, which are affected by both the rendering mode and stage quality.

Using CPU render mode utilizes the same software renderer used by the Flash Player installed on desktop computers and also produces the same high quality results. However, this comes at the cost of performance compared to using the GPU rendering pipeline.

Although fast, rendering vectors using the GPU will always result in an approximation of your source artwork. For fast moving content, this may be acceptable but for stationary objects the differences may be noticeable.

Essentially each rendering path will produce different results when dealing with vectors. CPU rendering is accurate but slower, while the GPU is faster but inaccurate. Both options, however, are typically more computationally expensive than using bitmaps.

Where appropriate, replace your complex vector artwork with bitmaps. However, be aware that bitmaps can significantly increase the size of your final `.ipa` file compared to vectors. The larger your IPA becomes, the longer your app will take to load and the more memory it will consume. Increased memory consumption itself can lead to degradation in performance.

Additionally, Apple currently imposes an over-the-air download limit of 20 MB. It is important your IPA doesn't exceed this limit as it prevents users from downloading your app over carrier networks and may affect sales.

Take a look at `chapter4\recipe4-final\recipe.fla` to see the exported PNGs being used in place of the original vector artwork.

There's more...

Intelligent use of bitmaps is vital in order to maximize the performance of your app. You may find the following options and information helpful in achieving this.

Export as Bitmap

For those using Flash Professional CS5.5, a more convenient option is available that allows you to instruct Flash to export bitmap representations of vector movie clips during publication. This not only provides you with optimized bitmap content for your app but also maintains the original vector artwork within the FLA.

To export a symbol as a bitmap, first select the symbol from the stage. Then from the **Properties** panel, expand the **DISPLAY** section and select **Export as Bitmap** from the **Render** field's drop-down box. If your clip requires transparency, then also ensure that the drop-down box directly beneath is set to **Transparent**.

Export as Bitmap is not available in Flash CS5.

Convert to Bitmap

An additional option named **Convert to Bitmap** is available from Flash Professional CS5.5 that converts vector symbols to bitmaps. Although **Export as Bitmap** does not alter your FLA's display list, this option replaces instances on the stage with a bitmap representation. The new bitmap representation is added to the library allowing you to make further edits using an image editor such as Adobe Photoshop.

To convert a symbol to a bitmap, simply right-click on an instance of it on the stage and select **Convert to Bitmap** from the context menu.

Convert to Bitmap is not available in Flash CS5.

Working with timeline animation

Vector-based timeline animations may further impact performance. This is especially true of complex tweens, which can be extremely expensive operations. On lower-end devices, such as the first and second generation iPhones and iPod touches, even relatively simple tweens can perform poorly. However, with the huge rendering improvements made since AIR 2.6 combined with the ever increasing hardware specification of each new generation of iOS device, this is becoming less of an issue. Remember, Apple itself no longer supports first and second generation devices.

If you are experiencing performance issues with a timeline animation, then consider exporting each frame of your animation as a PNG. Its length will be an important factor as bitmap-based animation can consume considerable memory and increase load time. In such cases you may need to make-do with a vector implementation or consider re-working the animation to make it suitable for mobile.

Targeting multiple screen sizes

The screen resolution varies across iOS devices. For example, the iPhone 3GS has a resolution of 320x480 whereas the iPhone 4 supports 640x960 pixels.

When targeting multiple screen sizes, consider creating different sized versions of your bitmaps—one for each screen resolution. This will avoid image quality degradation due to bitmap scaling and will also prevent any performance issues associated with scaling content.

Creating multiple versions of each bitmap will increase the final file size of your IPA but if performance is a priority, then it is likely to be worth the effort.

If you would rather avoid the overheads of bundling multiple bitmaps within your application, then it is also possible to scale vector artwork at runtime before storing a bitmap representation of it in memory. This technique is know as bitmap caching and is explored in detail in *Chapter 6*.

Pre-rendering filters and blends

Filters are often used in Flash projects to add visual effects such as drop shadows, beveled edges, and blur to display objects. Although filters can add impact to your application, they can seriously affect performance. This is especially true on iOS devices where the CPU speeds are limited compared to desktop computers. Additionally, in Flash Professional CS5.5, filters are no longer supported when using the GPU rendering pipeline.

It is recommended that you pre-render the graphical effects into the artwork, rather than applying filters at runtime using Flash. This will aid device performance and also ensure your effects work across both CPU and GPU rendering modes.

Rather than using an image editor to completely recreate the effects from scratch, you can use Flash Professional to create a bitmap representation of any filters applied to display objects on the stage. There are various ways to do this, including setting the instance's render property to **Export as Bitmap**, converting the whole library clip to a bitmap, or exporting a PNG image before re-importing it into Flash.

Non-normal blend modes are also expensive operations and should be 'baked' into your artwork in a similar fashion to filters.

See also

 ▸ *Adding content to the stage, Chapter 2*

 ▸ *Comparing vector and bitmap graphics, Chapter 6*

 ▸ *Using Cache as Bitmap, Chapter 6*

 ▸ *Targeting the Retina display, Chapter 8*

 ▸ *Supporting multiple resolutions, Chapter 8*

Resizing bitmaps

It is a common occurrence to see scaling being applied to bitmaps unnecessarily within Flash projects. Resizing bitmaps at runtime can be computationally expensive and degrades the image quality. Doing so can also result in a larger IPA file if the included artwork is actually larger than its intended display size.

Let us see how to resize existing bitmap artwork within Flash Professional.

Getting ready

From Flash Professional, open `chapter4\recipe5\recipe.fla` from the book's accompanying code bundle.

Again, you will be working with the familiar visuals from *Chapter 2* and *3*'s example Bubbles application. The assets for this recipe are made up of both vectors and bitmaps. The bubbles themselves are vectors, whereas the background image and the Flash logo are bitmaps. The bitmaps have been scaled to fit the screen. To see the comparison in size between the scaled instances on the stage and the original bitmaps stored in the library, you may want to drag both **background.png** and **flash-logo.png** onto the stage. Delete both from the stage before continuing.

Let us use Flash Professional to resize the bitmaps stored within the library, preventing the need for Flash to do this at runtime.

How to do it...

Resize the bitmaps by following the steps:

1. From the **Library** panel, double-click on **Bubble Huge**. This will move you to that symbol's timeline where you will see an instance of the **Huge Bubble with Logo** symbol.

2. Move inside this symbol by again double-clicking on it.

   On its timeline you will see two layers—**Bubble** and **Logo**. The **Logo** layer contains a bitmap representation of the Flash logo. This clip has been scaled down from 894x894 pixels to 200x200 pixels. Let us create a new version of this bitmap that is already scaled to the correct size.

3. From the **Library**, right-click on **flash-logo.png** and select **Edit with** from the context menu. When prompted, browse to and select an external editor such as Adobe Photoshop.

4. Within your editor, resize the image to 200x200 pixels and save it.

5.   Move back to Flash Professional.

You should now see the new version of the logo within the bubble, however, the logo will now be significantly smaller than the intended size. This is because the scale transformation that was originally applied to the 894x894 version is still being applied to the new bitmap.

6.   Lock the **Bubble** layer and click on the bitmap sitting on the **Logo** layer. From the **Properties** panel, change the width and height settings to the source bitmap's exact dimensions of 200x200.

7.   From the library, double-click on the **Background** movie-clip symbol.

This clip uses a bitmap named **background.png**, which is actually 640x960 pixels scaled down to 320x480. Again let us resize this bitmap within an image editor, preventing the need for it to be scaled within your app at runtime.

8.   Find **background.png** within the library. Right-click on it and select to edit the bitmap using the image editor of your choice. Resize the image to 320x480 and save it.

9.   Move back to Flash Professional. Using the **Selection Tool** (**V**), click on **background. png** sitting within the **Background** movie-clip symbol and set its width to 320 and its height to 480.

10. Save your FLA.

How it works...

You have successfully replaced the FLA's existing bitmaps with new versions that have been pre-rendered to the size they are intended to be viewed at. This will save valuable CPU cycles as there is no need to scale down the bitmaps at runtime. Resizing bitmaps can also reduce the overall size of your SWF significantly as long as those bitmaps were originally being scaled-down at runtime rather than being increased in size.

Take a look at `chapter4\recipe5-final\recipe.fla` to see the resized bitmaps being used in place of the original oversized bitmaps. When running on a more recent device, it may be difficult to notice any discernable difference in performance between the original version (`recipe5\recipe.fla`) and the final version (`recipe5-final\recipe.fla`), but for lower-end devices or more demanding projects, the gains can be significant.

There's more...

The following information will also be of benefit to you when resizing or optimizing assets.

Targeting multiple screen sizes

The screen resolution varies across iOS devices. For example, the iPhone 3GS has a resolution of 320x480 whereas the iPhone 4 supports 640x960 pixels.

When writing apps that target multiple screen sizes, you could be tempted to simply scale your bitmap content at runtime to fit each resolution. If you take this approach, then be aware that you may experience performance issues if your app attempts to render complex scenes at high frame rates. Additionally, the quality of your bitmaps will suffer as they are scaled.

Instead, consider creating different versions of each asset—one for each screen size you wish to support. Of course, having multiple versions of each asset will increase the final file size of your IPA but the end result will likely be worth the effort.

If you must resize your images at runtime, then you can take advantage of hardware acceleration to scale bitmaps with less impact on performance. You can find out more in *Chapter 6*.

Optimizing vector shapes

While this recipe has focused primarily on bitmaps, it is all too easy to create unnecessarily detailed vector content, which impacts rendering time and also bloats the size of your `.ipa` file.

To reduce the number of calculations required to draw your vector artwork, spend time removing unnecessary control points. With intelligent use of the **Subselection Tool** (**A**) and the **Delete Anchor Point Tool** (-), you can simplify the paths within your assets without any perceptual reduction in image quality.

The screen's pixel density makes it harder for a user to see much of the detail they would normally notice on a standard monitor. Removing unnecessary control points reduces the final size of your IPA and also improves rendering performance.

Stage quality

You can further increase performance by reducing the stage render quality used by your app. At present there are three quality settings available for iOS—low, medium, and high (AIR 2.0-2.7 supports only low and medium). By default, AIR for iOS uses the medium setting but you can change this in ActionScript by setting the `Stage.quality` property to one of the constants provided by the `flash.display.StageQuality` class.

For example, adding the following line of code to your document class will use the lowest render quality setting:

```
stage.quality = StageQuality.LOW;
```

The stage render quality is a global setting and is applied to all vector content within your application. However, bitmaps remain relatively unaffected and, with the exception of smoothing, will look identical across all quality settings. This conveniently allows you to get the highest level of performance from your vector assets without compromising the quality of any bitmaps within your application.

See also

- ▸ *Converting vectors to bitmaps*
- ▸ *Comparing vector and bitmap graphics, Chapter 6*
- ▸ *Using Cache as Bitmap Matrix, Chapter 6*
- ▸ *Targeting the Retina display, Chapter 8*
- ▸ *Supporting multiple resolutions, Chapter 8*

Masking content

Mask layers are frequently used throughout Flash projects to partially reveal content sitting on layers directly beneath the mask. The mask itself can be a filled shape, text, an instance of a graphic symbol, or a movie clip. Dynamic effects can even be created by applying shape or motion tweening to your masks.

This level of flexibility and sophistication can place a lot of demand on the CPU, leading to a drop in frame rate. Although desktop computers can handle most masking operations, the same effects will degrade the performance of your iOS apps. Wherever possible, limit your use of masks. For existing projects, rather than use masks, obscure your content with other clips that sit on top of it.

In this recipe we will do just that; removing a mask layer and instead using two movie clips to obscure the content that was previously clipped by the mask.

Getting ready

From the book's accompanying code bundle, open `chapter4\recipe6\recipe.fla` into Flash Professional.

The FLA shows a credits screen from a game. A mask layer is used to clip the credits text as it scrolls vertically upwards, ensuring that only text within a rectangular region in the center of the screen is shown.

To see the masked area for yourself, unlock the **Mask** layer within the FLA's timeline. Any text that scrolls into this region will be rendered on screen. Text that falls outside this region will be hidden. The text itself is a movie clip that sits on the **Credits** layer and is attached directly below the mask layer. Lock the layer again to re-apply the mask. The following screenshot shows the mask region and how the screen will look when the mask is applied to the credits text:

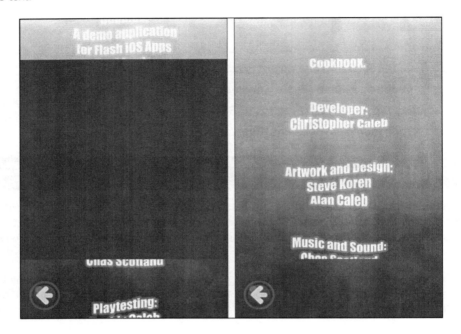

Test the FLA in ADL by selecting **Control | Test Movie | in AIR Debug Launcher (Mobile)** (*Ctrl + Enter | Cmd + Enter*).

Now publish the FLA for iOS and deploy the resulting IPA to your device. On older iOS devices such as first and second generation iPhones and iPod touches, you may find that the performance is seriously impaired. Masks are particularly problematic on older hardware. Remove the app from your device before proceeding.

Let us now go through the steps required to remove the mask and instead obscure the credits text using movie clips.

How to do it...

We will start by removing the mask layer.

1. Right-click on the **Mask** layer on the timeline and select **Delete Layers** from the context menu.

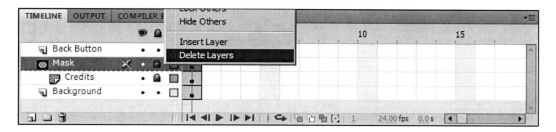

Now let us copy some new library symbols into your FLA.

2. Select **File | Open** and browse to `chapter4\recipe6\resources\resources.fla`. Click on **Open** to load the FLA.

3. Copy all the library symbols from `resources.fla` and paste them into the library of `recipe.fla`.

   The two new movie-clip symbols you copied—**Background Top** and **Background Bottom**—will be used to obscure any credits text that is outside the rectangular region that was previously defined by the mask.

4. Create a new layer directly above the **Credits** layer and name it **Background Front**.

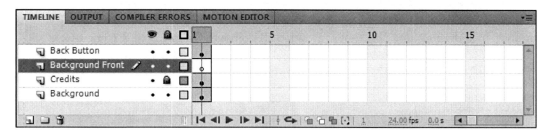

5. Drag an instance of **Background Top** from the library onto the **Background Front** layer. From the **Properties** panel, assign the position of x and y to 0 for the instance. If you are using Flash Professional CS5, then you should also expand the **DISPLAY** section and check the **Cache as bitmap** checkbox.

6. Also, drag an instance of **Background Bottom** from the library onto the **Background Front** layer. Set its x position to 0 and its y position to 385. Again, if you are using Flash Professional CS5, then within the **DISPLAY** section, check the **Cache as bitmap** checkbox.

7. Save your FLA and test using ADL (*Ctrl + Enter | Cmd + Enter*).

8. Finally, publish and deploy to your device. If you are using an older generation device, then the performance improvement will be significant.

How it works...

Although the implementation is different, the end result should be identical to the original mask layer implementation. However, using movie clips to obscure content is less computationally expensive compared to clipping with masks.

Obscuring is a fairly simple technique. In this example, two new clips were used that contained bitmap content from the FLA's background image. The credits text was then sandwiched between the original background image and the two new clips, giving the illusion that a mask was being applied to the text.

You may not be familiar with the **Cache as bitmap** render option. It is used in this example to take advantage of GPU acceleration for apps built using Flash Professional CS5. Cache as Bitmap and GPU acceleration will be covered in more detail in *Chapter 6*.

See also

▶ *Using Cache as Bitmap, Chapter 6*

▶ *Using Cache as Bitmap Matrix, Chapter 6*

Working with external SWFs

To reduce the initial load time, web-based Flash projects often keep resources such as graphics in separate .swf files that are loaded on demand. For example, a game that is split across multiple levels may have an external SWF for each level. When the player completes a level, the SWF containing the next level's resources is loaded at runtime.

Due to restrictions put in place by Apple, iOS applications cannot run interpreted code from an external source. This causes a problem for anyone hoping to load external SWFs that contain class files or ActionScript embedded within the timelines of library symbols. There is currently no way to create an external SWF that contains native ARM machine code.

If you are attempting to port a Flash project that loads external SWFs that contain ActionScript, then you will need to include the resources directly within your iOS app instead. Any resource files need to be published as SWC files rather than SWFs, allowing them to be statically linked and compiled with your iOS app.

Let us see how to do that.

Getting ready

We will require the use of various files from the book's accompanying code bundle. A resources FLA has been provided at `chapter4\recipe7\resources\assets.fla`. It is this FLA that we will publish as a `.swc` file and statically link to a second FLA, `chapter4\recipe7\recipe.fla`.

How to do it...

This recipe is broken into two main steps. First, we will publish a SWC from the resources FLA, then we will statically link the SWC to our application's FLA.

Publishing a SWC

Let us begin by creating a SWC from `assets.fla`.

1. Open `chapter4\recipe7\resources\assets.fla` into Flash Professional.

   This FLA contains a collection of resources intended to be loaded and used by `recipe.fla`. The FLA's stage is empty but within its library you will find movie-clip symbols with linkage IDs, allowing them to be instantiated and added to the display list at runtime.

   Now let us configure the FLA's publish settings, allowing a `.swc` file to be exported from its SWF.

2. Select **File | Publish Settings** from the drop-down menu.

   How you proceed depends on the version of Flash Professional that you are using. For Flash CS5.5, uncheck the **Flash (.swf)** checkbox and check on the **SWC** checkbox within the **PUBLISH** section. If you are using CS5, then click on the **Flash** tab before clicking on the **Export SWC** checkbox from the **SWF Settings** section.

3. Click on **OK** to set the changes and close the **Publish Settings** panel.

4. Save the changes to the FLA and then publish it by selecting **File | Publish** (*Alt + Shift + F12 | Shift + Cmd + F12*) from the drop-down menu. A file named `assets.swc` will be output to the same folder as your FLA.

Statically linking the SWC

Now, let us write a simple iOS app and statically link the assets SWC to it.

1. Start by opening `chapter4\recipe7\recipe.fla` into Flash Professional.

2. Create a document class. Name the class `Main` and add the following code to it:

   ```
   package {

       import flash.display.Sprite;

       public class Main extends Sprite {
   ```

```
        public function Main() {
          var background:Background = new Background();
          background.x = 0;
          background.y = 0;
          addChild(background);

          var bubble:BubbleHuge = new BubbleHuge();
          bubble.x = stage.stageWidth / 2;
          bubble.y = stage.stageHeight / 2;
          addChild(bubble);
        }
      }
    }
```

3. Save the document class.

4. Move back to your FLA and select **File | ActionScript Settings** from the drop-down menu. This will open the **Advanced ActionScript 3.0 Settings** panel where you can statically link assets.swc to your app.

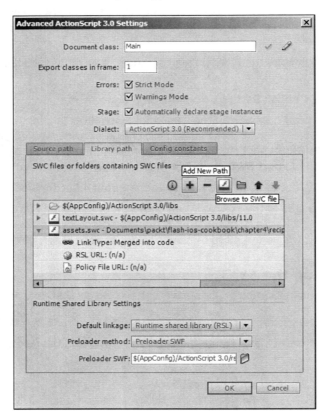

5. To do this, first click on the **Library path** tab, then click on the **Add New Path** icon, which is represented by a **+** symbol. Now click on the **Browse to SWC file** icon. Browse to and select your `assets.swc` file. It will be added to a list of SWC files to be included with your app when published. Expand the assets SWC entry by clicking on the icon to the left of its path. Ensure that its **Link Type** is set to **Merged into code**.

6. Close the **Advanced ActionScript 3.0 Settings** panel by clicking on the **OK** button at the bottom.

7. Save your FLA.

8. Publish and test your FLA within ADL (*Ctrl + Enter | Cmd + Enter*). The app should instantiate and add to its display list the **Background** and **Bubble Huge** symbols from the `assets.swc`.

9. Finally, publish and deploy the app for iOS and ensure that it works as expected on your device.

How it works...

We created a SWC file from the assets FLA and statically linked it to our iOS app. A SWC file is a package containing precompiled Flash symbols and ActionScript code. While SWC files can normally be loaded at runtime, you must statically link SWCs when writing apps that target iOS. This guarantees that Flash Professional compiles the SWC's ActionScript bytecode into native ARM machine code.

The document class in this recipe's example simply uses the linkage IDs associated with the assets SWC's library symbols to instantiate and add objects to the app's display list. Specifically the class creates and displays an instance of `Background` and an instance of `BubbleHuge` from `assets.swc`.

You should consider the total size of the resource files you will have to link to your iOS app. All statically linked content must be loaded up-front and will impact your app's initial load time and the amount of memory it consumes. With large projects, you run the risk of the app being closed by iOS if memory consumption is too high. The memory threshold will vary from device to device and will also depend upon the number of apps held in the background.

There's more...

Loading external SWF files isn't impossible but you are limited in what you can do.

The SWF cannot contain any ActionScript, including the assignment of linkage IDs to library symbols. This prevents you from being able to dynamically instantiate any of the SWF's library symbols from within your app. It is also not possible to lace ActionScript within your SWF's timeline to perform simple programmatic control of your animations.

You can however, place content on the SWF's stage; load the SWF into your app; then add the SWF to the display list. You can also embed sound within the external SWF's timeline and have it played back. Additionally, ActionScript calls can be made from your app to the external SWF, allowing programmatic control of instances within its display list. It is limited compared to what many Flash developers are used to but there are still uses for external SWFs in your iOS projects.

See also

- ▶ *Creating a basic document class, Chapter 3*
- ▶ *Linking classes to movie-clip symbols, Chapter 3*

5
Multi-touch and Gesture Support

In this chapter, we will cover:

- ▶ Setting the touch point input mode
- ▶ Detecting multiple touch points
- ▶ Dragging multiple display objects
- ▶ Tracking movement
- ▶ Setting the gesture input mode
- ▶ Handling a swipe gesture
- ▶ Panning an object
- ▶ Rotating an object
- ▶ Zooming an object

Introduction

The iPhone wasn't the first to use the technology, but its success kick-started the touch-screen revolution. Critical to that success was Apple's decision to include multi-touch support. Be it a single tap, swipe, or pinch; interaction with the iPhone's screen always feels intuitive and natural.

The Flash platform allows application developers to take full advantage of multi-touch when targeting iOS. In this chapter, we will explore how to work with multiple-touch points before covering how to detect and respond to gestures.

Setting the touch point input mode

The success of the iPhone has changed how people use mobile devices, with users now expecting to interact directly with a device by physically touching its screen. While a mouse is limited to the selection of a single point, iOS devices can detect multiple touches and track the movement of each of them simultaneously.

Flash provides full support for multi-touch but in order to take advantage of it you must first inform the platform of your intentions to receive and use touch-based events.

Let us see how this is done.

Getting ready

An FLA has been provided as a starting point for this recipe.

From the book's accompanying code bundle, open `chapter5\recipe1\recipe.fla` into Flash Professional.

Sitting on the stage is a dynamic text field named `output`. We will write some code to enable multi-touch input and write the success or failure of the request to the text field.

How to do it...

Perform the following steps:

1. Create a document class and name it `Main`.

2. Add the following two import statements:

```
import flash.display.MovieClip;
import flash.ui.Multitouch;
import flash.ui.MultitouchInputMode;
```

3. Now within the constructor add some code to enable multi-touch support:

```
public function Main() {
  if(Multitouch.supportsTouchEvents)
  {
    Multitouch.inputMode = MultitouchInputMode.TOUCH_POINT;
    output.text = ("inputMode = " + Multitouch.inputMode);
  }
  else
  {
    output.text = "Multi-touch events not supported.";
  }
}
```

4. Save the class file as `Main.as`.

5. Publish the FLA and deploy the IPA file to your iOS device.

When you run the app, the following text should be output to the screen:

inputMode = touchPoint

How it works...

Flash provides various multi-touch input modes, which determine the type of events your application can receive. In order to receive touch events, you need to set the `Multitouch.inputMode` property to `MultitouchInputMode.TOUCH_POINT`. Here is the line of code from your document class that does this:

```
Multitouch.inputMode = MultitouchInputMode.TOUCH_POINT;
```

In addition to setting `Multitouch.inputMode`, you can also query it to determine the currently selected input mode. For this recipe, the current input mode is written to the `output` text field to confirm that it was successfully set:

```
output.text = ("inputMode = " + Multitouch.inputMode);
```

Although Flash supports multi-touch across all iOS devices, the same is not true for all other operating systems and platforms. When writing cross-platform code, you may want to confirm support by checking the `Multitouch.supportsTouchEvents` property. In our code example, this is done before setting the input mode.

For more information regarding the multi-touch input mode, perform a search for `flash.ui.Multitouch` and `flash.ui.MultitouchInputMode` within Adobe Community Help.

It is also highly recommended that you spend time with Apple's iOS Human Interface Guidelines, where you will find best practices for driving the user experience through multi-touch. The documentation can be found on the iOS Dev Center at `http://developer.apple.com/devcenter/ios`.

There's more...

Let us look at some additional detail.

Available touch events

Setting the input mode for touch allows you to listen for touch-specific events being dispatched by objects of type `InteractiveObject` or objects that inherit `InteractiveObject`, such as `Sprite`, `MovieClip`, and `Stage`. On a multi-touch screen, each point of contact that can be made by a finger is known as a touch point.

The following touch events are available:

Touch events	Description
TOUCH_BEGIN	A touch point has been pressed.
TOUCH_END	A touch point has been released.
TOUCH_MOVE	A touch point is being moved. This occurs when a finger is being dragged across the screen.
TOUCH_TAP	A quick finger tap.
TOUCH_OVER	A touch point has moved over an interactive object.
TOUCH_OUT	A touch point has been moved away from an interactive object.
TOUCH_ROLL_OVER	A touch point has moved over an interactive object. Unlike TOUCH_OVER, this event will not fire for any children belonging to the object.
TOUCH_ROLL_OUT	A touch point has been moved away from an interactive object. Unlike TOUCH_OUT, this event will not fire for any children belonging to the object.

We will see some of these events in action during the next few recipes.

Determining the number of supported touch points

You can determine the number of touch points supported by your iOS device by examining the static `Multitouch.maxTouchPoints` property.

While you will find that five touch points are supported across the range of iOS devices, this property is of more practical use on cross-platform projects, where the number of touch points can vary wildly depending on the operating system and choice of input device. When targeting multiple platforms, optimize your content with this in mind.

Touch point hit targets

For elements that can be tapped within your application, ensure that a hit area that is at least the size of a fingertip is used. This equates to approximately 44x44 pixels on a standard resolution screen and 88x88 pixels on a Retina display.

Mouse events

The default input mode is `MultitouchInputMode.NONE`, which specifies that all user interaction with a touch-enabled device is interpreted as a mouse event. However, unlike `MultitouchInputMode.TOUCH_POINT`, only a single touch point can be processed at any one time.

Note that when the input mode is set to `MultitouchInputMode.TOUCH_POINT`, you can continue to listen for and respond to mouse events provided by `flash.events.MouseEvents`.

Testing in ADL

It is most likely that testing this recipe's code within ADL will result in the following message being output to the screen:

Multi-touch events not supported.

Not all desktop computers or operating systems support multi-touch. When using touch-based events within your code, it is advisable that you test directly on an iOS device.

See also

▶ *Creating a basic document class, Chapter 3*

▶ *Handling user interaction, Chapter 4*

▶ *Detecting multiple touch points*

▶ *Setting the gesture input mode*

Detecting multiple touch points

The term multi-touch refers to the ability to simultaneously detect and track two or more distinct points of contact on a touch-screen. Touch events are similar to the mouse events provided by Flash, except you can listen for and respond to multiple touch events all at once.

Let us revisit the Bubbles app from *Chapter 3* and add multi-touch interaction to it. We will add functionality to let the user trap multiple bubbles by holding a finger on top of each.

Getting ready

A version of the Bubbles FLA has been provided for you to work from.

From Flash Professional, open `chapter5\recipe2\recipe.fla` from the book's accompanying code bundle.

How to do it...

We will be making changes to both the FLA's document class and `Bubble.as`.

Updating the Bubble class

Let us start by adding some code to `Bubble.as` that prevents any of the bubble instances from moving if being held:

1. Open the `Bubble.as` class.

2. Add the following member variable:

```
private var _held:Boolean = false;
```

3. Now write a getter and a setter method for the `_held` variable:

```
public function set held(h:Boolean):void {
  _held = h;
}

public function get held():Boolean {
  return _held;
}
```

4. Move to the `update()` method and write a few lines of code at the start to prevent the bubble's update logic from running if it is being held:

```
public function update():void {
  if(_held)
  {
    return;
  }
}
```

5. Finally, within the constructor, disable user input for any child display objects within the bubble—we are only interested in receiving events for the bubble's container:

```
public function Bubble() {
  mouseChildren = false;
}
```

6. Save `Bubble.as`.

Responding to multiple touch events

Now within the FLA's document class, let us listen for multi-touch events and trap any bubbles that are being touched:

1. Open the `Main.as` document class.

2. Include the following three import statements:

```
import flash.ui.Multitouch;
import flash.ui.MultitouchInputMode;
import flash.events.TouchEvent;
```

3. Within the constructor, set the input mode, and listen for `TouchEvent.TOUCH_BEGIN` and `TouchEvent.TOUCH_END` being dispatched from the stage:

```
public function Main() {
  Multitouch.inputMode = MultitouchInputMode.TOUCH_POINT;
  stage.addEventListener(TouchEvent.TOUCH_BEGIN, touchBegin);
  stage.addEventListener(TouchEvent.TOUCH_END, touchEnd);

  application = NativeApplication.nativeApplication;
```

4. Write a handler for the `TOUCH_BEGIN` event:

```
private function touchBegin(e:TouchEvent):void {
  var b:Bubble = e.target as Bubble;
  if(b != null)
  {
    b.held = true;
  }
}
```

5. And add a handler for the `TOUCH_END` event too:

```
private function touchEnd(e:TouchEvent):void {
  var b:Bubble = e.target as Bubble;
  if(b != null)
  {
    b.held = false;
  }
}
```

6. Save `Main.as`.

7. Publish the FLA and deploy the IPA file to your device.

Run the app and hold your fingers on multiple bubbles to stop them from floating upwards. Lifting your finger off a bubble will release it again.

How it works...

This recipe took advantage of multi-touch to allow the detection of touch points across multiple objects simultaneously.

Touch was enabled with the following line of code within the `Main` class' constructor:

```
Multitouch.inputMode = MultitouchInputMode.TOUCH_POINT;
```

Touch events can be dispatched by any `InteractiveObject` or sub-class of `InteractiveObject`, such as `Sprite`, `MovieClip`, and `Stage`.

Listeners for the following two events were added to the stage:

▶ `TouchEvent.TOUCH_BEGIN`

▶ `TouchEvent.TOUCH_END`

The `TOUCH_BEGIN` event is fired when the user presses a finger onto any child interactive object of the stage. This is the case even if other areas of the screen's surface are already being touched. When the user lifts their finger from an interactive object, the `TOUCH_END` event is dispatched.

In this recipe, the stage's child objects consist of bubble instances and a single background movie clip. The event handlers simply check to see if the event was dispatched from a `Bubble` instance, and if so the bubble's `held` property is set. For the `TOUCH_BEGIN` event, the bubble's `held` property is set to `true`, thus freezing it. When the `TOUCH_END` event is received, the bubble's held property is set to `false`, allowing it to start moving upwards again.

You can obtain more information regarding the `flash.events.TouchEvent` class from Adobe Community Help.

Handling roll out

Sometimes the user's finger may slide away from the bubble rather than being cleanly lifted from it. When this happens in this recipe's example code, the held bubble doesn't receive the `TOUCH_END` event and therefore doesn't start floating upwards again.

You can rectify this by listening for `TouchEvent.TOUCH_ROLL_OUT` being dispatched from each of the bubble instances. Simply add the following line within the `Main` class' constructor:

```
for(var i:uint = 0; i < bubbles.length; i++)
{
  bubbles[i].speed = speeds[i];
  bubbles[i].addEventListener(TouchEvent.TOUCH_ROLL_OUT,
    touchEnd);
}
```

Now when the user slides his or her finger away from a bubble, the `touchEnd()` handler will get called and the bubble will start moving again.

> You can carry your code from this recipe into the next. If you have added an event listener for `TouchEvent.TOUCH_ROLL_OUT`, then remove it again before continuing as it isn't required and will produce odd behavior if left in.

There's more...

Each event object that your handler receives contains a number of properties related to that touch event. You may find the following properties useful when detecting multiple touch points.

Primary touch point

When touching a screen at multiple locations, the primary touch point is deemed to be the location that was first touched. When your event handler receives a `TouchEvent` object, you can query its `isPrimaryTouchPoint` property to determine this.

Touch point ID

A unique ID is assigned to every new touch point and is used across all events associated with that point of contact. You can determine the touch point that an event is associated with by examining its `touchPointID` property.

Local touch coordinates

You can use the `localX` and `localY` properties to determine the coordinates at which a touch event occurred relative to the interactive object. Bear in mind that these two properties won't provide pixel-perfect accuracy on touch-screen devices due to the nature of the technology and the surface area that is covered by a finger tip.

Global touch coordinates

You can also obtain the position at which an event occurred in global stage coordinates. Simply inspect the value of the event's `stageX` and `stageY` properties.

See also

▸ *Linking classes to movie-clip symbols, Chapter 3*

▸ *Using an update loop, Chapter 3*

▸ *Setting the touch point input mode*

▸ *Dragging multiple display objects*

Dragging multiple display objects

With touch-enabled screens, the act of dragging a display object with a finger is very intuitive. Adobe AIR provides API calls that allow this type of interaction without much effort. In addition, the multi-touch capabilities of iOS can be harnessed to allow multiple objects to be dragged at once.

We will continue where we left off in the *Detecting multiple touch points* recipe and add the ability to drag the bubbles around the screen.

Getting ready

If you haven't already done so, complete the *Detecting multiple touch points* recipe before proceeding.

You can continue to work with the code you wrote during that recipe. Alternatively, from the book's accompanying code bundle, open `chapter5\recipe3\recipe.fla` into Flash Professional and work from there.

How to do it...

Open the FLA's document class and perform the following steps:

1. Declare the following member variable:

```
private var touching:Array;
```

   This array will be used to map touch points to `Bubble` instances.

2. Within the constructor, set the `touching` member variable to an empty array:

```
public function Main() {
    touching = [];
    Multitouch.inputMode = MultitouchInputMode.TOUCH_POINT;
    stage.addEventListener(TouchEvent.TOUCH_BEGIN, touchBegin);
    stage.addEventListener(TouchEvent.TOUCH_END, touchEnd);
```

3. Move to the `touchBegin()` event handler and make the following changes:

```
private function touchBegin(e:TouchEvent):void {
    var b:Bubble = e.target as Bubble;
    if(b != null && !b.held)
    {
        b.held = true;
        b.startTouchDrag(e.touchPointID);
        touching[e.touchPointID] = b;
    }
}
```

4. Now alter the `touchEnd()` handler too:

```
private function touchEnd(e:TouchEvent):void {
    var b:Bubble = touching[e.touchPointID];
    if(b != null)
    {
        b.held = false;
        b.stopTouchDrag(e.touchPointID);

        delete touching[e.touchPointID];
        touching[e.touchPointID] = null;
    }
}
```

5. Save `Main.as`.

6. Publish the FLA and deploy the IPA to your device.

When you run the app, you will now be able to stop and drag the bubbles. You can even drag multiple bubbles simultaneously. Give it a try.

How it works...

Much of the work in this recipe is performed by `startTouchDrag()` and `stopTouchDrag()`. Both methods are defined by `flash.display.Sprite` and are also available to classes that inherit it, including our `Bubble` class.

The `startTouchDrag()` method allows the user to drag a bubble across the screen. It does this by associating a touch point ID with a bubble, continuously updating the bubble's position to reflect that of the touch point.

On the other hand, the `stopTouchDrag()` method stops the bubble from being dragged by the specified touch point ID.

Let us take a look at the `touchBegin()` event handler where `startTouchDrag()` is called. Two lines of code that are of particular interest have been highlighted:

```
private function touchBegin(e:TouchEvent):void {
  var b:Bubble = e.target as Bubble;
  if(b != null && !b.held)
  {
    b.held = true;
    b.startTouchDrag(e.touchPointID);
    touching[e.touchPointID] = b;
  }
}
```

First, the interactive object that was touched is obtained by querying the event's `target` property and an attempt is made to cast it to a `Bubble` object. If the object is a bubble, then its `startTouchDrag()` method is called with the event's touch point ID being passed as an argument.

Every point of contact made with the screen is assigned a unique ID that can be used by methods such as `startTouchDrag()` and `stopTouchDrag()`. You can determine the touch point that an event is associated with by examining its `touchPointID` property. We take advantage of these unique IDs within our code to associate a bubble with a touch point. You can see this mapping taking place near the end of the `touchBegin()` event handler:

```
private function touchBegin(e:TouchEvent):void {
  var b:Bubble = e.target as Bubble;
  if(b != null && !b.held)
  {
    b.held = true;
    b.startTouchDrag(e.touchPointID);
    touching[e.touchPointID] = b;
  }
}
```

The handler makes use of the `touching` member variable to store a reference to the bubble that is being dragged by the user. The bubble instance is placed in the `touching` array, with the event's touch point ID being used as the index position.

Let us now take a look at the `touchEnd()` event handler, where we obtain from the `touching` array, the bubble that has just been released by the user:

```
private function touchEnd(e:TouchEvent):void {
  var b:Bubble = touching[e.touchPointID];
  if(b != null)
  {
    b.held = false;
    b.stopTouchDrag(e.touchPointID);

    delete touching[e.touchPointID];
    touching[e.touchPointID] = null;
  }
}
```

In the above method, the event's `touchPointID` is obtained and used to retrieve the associated bubble from the `touching` array. If a bubble instance was retrieved, then its `stopTouchDrag()` method is called with the event's touch point ID being passed as an argument. This will stop the bubble being dragged by the user's finger.

Finally, at the end of the method, the bubble reference is removed from the `touching` array as it is no longer required:

```
private function touchEnd(e:TouchEvent):void {
  var b:Bubble = touching[e.touchPointID];
  if(b != null)
  {
    b.held = false;
    b.stopTouchDrag(e.touchPointID);

    delete touching[e.touchPointID];
    touching[e.touchPointID] = null;
  }
}
```

That is all there is to it. With the use of the `Sprite` class' `startTouchDrag()` and `stopTouchDrag()` methods and by tracking touch point IDs, we were able to manage the dragging of multiple interactive objects.

You can obtain more information regarding the `flash.display.Sprite` class from Adobe Community Help.

There's more...

Following is some more information regarding `startTouchDrag()`.

startTouchDrag() parameters

The `startTouchDrag()` method expects three arguments with only the first being mandatory:

- ▶ `touchPointID`: The ID of the touch point that will be used to drag the sprite.
- ▶ `lockCenter`: Whether to lock the center of the sprite to the touch point (`true`), or lock to the point where contact was made with the sprite (`false`). Defaulted to `false`.
- ▶ `bounds`: A `Rectangle` that defines a constraint region for the sprite that is being dragged. Defaulted to `null` meaning there is to be no constraint region.

This recipe's example code only used the first argument. Meaning the center of the bubble wasn't locked to the user's finger and the user was free to drag the bubble anywhere on the screen.

To force the bubble's center to lock to the user's finger, simply pass `true` as the second argument:

```
b.startTouchDrag(e.touchPointID, true);
```

The following example also constrains the bubble to a 200x200 pixel region at the top-left corner of the screen:

```
b.startTouchDrag(
    e.touchPointID, true, new Rectangle(0, 0, 200, 200));
```

Try applying each example to your code.

See also

- ▶ *Setting the touch point input mode*
- ▶ *Tracking movement*

Tracking movement

One important touch-based event that we haven't looked at yet in detail is `TouchEvent.TOUCH_MOVE`. This event is fired whenever the user moves a finger across the screen and can be queried to determine the contact point's coordinates. Every time the user's finger changes position, a new `TOUCH_MOVE` event is dispatched.

Although `startTouchDrag()` and `stopTouchDrag()` are recommended for dragging objects, you can instead update an object's position in response to TOUCH_MOVE events.

Let us make some changes to the code from the *Dragging multiple display objects* recipe to do this.

Getting ready

If you haven't already done so, complete the *Dragging multiple display objects* recipe before proceeding.

You can continue to work with your code from that recipe. Alternatively, from the book's accompanying code bundle, open `chapter5\recipe4\recipe.fla` into Flash Professional and work from there.

How to do it...

Perform the following steps within the FLA's document class:

1. Move to the constructor and add a listener for `TouchEvent.TOUCH_MOVE`:

```
public function Main() {
  touching = [];
  Multitouch.inputMode = MultitouchInputMode.TOUCH_POINT;
  stage.addEventListener(TouchEvent.TOUCH_BEGIN, touchBegin);
  stage.addEventListener(TouchEvent.TOUCH_END, touchEnd);
  stage.addEventListener(TouchEvent.TOUCH_MOVE, touchMove);
```

2. Remove the call to `startTouchDrag()` from the `touchBegin()` handler by deleting the highlighted line of code from the `if` statement:

```
private function touchBegin(e:TouchEvent):void {
  var b:Bubble = e.target as Bubble;
  if(b != null && !b.held)
  {
    b.held = true;
    b.startTouchDrag(e.touchPointID, true);
    touching[e.touchPointID] = b;
  }
}
```

3. Also remove the call to `stopTouchDrag()` from the `touchEnd()` handler by deleting the highlighted line of code from the `if` statement:

```
private function touchEnd(e:TouchEvent):void {
  var b:Bubble = touching[e.touchPointID];
  if(b != null)
  {
    b.held = false;
    b.stopTouchDrag(e.touchPointID);
```

```
        delete touching[e.touchPointID];
        touching[e.touchPointID] = null;
      }
    }
```

4. Now write the `touchMove()` event handler:

```
private function touchMove(e:TouchEvent):void {
  var b:Bubble = touching[e.touchPointID] as Bubble;
  if(b != null)
  {
    b.x = e.stageX;
    b.y = e.stageY;
  }
}
```

5. Save `Main.as`.

6. Publish the FLA and deploy the IPA to your device.

This example should behave in an identical way to the previous recipe.

How it works...

Although dragging was previously taken care of by `startTouchDrag()` and `stopTouchDrag()`, for this recipe we manually update the position of the bubbles by responding to `TouchEvent.TOUCH_MOVE`.

The bulk of the work is performed within the `touchMove()` event handler, which is shown again as follows:

```
private function touchMove(e:TouchEvent):void {
  var b:Bubble = touching[e.touchPointID] as Bubble;
  if(b != null)
  {
    b.x = e.stageX;
    b.y = e.stageY;
  }
}
```

Using the event's touch point ID, a reference to the bubble associated with it (if any) is retrieved from the `touching` array. The bubble's x and y properties are then updated to reflect the on-screen position of the user's finger, which is retrieved from the event's `stageX` and `stageY` properties.

Every time one of the user's fingers changes position on the device's screen, the `TOUCH_MOVE` event is dispatched, and any bubble associated with that contact point is re-positioned to match the finger's position.

While this recipe has concentrated on the use of TOUCH_MOVE to perform dragging, the event can be applied to many other tasks. For example, it could be used to track finger movement for a paint application or to trace a path for a game character to follow.

If you are implementing dragging within your app, it is recommended that you use startTouchDrag() and stopTouchDrag() instead, which has performance benefits over listening for TOUCH_MOVE events. However, now that you are comfortable working with the TOUCH_MOVE event, you should be able to put it to various other uses.

See also

> ▸ *Setting the touch point input mode*
> ▸ *Dragging multiple display objects*

Setting the gesture input mode

Along with handling simple multi-touch events, AIR for iOS provides support for gestures such as zoom, rotation, and swipe. A gesture is a single event that is made up from a sequence of simpler multi-touch events. Although you can capture multi-touch events and translate them into gestures yourself, the Flash platform also provides support for the most common ones, reducing your workload.

In order to receive gesture events, you must select the appropriate input mode.

Let us see how this is done.

Getting ready

From Flash Professional, open chapter5\recipe5\recipe.fla from the book's accompanying code bundle.

Sitting on the stage is a dynamic text field named output. We will write some code to enable gesture input and write the success or failure of the request to the text field.

How to do it...

Perform the following steps:

1. Create a document class and name it Main.
2. Add the following two import statements:

```
import flash.display.MovieClip;
import flash.ui.Multitouch;
import flash.ui.MultitouchInputMode;
```

3. Now within the constructor, add some code to enable gesture support:

```
public function Main() {
  if(Multitouch.supportsGestureEvents)
  {
    Multitouch.inputMode = MultitouchInputMode.GESTURE;
    output.text = ("inputMode = " + Multitouch.inputMode);
  }
  else
  {
    output.text = "Gesture events not supported.";
  }
}
```

4. Save the class file as `Main.as`.

5. Publish the FLA and deploy the IPA file to your iOS device.

When you run the app, the following text should be output on the screen:

inputMode = gesture

How it works...

Flash provides various multi-touch input modes, which determine the type of events your application can receive. In order to receive gesture events, you need to set the `Multitouch.inputMode` property to `MultitouchInputMode.GESTURE`. The following is the line of code from your document class that does this:

```
Multitouch.inputMode = MultitouchInputMode.GESTURE;
```

In addition to setting `Multitouch.inputMode`, you can also query it to determine the currently selected input mode. In this recipe's code example, the current input mode is written to the `output` text field to confirm that it was successfully set:

```
output.text = ("inputMode = " + Multitouch.inputMode);
```

Although Flash provides gesture support across all iOS devices, when writing cross-platform code you may want to confirm support by checking the `Multitouch.supportsGestureEvents` property. In our code example, this is done before setting the input mode.

It should be noted that when the input mode is set for handling gestures you will be unable to receive basic touch events from the `TouchEvent` class. If you need to receive both touch and gesture events at the same time, then you will need to select the `MultitouchInputMode.TOUCH_POINT` input mode and capture multiple touch events before synthesizing them into gesture events yourself.

For more information regarding the gesture input mode, perform a search for `flash.ui.Multitouch` and `flash.ui.MultitouchInputMode` within Adobe Community Help.

Apple places a lot of importance on the correct use of gestures in order to provide consistency across applications. Apple's iOS Human Interface Guidelines contains a list of standard gestures and the actions users typically perform with them. When supporting gestures within your own applications, try not to deviate from the expected behavior.

There's more...

The following are some additional details regarding gestures.

Available gesture events and types

Setting the input mode for gestures allows you to listen for gesture-specific events being dispatched by objects of type `InteractiveObject` or objects that inherit `InteractiveObject`, such as `Sprite`, `MovieClip`, and `Stage`.

As with touch point input, gestures can also take advantage of multiple touch points.

The following gesture events are available:

  ▶ `GestureEvent.GESTURE_TWO_FINGER_TAP`: Dispatched when two fingers are used to tap the screen.

  ▶ `TransformGestureEvent.GESTURE_PAN`: An attempt is made to move content that is typically too large to fit on screen. The pan gesture is fired when two fingers are being moved across on-screen content.

  ▶ `TransformGestureEvent.GESTURE_ROTATE`: Dispatched when two touch points are rotated around each other. This gesture is typically used to rotate on-screen content.

  ▶ `TransformGestureEvent.GESTURE_SWIPE`: A quick stroke of a finger across the screen. Swipe gestures are commonly used to scroll lists or quickly flick between pages of information.

  ▶ `TransformGestureEvent.GESTURE_ZOOM`: Two touch points are either being moved towards or away from one another. This gesture is commonly used to zoom on-screen content.

We will see some of these events in action throughout the remainder of this chapter.

Determining the supported gestures

You can obtain a list of gestures supported by your iOS device using the static `Multitouch.supportedGestures` property. A vector array of strings will be returned, where each string represents a gesture event.

Mouse events

The default input mode is `MultitouchInputMode.NONE`, which specifies that all user interaction with a touch-enabled device is interpreted as a mouse event. However, unlike `MultitouchInputMode.GESTURE` and `MultitouchInputMode.TOUCH_POINT`, only a single touch point can be processed at any one time.

Note that when the input mode is set to `MultitouchInputMode.GESTURE`, you can continue to listen for and respond to mouse events provided by `flash.events.MouseEvents`.

Testing in ADL

It is most likely that testing this recipe's code within ADL will result in the following message being output on the screen:

Gesture events not supported.

Not all desktop computers or operating systems support gesture-based events. When using gestures within your code, it is advisable that you test directly on an iOS device.

See also

 ► *Handling user interaction, Chapter 4*
 ► *Setting the touch point input mode*
 ► *Handling a swipe gesture*
 ► *Panning an object*

Handling a swipe gesture

The introduction of touch-screens has made the process of moving between pages of information more natural. The iPhone made simple touch gestures, such as swiping, popular. For example, many photo viewer applications allow the user to quickly flick their finger across the screen in order to view the next image in a sequence.

The `TransformGestureEvent.GESTURE_SWIPE` event is available, allowing both vertical and horizontal swiping gestures to be detected and acted upon.

Let us see how this is done.

Getting ready

From Flash Professional, open `chapter5\recipe6\recipe.fla` from the book's accompanying code bundle.

Sitting on the stage is a container movie clip named content, which is over twice the width of the stage. Inside the container are two distinct bubbles, with only a single bubble able to fit on screen at any one time. We will write code to let the user swipe horizontally between the two bubbles.

How to do it...

Perform the following steps to listen for and respond to a horizontal swipe gesture:

1. Create a document class and name it Main.

2. Include the following import statements:

```
import flash.display.MovieClip;
import flash.events.TransformGestureEvent;
import flash.ui.Multitouch;
import flash.ui.MultitouchInputMode;
import fl.transitions.Tween;
import fl.motion.easing.Sine;
```

3. Add the following code within the class' constructor:

```
public function Main() {
    Multitouch.inputMode = MultitouchInputMode.GESTURE;
    stage.addEventListener(TransformGestureEvent.GESTURE_SWIPE,
        swipe);
}
```

4. Now add the swipe gesture's event handler:

```
private function swipe(e:TransformGestureEvent):void {
    var t:Tween;
    if(e.offsetX == -1)
    {
        t = new Tween(content, "x",
            Sine.easeOut, content.x, -465, 0.25, true);
    }
    else if(e.offsetX == 1)
    {
        t = new Tween(content, "x",
            Sine.easeOut, content.x, -35, 0.25, true);
    }
}
```

5. Save the class file as Main.as.

6. Publish the FLA and deploy the IPA to your device.

Quickly swipe your finger from right to left to move to the second bubble, and left to right to move back to the first.

How it works...

Gesture events can be dispatched by any `InteractiveObject` or sub-class of `InteractiveObject`, such as `Sprite`, `MovieClip`, and `Stage`.

In this recipe, we took advantage of the gesture input mode to listen for and respond to `TransformGestureEvent.GESTURE_SWIPE`.

Support for gesture-based input was enabled with the following line of code:

```
Multitouch.inputMode = MultitouchInputMode.GESTURE;
```

A listener was then added for the `GESTURE_SWIPE` event:

```
stage.addEventListener(TransformGestureEvent.GESTURE_SWIPE,
    swipe);
```

Notice the listener was actually added to the stage, allowing the user to swipe anywhere on screen and not just on the `content` movie clip.

It is within the `swipe()` handler where we respond to the user's swipe gesture and slide the `content` movie clip either to its far-left or far-right.

To decide which direction to slide the movie clip, we inspect the `TransformGestureEvent` object's `offsetX` property. A value of `1` indicates that the user swiped to the right, whereas a value of `-1` indicates the user swiped to the left. You can see the code for this highlighted as follows:

```
private function swipe(e:TransformGestureEvent):void {
  var t:Tween;
  if(e.offsetX == -1)
  {
    t = new Tween(content, "x",
      Sine.easeOut, content.x, -465, 0.25, true);
  }
  else if(e.offsetX == 1)
  {
    t = new Tween(content, "x",
      Sine.easeOut, content.x, -35, 0.25, true);
  }
}
```

Finally the actual scrolling of the content is performed. The `fl.transitions.Tween` class is used to slide the `content` movie clip into position. To perform a gradual acceleration and deceleration during the sliding transition, the `fl.motion.easing.Sine` class was used. Refer to Adobe Community Help for more information regarding these two classes.

There's more...

The following is one more property of `TransformGestureEvent` that is relevant to swipe gestures.

Swiping vertically

Although it wasn't covered in this recipe's example code, you can just as easily detect a vertical swipe by querying the event's `offsetY` property. A value of `-1` will be returned for an upwards swipe, whereas `1` will be returned for a downwards swipe.

Although both horizontal and vertical swiping motions are represented by separate properties, AIR for iOS does not support diagonal swiping gestures. A user can either swipe horizontally or vertically.

See also

- ▶ *Setting the gesture input mode*
- ▶ *Panning an object*

Panning an object

Given the size constraints of screens on iOS devices, such as the iPhone and iPod touch, a user may need to pan or scroll to reveal content that is sitting out of view. The Flash platform provides the `TransformGestureEvent.GESTURE_PAN` event that you can listen for in order to detect a pan gesture on any interactive object. The gesture is initiated by the user placing two fingers on an object then sliding them across the screen to move it.

This recipe will show you how to take advantage of the pan gesture in your projects.

Getting ready

From Flash Professional, open `chapter5\recipe7\recipe.fla` from the book's accompanying code bundle.

Sitting on the stage is a movie clip named `bubble`, which is too large to fit fully on screen. We will write some ActionScript to let the user pan the movie clip in order to see parts that are hidden from view.

How to do it...

Perform the following steps:

1. Create a document class and name it `Main`.

2. Add the following three import statements:

```
import flash.display.MovieClip;
import flash.events.TransformGestureEvent;
import flash.ui.Multitouch;
import flash.ui.MultitouchInputMode;
```

3. Within the constructor, set the input mode and listen for `TransformGestureEvent.GESTURE_PAN`:

```
public function Main() {
  Multitouch.inputMode = MultitouchInputMode.GESTURE;
  bubble.addEventListener(TransformGestureEvent.GESTURE_PAN,
    pan);
}
```

4. Write a handler for the `GESTURE_PAN` event:

```
private function pan(e:TransformGestureEvent):void {
  bubble.x += e.offsetX;
  bubble.y += e.offsetY;
}
```

5. Save the class file as `Main.as`.

6. Publish the FLA and deploy the IPA to your device.

Touch the on-screen bubble with two fingers then slide them across the screen to pan the content.

How it works...

In order to respond to a panning gesture, a listener for `TransformGestureEvent.GESTURE_PAN` was added:

```
bubble.addEventListener(TransformGestureEvent.GESTURE_PAN,
  pan);
```

The GESTURE_PAN event is repeatedly dispatched as the user slides both fingers across the screen. The actual panning of the content takes place within the pan() event handler. Here, we use the offsetX and offsetY properties of the TransformGestureEvent object that was passed to the method:

```
private function pan(e:TransformGestureEvent):void {
    bubble.x += e.offsetX;
    bubble.y += e.offsetY;
}
```

Together, both properties provide the horizontal and vertical distance that the user's fingers have travelled since the last GESTURE_PAN event. We simply use these offsets to reposition the bubble movie clip.

For more information, perform a search for flash.events.TransformGestureEvent within Adobe Community Help.

There's more...

The following are a couple of final things regarding panning, including a property of the TransformGestureEvent class that you may find of interest.

Gesture phases

Some gesture events are split into three distinct phases known as beginning, update, and end. If your application is required to respond to a gesture event's individual phase, then you can query the event's phase property. Each phase is represented by a constant provided by the flash.events.GesturePhase class.

For example, when a user is panning on-screen content, the GESTURE_PAN event will go through each of these phases:

- GesturePhase.BEGIN: The user touches the screen with both fingers and starts to move them across the screen
- GesturePhase.UPDATE: The user is moving both fingers across the screen
- GesturePhase.END: The user lifts one or both fingers from the screen

Let us look at a simple example where the bubble movie clip from this recipe is expanded in size at the beginning of a gesture phase, then shrinks back to its original size at the end. During the update phase, the user will be able to pan the content as before:

```
private function pan(e:TransformGestureEvent):void {
    if(e.phase == GesturePhase.BEGIN)
    {
        bubble.scaleX += 0.2;
        bubble.scaleY += 0.2;
    }
```

```
    else if(e.phase == GesturePhase.END)
    {
      bubble.scaleX -= 0.2;
      bubble.scaleY -= 0.2;
    }
    else if(e.phase == GesturePhase.UPDATE)
    {
      bubble.x += e.offsetX;
      bubble.y += e.offsetY;
    }
  }
}
```

Make the changes to your code and add an import statement for `flash.events.GesturePhase`. Deploy the IPA to your device and try panning the on-screen content to get a feel of it when each of the gesture's phases occur.

 You can carry your code from this recipe into the next. If you have made the changes above, then remove them before continuing as they aren't required.

Neither the swipe nor two-finger tap gesture have multiple phases. When working with either of these gestures, the `phase` property will always return `GesturePhase.ALL`.

Single finger panning

The `GESTURE_PAN` event only detects panning that is initiated and controlled using two fingers. Single finger panning, which is the expected behavior on iOS, can be achieved using the `startTouchDrag()` and `stopTouchDrag()` methods provided by `flash.display.Sprite`. For details refer to the *Dragging multiple display objects* recipe earlier in this chapter.

See also

- ▸ *Setting the gesture input mode*
- ▸ *Dragging multiple display objects*
- ▸ *Rotating an object*

Rotating an object

Rotation is another popular gesture used within iOS apps. It is performed by placing two fingers on your device's screen and rotating either one contact point around the other, or both around each other. To allow the rotation of content, you can listen for and respond to the `TransformGestureEvent.GESTURE_ROTATE` event.

We will continue from the *Panning an object* recipe and add the ability to rotate the on-screen content.

Getting ready

If you haven't already done so, complete the *Panning an object* recipe before proceeding.

You can continue to work with the code you wrote during that recipe. Alternatively, open `chapter5\recipe8\recipe.fla` from the book's accompanying code bundle and work from there. You will also find the FLA's document class in the same folder.

How to do it...

Perform the following steps within the FLA's document class:

1. Within the constructor, listen for `TransformGestureEvent.GESTURE_ROTATE`:

```
public function Main() {
    Multitouch.inputMode = MultitouchInputMode.GESTURE;
    bubble.addEventListener(TransformGestureEvent.GESTURE_PAN,
        pan);
    bubble.addEventListener(TransformGestureEvent.GESTURE_ROTATE,
        rotate);
}
```

2. Add a handler that responds to the event:

```
private function rotate(e:TransformGestureEvent):void {
    bubble.rotation += e.rotation;
}
```

3. Save your changes.

4. Publish the FLA and test it on your device.

You should now be able to rotate the on-screen content as well as being able to pan it.

> If you are testing on an older device, then you may find that the app performs poorly with the frame rate falling quite short of its target. This will be particularly true if you are developing with Flash Professional CS5. Don't worry; there are ways to dramatically improve the performance, which we will cover in *Chapter 6, Graphics and Hardware Acceleration*.

How it works...

Only a few simple steps were required to add rotation support.

First, a listener for the `TransformGestureEvent.GESTURE_ROTATE` event was added to the `bubble` movie clip:

```
bubble.addEventListener(TransformGestureEvent.GESTURE_ROTATE,
    rotate);
```

Finally, the actual event handler queried the event's `rotation` property in order to determine how much to rotate the movie clip:

```
private function rotate(e:TransformGestureEvent):void {
    bubble.rotation += e.rotation;
}
```

The `rotation` property specifies the change in rotation, measured in degrees, since the previous gesture event. This value was then added to the bubble's current angle of rotation in order to correctly update it.

See also

- ▸ _Setting the gesture input mode_
- ▸ _Zooming an object_
- ▸ _Using Cache as Bitmap Matrix, Chapter 6_

Zooming an object

The final gesture we will look at in this chapter is "zoom", which allows a user to scale content. It is typically performed by pinching the screen with two fingers. Drawing your fingers closer will zoom-out while pulling them apart will zoom-in. The Flash platform provides the `TransformGestureEvent.GESTURE_ZOOM` event that you can listen for and respond to.

Getting ready

If you haven't already done so, complete the _Rotating an object_ recipe before performing this one.

You can continue to work with the code you wrote during that recipe. Alternatively, work from the FLA and document class found in the book's accompanying code bundle at `chapter5\recipe9\`.

How to do it...

Make these changes to the FLA's document class:

1. Within the constructor, listen for the GESTURE_ZOOM event:

```
public function Main() {
    Multitouch.inputMode = MultitouchInputMode.GESTURE;
    bubble.addEventListener(TransformGestureEvent.GESTURE_PAN,
        pan);
    bubble.addEventListener(TransformGestureEvent.GESTURE_ROTATE,
        rotate);
    bubble.addEventListener(TransformGestureEvent.GESTURE_ZOOM,
        zoom);
}
```

2. Now, add an event handler for the zoom gesture:

```
private function zoom(e:TransformGestureEvent):void {
    bubble.scaleX *= e.scaleX;
    bubble.scaleY *= e.scaleY;
}
```

3. Save the class file.
4. Publish the FLA and deploy the IPA to your device.

You should now be able to pan, rotate, and zoom the bubble using the gestures provided by the Flash platform.

 If you are testing on an older device, then you may find that the app performs poorly with the frame rate falling quite short of its target. This will be particularly true if you are developing with Flash Professional CS5. Don't worry; there are ways to dramatically improve the performance, which we will cover in *Chapter 6, Graphics and Hardware Acceleration*.

How it works...

As with the other gestures covered in this chapter, implementing pinch zoom isn't difficult.

An event listener for TransformGestureEvent.GESTURE_ZOOM was added followed by the event's handler, which was responsible for actually zooming into the bubble movie clip.

The following is the line of code that was used to register the listener:

```
bubble.addEventListener(TransformGestureEvent.GESTURE_ZOOM,
    zoom);
```

And you can see the bubble's `scaleX` and `scaleY` properties being set within the `zoom()` event handler as follows:

```
private function zoom(e:TransformGestureEvent):void {
  bubble.scaleX *= e.scaleX;
  bubble.scaleY *= e.scaleY;
}
```

The `TransformGestureEvent` object's `scaleX` and `scaleY` properties specify the change in horizontal and vertical scale since the previous gesture event. To apply these values to a display object, simply multiply the display object's `scaleX` and `scaleY` properties with the event object's `scaleX` and `scaleY` properties respectively. You can see this being done in the code earlier.

It may not be immediately obvious, but the bubble's library symbol has its registration point set at its center. When scaling content, make sure the artwork within your container clip is centered otherwise the user may be presented with unexpected behavior when performing a zoom gesture.

See also

- ▸ *Setting the gesture input mode*
- ▸ *Using Cache as Bitmap Matrix, Chapter 6*

6

Graphics and Hardware Acceleration

In this chapter, we will cover:

- ▶ Comparing vector and bitmap graphics
- ▶ Understanding GPU-Blend mode
- ▶ Understanding GPU-Vector mode
- ▶ Using Cache as Bitmap
- ▶ Using Cache as Bitmap Matrix
- ▶ Accessing bitmaps with ActionScript
- ▶ Loading bitmaps at runtime
- ▶ Working with sprite sheets
- ▶ Performing bitmap animation with ActionScript

Introduction

The release of CS5 made it possible for Flash developers to create exciting content for iOS devices without changing their workflow. However, with only a fraction of the computing power of a modern day desktop or laptop, developing for devices such as the iPhone requires special design and coding considerations.

One of the largest bottlenecks is graphics rendering and it has become an area of frustration for many. It is simply not realistic to build the same graphics-heavy FLAs that you normally would for desktop delivery and expect them to run well on mobile. Even seemingly simple graphical operations can perform badly on iOS devices if poorly implemented.

By making available the same powerful drawing and animation tools that you are already familiar with, the Flash IDE can actually lull you into a false sense of security. For example, complex vector artwork, masks, timeline animations, deeply-nested display lists, and alpha transparencies are all easy to create but can negatively impact the performance of your app. Targeting mobile requires careful planning, profiling, and an understanding of the hardware you are developing for.

In this chapter, we will explore many techniques for optimizing render performance. We will cover both Flash's rendering pipeline and the hardware constraints that you will be working within. In addition, we will see how to take advantage of hardware acceleration, offloading much of the rendering workload from the CPU to the Graphics Processing Unit (GPU).

Comparing vector and bitmap graphics

Although Flash provides bitmap support, it is primarily thought of as a vector animation tool. Vector content can be created and edited directly within the IDE, making vectors an obvious choice above bitmaps, which must be edited externally.

However, given the hardware constraints of mobile devices such as the iPhone, are vectors appropriate or should you consider using bitmaps in order to maximize performance?

Getting ready

Two FLAs have been provided for this recipe and can be found within the book's accompanying code bundle at `chapter6\recipe1\`.

Both perform a simple render performance test. Each attempts to render ten instances of an animating movie clip. After five seconds, the test will end and the average number of frames per second (FPS) that was achieved will be shown. The higher that number, the faster the rendering performance of the test.

The first FLA—`recipe-vectors.fla`—uses vector artwork for each of the movie clip's animation frames. The second—`recipe-bitmaps.fla`—uses a bitmap representation for each.

How to do it...

Perform the following steps in order to run both tests on your device:

1. Open `recipe-vectors.fla` into Flash Professional.

2. Within the library, you will find a symbol named **Monkey**, which contains a four-frame vector animation. Double-click on the symbol and explore its display list. Its construction is typical for a Flash project, containing many nested clips of vector artwork.

3. Publish the FLA and deploy `c6-r1-v.ipa`. On your device's home screen, find the app named **c6 r1 v** and launch it. Wait for five seconds and then take a note of the frame rate that was achieved.

4. Now open `recipe-bitmaps.fla`. Double-click on the **Monkey** library symbol and explore its timeline. This FLA performs the same test as the first, except it uses a bitmap for each animation frame rather than vectors.

5. Publish the FLA and deploy `c6-r1-b.ipa` to your device. Launch **c6 r1 b** and take a note of the frame rate.

How it works...

The rendering performance of each will vary across iOS devices but no matter what device you use, the bitmap-based animation will outperform the vector-based equivalent.

To confirm this, let us take a look at the results of the two FLAs compiled from Flash Professional CS5 and run across a handful of devices. The following chart shows the average frame rate, measured in frames per second, that was achieved by each test:

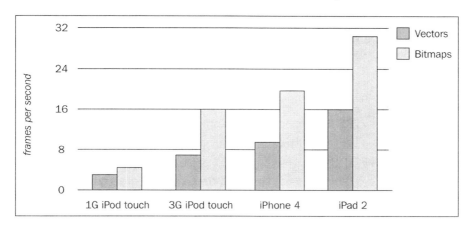

The results shown in this chart are an average taken from five runs of each test. Each device was running iOS 5 with the exception of the first-generation iPod touch, which had iOS 3.1 installed.

Use these results as a rough guide as they may vary slightly across runs.

So why do bitmaps render to the screen faster than vectors?

Vector graphics are represented by a combination of strokes, fills, colors, and gradients, with expensive mathematical calculations required in order to render them. Bitmaps on the other hand are simply a pixel-by-pixel representation of each color required by an image. With every single point of a bitmap already known, it can quickly be plotted to the screen.

So does this mean you should exclusively use bitmaps in place of vectors when developing for iOS? Not necessarily. Unlike bitmaps, vector artwork can be scaled and translated without losing fidelity. This is due to the fact that vector graphics are represented mathematically. Another advantage of vectors is file size. In many cases, vectors consume significantly less space than their bitmap counterparts.

However, if frame rate is critical to the success of your application, then you should always attempt to select the fastest rendering option. Also, be aware that doing so may come at the expense of increased memory usage, larger file sizes, and extended development times.

There's more...

Whether you opt to use vectors or bitmaps, adjusting the rendering quality can aid performance.

Stage quality

You can further increase performance by reducing the rendering quality used by your app. This is especially useful if you are attempting to maximize your frame rate while manipulating complex vector artwork.

Using ActionScript, set the `Stage.quality` property to one of the following constants:

 ▶ `StageQuality.HIGH`: Provides bitmap smoothing and anti-aliasing
 ▶ `StageQuality.MEDIUM`: Provides bitmap smoothing and uses lower quality anti-aliasing
 ▶ `StageQuality.LOW`: Does not smooth bitmaps or anti-alias graphics

All three quality settings are available from AIR 3.0 with only low and medium quality being supported by AIR 2.0-2.7. All versions of AIR for iOS use `StageQuality.MEDIUM` as the default setting.

Render quality is applied globally to all content within your application. Bitmaps, however, remain relatively unaffected and, with the exception of smoothing, will look identical across all quality settings. This conveniently allows you to get the highest level of performance from your vector assets without compromising the quality of any bitmaps within your application. You can repeatedly change the quality setting throughout your app's lifetime to best suit its needs at any particular moment.

Try reducing the stage's render quality within this recipe's FLAs. Simply open the `Main.as` document class shared by both and add the following line of code at the start of the constructor:

```
stage.quality = StageQuality.LOW;
```

Additionally, add the following import statement:

```
import flash.display.StageQuality;
```

Publish and re-deploy both `.ipa` files.

Rendering should now be faster although the quality of the vector artwork will be noticeably reduced. For many situations, this sacrifice may be acceptable, especially on a compact mobile device screen where any reduction in quality may be hard to spot.

See also

▸ _Converting vectors to bitmaps, Chapter 4_

▸ _Resizing bitmaps, Chapter 4_

Understanding GPU-Blend mode

Unlike developing for the Flash desktop player, two rendering modes are available to those targeting AIR for iOS. Exactly the same software renderer that is present in the desktop player is provided as the first option and is handled by the device's CPU. The second allows you to take advantage of the device's GPU and can significantly improve rendering performance in certain circumstances.

A rendering mode must be selected before compiling your FLA for iOS and cannot be changed at runtime. It is, therefore, important to understand the differences between both modes and make a decision early on regarding which one you would like to support. The choice of renderer can dictate how you architect your application.

Although both Flash Professional CS5 and CS5.5 provide an option to perform rendering on the GPU, how that rendering mode is actually implemented is different.

In this recipe, we will publish and deploy some example FLAs to help you understand the differences between the two modes. In particular, we will focus on the GPU-rendering mode provided by Flash Professional CS5.

Getting ready

Two FLAs have been provided with the book's accompanying code bundle—`render-test-cpu.fla` and `render-test-gpu.fla`—and can be found at `chapter6\recipe2\`.

Both FLAs are identical, with each randomly re-positioning ten movie-clip instances on every frame update. After five seconds, the test will end and the average number of frames per second (FPS) that was achieved will be shown. The higher that number, the faster the rendering performance of the test.

For this recipe, the FLAs should only be compiled using Flash Professional CS5. However, if you are using CS5.5, read through the material covered here before moving to the next recipe.

How to do it...

Let us select a rendering mode for each FLA and see how they perform on an actual device.

1. Open `render-test-cpu.fla` within Flash Professional CS5.

2. Select **File | iPhone OS Settings**.

3. From the **iPhone OS Settings** panel, select **CPU** from the **Rendering** field's drop-down box. Click on **OK** to confirm the change.

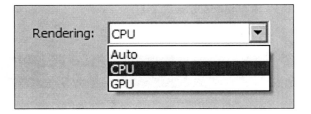

4. Save the FLA.

5. Publish the FLA and deploy `c6-r2-cpu.ipa` to your device. On your device's home screen, find the app named **c6 r2 cpu** and launch it. Take a note of the frame rate that was achieved by the test and then close the app.

6. Now, open `render-test-gpu.fla`.

7. Select **File | iPhone OS Settings**. This time, set the panel's **Rendering** field to **GPU**.

8. Click on **OK** to close the panel.

9. Save the FLA.

10. Publish and deploy `c6-r2-gpu.ipa` to your device. Launch the app labeled **c6 r2 gpu**. Take a note of the frame rate that was achieved.

How it works...

From the iPhone OS Settings panel, we set a different rendering mode for each of the FLAs. Both FLAs performed an identical test but used a different rendering path. The first used the CPU to render all graphical content, while we selected the GPU for the second.

The following chart shows the results of running the tests on a selection of devices. The results show the frame rate, measured in frames per second, that was achieved by each test.

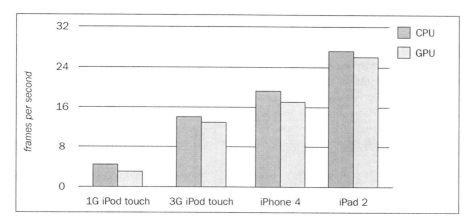

 The results shown in this chart are an average taken from five runs of each test. Each device was running iOS 5 with the exception of the first-generation iPod touch, which had iOS 3.1 installed.

Use these results as a rough guide as they may vary slightly across runs.

As you can see, the actual results vary across device but surprisingly there is very little difference in performance between the two modes, with CPU being slightly faster. You likely expected GPU rendering to be significantly better than CPU but to understand why this was not the case, we need to examine the rendering process in a little more detail. In particular, we need to look at how GPU rendering is implemented by AIR 2.0 in Flash Professional CS5.

The rendering process

Rendering is split into the following two distinct parts:

► Rasterization
► Scene composition

During **rasterization**, every element within your display list is drawn to a separate off-screen pixel buffer.

Once rasterization is complete, those pixel buffers are taken and are arranged to recreate the scene represented by the display list. This is known as **scene composition**.

Regardless of whether you are using Flash CS5 or CS5.5, both CPU and GPU modes will perform this rendering process. How each rendering mode achieves this, however, is different.

CPU mode and GPU-Blend mode

When using CPU mode, both rasterization and scene composition are performed entirely in software by the CPU.

In Flash CS5, when GPU mode is selected, the device's GPU will be used to compose the scene. Rasterization, however, is still performed by the CPU, with each of the off-screen pixel buffers being uploaded to the GPU for composition. In other words, the rendering process is only partially performed on the GPU. This is shown in the following illustrations. This implementation is known as GPU Blend and differs from that used by CS5.5:

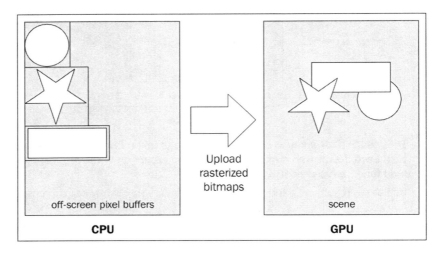

The following table should help clarify the difference between CPU and GPU-Blend mode used by AIR 2.0 in Flash CS5:

Render mode	Rasterization	Scene composition
CPU	CPU	CPU
GPU Blend	CPU	GPU

The GPU found on iOS devices can compose a scene much faster than the CPU. However, the process of uploading the pixel buffers from the CPU to the GPU can be expensive because of the amount of data that has to be sent. Therefore, to benefit from GPU acceleration when using Flash CS5, you must minimize the amount of bitmap traffic going from the CPU to the GPU. In other words, you need to reduce the frequency with which display objects are re-rasterized.

Redrawing dirty regions

Re-rasterization takes place when content within a scene changes. Whenever changes occur, Flash takes a note of the rectangular regions within the scene that need to be redrawn. These are known as the dirty regions and are used as an alternative to simply rendering the entire screen again. This is illustrated in the following diagram where the star-shaped clip moves position:

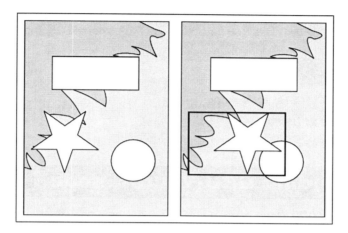

In this example, the star movie clip changes position between frames and by doing so creates a dirty region. The dirty region is represented as a rectangular area that encompasses the space consumed by the star's previous and current location. The circle, background image, and the star itself all touch this dirty region meaning all three need to be re-rasterized. Any display objects that intersect a dirty region need to be re-rasterized.

When using GPU Blend, the bitmap data for each of the re-rasterized display objects needs to be uploaded to the GPU in order for compositing to take place. As stated, uploading to the GPU can be expensive.

For scenes that change frequently, the performance of your app may suffer when using GPU acceleration. This is why `render-test-gpu.fla` doesn't perform as well as you might expect. There are so many changes per frame that the bandwidth penalty from transferring the re-drawn pixel buffers to the GPU actually negates much of the performance gained from utilizing the GPU.

There are techniques that can be employed to cache bitmap data directly on the GPU rather than continuously re-rasterizing and uploading from the CPU. We will discuss these shortly, but it should be clear that taking full advantage of AIR 2.0's hardware acceleration isn't as simple as changing the rendering mode within the iPhone OS Settings panel.

There's more...

One more thing, which you may have noticed when selecting a rendering mode is as follows:

Auto rendering

As well as CPU and GPU, there is an additional rendering option named **Auto** that is available. At this moment in time, **Auto** actually defaults to the CPU renderer and is, therefore, no different to selecting **CPU**. This is true for both Flash Professional CS5 and CS5.5.

See also

▸ *Understanding GPU-Vector mode*

▸ *Using Cache as Bitmap*

▸ *Using Cache as Bitmap Matrix*

Understanding GPU-Vector mode

In the *Understanding GPU-Blend mode* recipe, we spent time covering the intricacies of the GPU-rendering mode provided by Flash Professional CS5. Although GPU rendering is also supported for those using Flash Professional CS5.5, its implementation differs from CS5's.

In this recipe, we will cover how to select a rendering mode using CS5.5 and also use the same tests from the *Understanding GPU-Blend mode* recipe in order to see the performance difference between both GPU renderers.

Getting ready

Two FLAs have been provided—`render-test-cpu.fla` and `render-test-gpu.fla`—and can be found in the book's accompanying code bundle at `chapter6\recipe3\`.

Both FLAs are identical, with each randomly re-positioning ten movie-clip instances on every frame update. After five seconds, the test will end and the average number of frames per second (FPS) that was achieved will be shown. The higher that number, the faster the rendering performance of the test.

The FLAs should only be compiled using Flash Professional CS5.5. However, it is recommended that those using CS5 read through the material covered here rather than skipping to the next recipe.

How to do it...

Let us select a different rendering mode for each FLA and see the performance differences between the two on an actual device.

1. Open `render-test-cpu.fla` within Flash Professional CS5.5.

2. Select **File | AIR for iOS Settings** from Flash's drop-down menu.

3. From the AIR for iOS Settings panel, select **CPU** from the **Rendering** field's drop-down box. Click on **OK**.

4. Save the FLA.

5. Publish the FLA and deploy `c6-r3-cpu.ipa` to your device. From the home screen, launch the app labeled **c6 r3 cpu**. Let the app run for five seconds and then take a note of the frame rate.

6. Now, open `render-test-gpu.fla`.

7. Move to the **AIR for iOS Settings** panel and this time set the **Rendering** field to **GPU**.

8. Save the FLA.

9. Publish and deploy `c6-r3-gpu.ipa` to your device. Launch **c6 r3 gpu** and take a note of the app's frame rate.

How it works...

From the AIR for iOS Settings panel, we set a different rendering mode for each of the test FLAs. Both FLAs performed an identical test but used different rendering paths. The first used the CPU to render all graphics content, while we selected the GPU for the second.

The following chart shows the results of running the tests on a selection of devices. Each result shows the average frame rate that was achieved by each test.

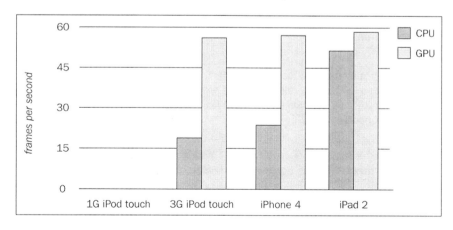

The results shown throughout this recipe are an average taken from five runs of each test. Each device was running iOS 5.

Use these results as a rough guide as they may vary slightly across runs.

It should be apparent that impressive performance gains can be made when setting GPU rendering within Flash Professional CS5.5. This is in stark contrast to the results from the *Understanding GPU-Blend mode* recipe where Flash Professional CS5 was used. Take the **iPhone 4** as an example. While there was no benefit from using the GPU when publishing from CS5, the same test published from CS5.5 exhibited a 252% increase in render performance—23 frames per second using the CPU compared to 58 using the GPU.

The following chart lets you easily compare the GPU rendering results for `render-test-gpu.fla` across both versions of Flash Professional:

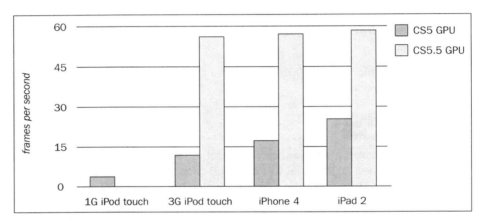

When published from CS5 and run on an iPhone 4, only an average of 17 frames per second were achieved over a five second period. Publishing the FLA using CS5.5 managed 58 frames per second on the same device. Quite an improvement!

You may have noticed in this chart that the GPU test compiled from Flash CS5.5 was not run on the first-generation iPod touch. Support for ARM v6 devices such as the first-generation iPod touch was dropped in AIR 2.6.

So why does GPU rendering produce such huge gains in CS5.5 compared to CS5? It is down to changes in how GPU rendering has been implemented since AIR 2.6, which we will now cover.

GPU-Vector mode

GPU Blend, which is the GPU-render mode supported in Flash CS5, only actually performs scene composition on the GPU—rasterization takes place entirely on the CPU. The GPU-render mode supported by CS5.5, however, performs both rasterization and scene composition on the GPU, removing the need to transfer bitmap data from the CPU to the GPU. This implementation is known as GPU Vector and is many times faster than GPU Blend.

When GPU rendering is selected, GPU Vector will be used by AIR for iOS apps published from Flash Professional CS5.5, while apps published from CS5 will use GPU Blend.

The following table summarizes the various rendering modes and from which version of Flash and AIR each is available:

Render mode	Rasterization	Scene composition	Flash	AIR
CPU	CPU	CPU	CS5 and CS5.5	2.0 - 3.x
GPU Blend	CPU	GPU	CS5	2.0
GPU Vector	GPU	GPU	CS5.5	2.6 - 3.x

When working with Flash Professional CS5, obtaining a high frame rate from even a modest FLA can be difficult without an understanding of GPU Blend and knowing how to minimize bitmap traffic between the CPU and GPU. On the other hand, those working with Flash Professional CS5.5 need not worry so much. GPU-Vector mode removes much of the hardship, making the process of writing AIR for iOS apps closer to writing for the desktop.

Use GPU mode ahead of CPU as it yields better performance. This is true for both CS5 and CS5.5, although those using CS5 will need to work a little harder in order to take advantage of the hardware acceleration provided by the GPU.

GPU Vector is a very strong reason for upgrading from Flash Professional CS5 to CS5.5. Of course, if you are targeting older iOS devices such as the second-generation iPod touch or iPhone 3G, then you will still need to rely upon CS5 and GPU Blend.

There's more...

The blazing-fast performance of GPU-Vector mode does come at a cost.

Rendering vectors using GPU-Vector mode

Performance isn't the only noticeable difference between GPU-Blend and GPU-Vector modes. Whereas GPU Blend and CPU will produce identical renditions of vector artwork, GPU Vector won't always be so accurate.

The GPU is optimized for rendering bitmaps and doesn't provide the same fidelity as the software renderer when recreating the complex vector shapes used by Flash. GPU-Vector mode requires that Flash's vector shapes be converted to simpler triangles that can be rendered quickly by the GPU. GPU Blend on the other hand, performs all rasterization on the CPU, allowing it to take advantage of the software renderer at the expense of performance.

When using Flash Professional CS5.5, be aware that rendering vector artwork on the GPU won't be as precise as rendering on the CPU. CPU rendering is accurate but slow, whereas the GPU is faster but inaccurate. However, any differences between the two can be difficult to spot.

Using GPU-Vector mode with Flash Professional CS5

Although Flash Professional CS5 only supports AIR 2.0, it is actually possible to take advantage of the GPU-Vector rendering mode supported by AIR 2.6 and above. To do this, you will need to first publish a SWF from Flash CS5, then package the SWF into a native iOS app from the command line using the AIR Development Tool (ADT). ADT is included with the latest AIR SDK and can be downloaded from `www.adobe.com/products/air/sdk`.

Command line packaging is outside the scope of this book; however, Adobe does provide detailed documentation on the subject at: `http://help.adobe.com/en_US/air/build/WS901d38e593cd1bac35eb7b4e12cddc5fbbb-8000.html`.

Stage 3D

In addition to AIR's existing rendering modes, Adobe has recently released a new rendering model named Stage 3D (previously codenamed Molehill), which leverages GPU hardware to provide advanced 2D and 3D capabilities.

At the time of writing, Stage 3D is only available for Flash and AIR on the desktop. However, Adobe is actively working to bring it to mobile. When it arrives, Stage 3D's performance should far exceed what is currently possible with AIR for iOS's existing rendering pipelines.

You can find out more about Stage 3D from Adobe Developer Connection at `www.adobe.com/devnet/flashplayer/stage3d.html`.

See also

- ▶ *Using Cache as Bitmap*
- ▶ *Using Cache as Bitmap Matrix*

Using Cache as Bitmap

Rasterization can be expensive and should be minimized. For display objects that only experience translation along the X and Y axes, there is a technique available that removes the need for that object to be re-rasterized. This technique is known as Cache as Bitmap and in most circumstances can accelerate the rendering performance of your application.

Cache as Bitmap takes a display object and generates a bitmap representation of it internally. The cached bitmap is then used for rendering rather than re-rasterizing the original display object. This can result in huge performance gains, particularly when working with complex vector artwork, which can be CPU-intensive to rasterize.

Normally, when a display object changes position, it needs to be re-rasterized. When cached, however, any two-dimensional translations will no longer result in that object being redrawn. Instead, its cached bitmap will be used.

Let us see how to apply Cache as Bitmap using both ActionScript and the Flash IDE.

Getting ready

Before continuing you should be aware of the difference between vector and bitmap graphics, and also have a firm understanding of the various rendering paths available when developing AIR for iOS apps. If you haven't already done so, complete the following recipes:

- *Comparing vector and bitmap graphics*
- *Understanding GPU-Blend mode*
- *Understanding GPU-Vector mode*

An FLA has been provided for this recipe and can be found within the book's accompanying code bundle at `chapter6\recipe4\recipe.fla`.

Its document class positions ten instances of a **Monkey** movie clip on top of a **Background** movie clip. On every frame update, the ten monkeys are randomly repositioned. After a period of five seconds, the average frame rate that was achieved is displayed.

The movie clips used for this recipe are constructed from vector graphics as opposed to bitmaps. Also, this recipe's FLA has been set to use GPU rendering.

How to do it...

We will first see how the existing version of the FLA performs before taking advantage of bitmap caching.

1. Open `recipe.fla`.
2. Publish the current version of the FLA and deploy it to your device.

3. Launch the app from your device's home screen.

4. Take a note of the frame rate; then delete the app from your device.

5. Now, move back to `recipe.fla` within Flash.

   Let us apply Cache as Bitmap to the display objects used by the FLA. Using the **Selection Tool (V)**, click on the **Background** movie clip sitting on the stage. From the **Properties** panel, expand the **DISPLAY** section and enable Cache as Bitmap. If you are using Flash Professional CS5, then this is done by checking the **Cache as bitmap** checkbox. For CS5.5, select **Cache as Bitmap** from the **Render** field's drop-down box.

6. Open the FLA's document class and add the following line of code within the constructor:

   ```
   for(var i:uint = 0; i < 10; i++)
   {
      var monkey:MovieClip = new Monkey();
      monkey.x = Math.random() * stage.stageWidth;
      monkey.y = Math.random() * stage.stageHeight;
      monkey.cacheAsBitmap = true;

      monkeys.push(monkey);

      addChild(monkey);
   }
   ```

7. Save the class.

8. Publish and deploy the new version to your device.

9. Compare the frame rate against the previous version of the app. The app's performance should be noticeably improved.

How it works...

The `DisplayObject` class provides the `cacheAsBitmap` property, which is available from any class that extends `DisplayObject`, such as `Sprite` and `MovieClip`.

We used ActionScript to set the `cacheAsBitmap` property for each of the **Monkey** instances:

```
monkey.cacheAsBitmap = true;
```

For the **Background** movie clip sitting on the stage, caching was activated through the **Properties** panel.

To understand why bitmap caching can be beneficial, let us start by examining what happens within this recipe's example when Cache as Bitmap isn't set.

On each frame update, the position of the ten **Monkey** movie-clip instances is changed, forcing a dirty region to be created for each of the ten clips. Although the **Background** movie clip doesn't change position, it falls within the dirty regions. Therefore, on each frame update, the **Background** and all ten **Monkey** instances need to be re-rasterized before being composited into the scene.

By taking advantage of Cache as Bitmap, the rendering time for each frame can be reduced. After setting Cache as Bitmap, each clip is initially rasterized and an internal representation is stored. Now on each frame update, there will be no need to re-rasterize any of the **Monkey** movie clips or the **Background** movie clip, as a cached bitmap representation of each is available and can be used during scene composition.

On every frame update other than the first, we have managed to completely skip rasterization.

Whether using Flash Professional CS5 or CS5.5, you should have experienced a significant performance increase by using Cache as Bitmap. The following chart gives you the results from publishing this recipe's example using CS5 and testing it on a handful of devices:

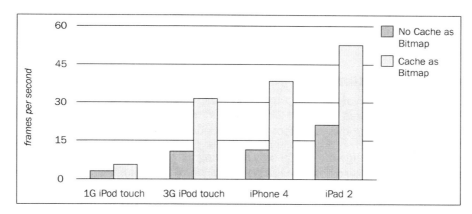

And the following chart shows the same test published using CS5.5 and AIR 3.0:

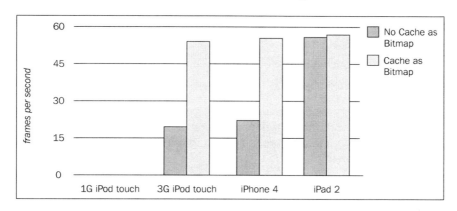

>
> The results shown in these charts are an average taken from five runs of each test. Each device was running iOS 5 with the exception of the first-generation iPod touch, which had iOS 3.1 installed.
>
> Use these results as a rough guide as they may vary slightly across runs.

As you can see from the charts, Cache as Bitmap can significantly increase your application's frame rate when using complex vector artwork. This does come at the expense of memory; however, as an additional bitmap for each display object must be stored.

Although we utilized GPU rendering in this recipe, using Cache as Bitmap in conjunction with CPU rendering will also lead to performance increases when dealing with complex vector artwork. Caching directly on the GPU, however, produces the largest performance increase.

There's more...

Cache as Bitmap is extremely powerful and when used correctly can be hugely beneficial. However, it is not always apparent when to use it and there are several pitfalls that you should be aware of.

Other transformation changes

Bitmap caching is only advantageous if the cached bitmap does not have to be frequently re-generated. While changes along the X or Y axes are fine, other changes will invalidate the cached bitmap, forcing the display object to be re-cached.

For objects that don't change often, you may be willing to take the performance hit. However, frequent changes are likely to degrade the performance of your application, as each new change is rasterized and then copied back into the internal pixel buffer.

The following is a list of changes that will force a display object to be re-cached:

- Visibility
- Alpha transparency
- Transformation—Scale and Rotation
- Playhead movement within the object's timeline
- Any change to a child object

Constantly re-caching is very expensive and will slow your application. If you need to make frequent changes to an object, then either avoid using Cache as Bitmap, or deactivate it during such periods. Improper use of Cache as Bitmap will reduce the render performance of your application rather than improve it.

Caching display objects that contain children

Be careful when setting Cache as Bitmap on display objects that contain children.

An internal bitmap will be created of the entire container including all of its child objects. If any of those children change relative to the container, then the whole container clip will need to be re-cached. This is true even if a child object only changes its x or y position. It is only the container clip that can be successfully translated without invalidating the cached bitmap.

For nested clips, apply Cache as Bitmap to the lowest leaf node that changes relative to its container. Don't apply Cache as Bitmap to the container itself.

This is a common mistake and can cripple the performance of your application.

Taking advantage of GPU Blend

If you are using Flash Professional CS5 and wish to take advantage of GPU rendering, then the use of Cache as Bitmap is essential for GPU Blend to be effective. It isn't just vectors that can benefit either—bitmap performance can be accelerated too.

Where cached bitmaps are stored is important. When using GPU rendering, the cached bitmaps will be stored directly on the GPU as textures. This is of particular importance when using GPU Blend as it removes the bandwidth bottleneck experienced when bitmap data is repeatedly transferred from the CPU to the GPU.

By using bitmap caching in conjunction with GPU Blend, rendering performance will be vastly increased. The only time bitmap data will be transferred from the CPU to the GPU will be when each display object is initially cached, or when a cached bitmap needs to be regenerated.

For GPU Blend, Cache as Bitmap will accelerate both display objects that use vectors and those that use bitmaps. Where possible, try to take advantage of it.

Bitmaps and GPU Vector

While applying Cache as Bitmap to bitmaps provides acceleration for GPU Blend, the same isn't true for GPU Vector and will actually slightly degrade performance.

When you cache a display object, you are essentially creating a pixel buffer. However, that is exactly what a bitmap is anyway. By caching bitmaps when using GPU Vector, you are simply creating a secondary copy of your bitmap, which will only consume more memory and take time to perform the second copy.

In GPU-Blend mode, Cache as Bitmap is used to copy the bitmaps to GPU memory. In GPU-Vector mode, the bitmaps are already in GPU memory, removing the need for Cache as Bitmap.

Using vectors ahead of bitmaps

When working with vector artwork, Cache as Bitmap can be used to produce the performance benefits typically associated with bitmaps. Simply create your artwork using Flash's drawing tools and then set Cache as Bitmap for each movie clip that contains that vector artwork. The clips will be rasterized and the cached bitmap versions will be used from that point onwards.

This technique is almost as fast as simply using a bitmap representation of your artwork. The only difference being is that a vector version first has to be converted to a bitmap, which will result in a slight performance hit when the object first appears on screen. If the size of your IPA is a concern or you genuinely need to use vector artwork, then this option is ideal.

See also

▶ *Adding content to the stage, Chapter 2*

▶ *Masking content, Chapter 4*

▶ *Using Cache as Bitmap Matrix*

Using Cache as Bitmap Matrix

Cache as Bitmap is extremely useful for display objects that are only affected by two-dimensional translation. However, it is also possible to benefit from bitmap caching when applying other changes to a display object such as scaling and rotation. This is achieved by using a transform matrix in conjunction with a cached bitmap and is known as Cache as Bitmap Matrix.

Let us work through an example.

Getting ready

An FLA has been provided as a starting point. From the book's accompanying code bundle, open `chapter6\recipe5\recipe.fla` into Flash Professional.

Ten instances of a **Monkey** movie clip are positioned on top of a **Background** movie clip. All ten movie clips are continuously rotated and after five seconds, the average frame rate that was achieved is displayed.

The movie clips used for this recipe are constructed from vector graphics and the FLA has been set to use GPU rendering.

How to do it...

Work through the following steps to see the performance benefit Cache as Bitmap Matrix provides for each of the rotating movie clips.

1. Publish the current version of the FLA and deploy it to a device.

2. Launch the app and take a note of the frame rate that is reported after five seconds.

3. Delete the app from your device.

4. Move back to `recipe.fla` within Flash Professional.

5. Open the FLA's `Main.as` document class and add the following lines of code within the constructor:

```
var matrix:Matrix = new Matrix();
for(var i:uint = 0; i < 10; i++)
{
   var monkey:MovieClip = new Monkey();
   monkey.x = Math.random() * stage.stageWidth;
   monkey.y = Math.random() * stage.stageHeight;
   monkey.rotation = Math.random() * 360;
   monkey.cacheAsBitmap = true;
   monkey.cacheAsBitmapMatrix = matrix;

   monkeys.push(monkey);

   addChild(monkey);
}
```

6. Finally, add an import statement for the `Matrix` class:

```
import flash.geom.Matrix;
```

7. Save the document class.

8. Publish and deploy to your device.

9. Compare the number of frames rendered against the previous version of the app. It should be improved.

How it works...

Cache as Bitmap Matrix prevents a display object's cached bitmap from becoming invalid when any two-dimensional transformation is applied. The same is also true for a change in visibility or alpha transparency. Therefore, for any of these changes, the cached bitmap won't be regenerated; the changes will instead be applied directly to the cached bitmap's internal pixel buffer, which is advantageous as the display object won't need to be re-rasterized.

Unlike Cache as Bitmap, Cache as Bitmap Matrix cannot be set from Flash's **Properties** panel. Instead, use ActionScript to set the `cacheAsBitmapMatrix` property provided by the `DisplayObject` class.

The `cacheAsBitmapMatrix` property is set by passing it a `Matrix` object and is used to generate the cached bitmap. For this recipe, we passed the identity matrix, which forced the display objects to be rasterized without any change in appearance.

In mathematics, a matrix is a rectangular array of numbers, which can be used to apply a transformation to points in 2D or 3D space. A matrix can be used to apply various graphical transformations to Flash display objects, such as translation, rotation, scaling, and skewing. An identity matrix is a special matrix that does not alter the appearance of any points that it is applied to.

The `flash.geom.Matrix` class is provided by the Flash API, making it easy to create matrices that can be used to perform transformations upon your display objects. When instantiating a `Matrix` object, an identity matrix is created if you do not provide any parameters to the constructor.

The `cacheAsBitmapMatrix` property cannot be used on its own and must always be set in conjunction with the `cacheAsBitmap` property. You can see this in the following code snippet taken from this recipe's example code:

```
monkey.cacheAsBitmap = true;
monkey.cacheAsBitmapMatrix = matrix;
```

If you have already applied Cache as Bitmap on a display object, then there is no penalty for also applying Cache as Bitmap Matrix. In fact, this is the recommended practice as it will prevent performance penalties if changes other than to an object's `x` and `y` properties are made.

The following table shows the benefits of using Cache as Bitmap Matrix by highlighting changes that won't invalidate the cached bitmap.

	Translate	Scale	Rotate	Skew	Alpha	Visibility
`cacheAsBitmap`	✓					
`cacheAsBitmap` and `cacheAsBitmapMatrix`	✓	✓	✓	✓	✓	✓

When scaling or rotating a vector display object that has been cached, there may be a loss of fidelity as the transformations will be applied to the cached bitmap rather than to the original vector artwork. Therefore, the final rendition will exhibit the artifacts associated with scaling or rotating bitmap images.

Setting the `cacheAsBitmapMatrix` property generates a cached bitmap even if the display object is off-screen or has its `visible` property set to `false`.

If you are curious about matrices, then perform a search for `flash.geom.Matrix` within Adobe Community Help. For a better understanding of matrix mathematics, refer to Wikipedia: `http://en.wikipedia.org/wiki/Matrix_(mathematics)`.

There's more...

Now, let us explore Cache as Bitmap Matrix in more detail.

Selecting a matrix transformation

The matrix transformation you set the `cacheAsBitmapMatrix` property to will be used to generate the cached bitmap.

For example, you may choose to use a scale matrix to create a cached version of a vector movie clip that is actually twice the movie clip's original size. Although the cached bitmap would consume more memory, it would allow the movie clip to maintain its fidelity when being scaled to a maximum of twice its size. Alternatively, you could cache a version that is half the size of the original, reducing memory overheads at the expense of fidelity.

It is important to note that creating a cached bitmap that is different in size to the actual display object doesn't alter the size of the object on screen. In other words, if your display object is 100x100 pixels in size and its cached bitmap is 50x50 pixels, the object will remain 100x100 pixels in size on screen. AIR will take the 50x50 cached bitmap and actually double its dimensions to ensure it is shown at the correct size.

The following code example shows how to create a cached bitmap that is half the size of the actual display object:

```
var matrix:Matrix = new Matrix();
matrix.scale(0.5, 0.5);
displayObject.cacheAsBitmap = true;
displayObject.cacheAsBitmapMatrix = matrix;
```

However, generally the identity matrix will suffice:

```
displayObject.cacheAsBitmap = true;
displayObject.cacheAsBitmapMatrix = new Matrix();
```

Changing the Matrix object

A common pitfall is attempting to apply two-dimensional transformations to a display object by altering the `cacheAsBitmapMatrix` transform. Making changes to this matrix will actually invalidate the cache, forcing a new bitmap to be generated.

To apply transforms such as scaling and rotation to your display object, simply use its two-dimensional transformation properties such as `scaleX`, `scaleY`, and `rotation`.

For most use cases, the `cacheAsBitmapMatrix` property should be set once for a display object, and then left untouched.

Reusing the Matrix object

If you are applying the same transformation matrix to a series of display objects, then create a single instance of the `Matrix` object and re-use it. It is a common mistake to recreate the `Matrix` object each time:

```
for(var i:uint = 0; i < 100; i++)
{
    displayObjects[i].cacheAsBitmap = true;
    displayObjects[i].cacheAsBitmapMatrix = new Matrix();
}
```

This code will compile and run but will create 100 copies of the identity matrix. This will unnecessarily consume memory and degrade performance due to the number of memory allocations and eventual garbage collection.

Instead, create the matrix outside of your loop and re-use it as shown in the following code snippet:

```
var matrix:Matrix = new Matrix();
for(var i:uint = 0; i < 100; i++)
{
    displayObjects[i].cacheAsBitmap = true;
    displayObjects[i].cacheAsBitmapMatrix = matrix;
}
```

3D properties

When a display object has a 3D property applied to it, that object automatically becomes cached and you have no control over the transformation matrix that is used to generate the cached bitmap. The `cacheAsBitmapMatrix` property can only be used with display objects that don't have any 3D properties set. If you set a 3D property, such as `z` or `rotationX`, on a display object that has bitmap caching applied, then your cached bitmap will be deactivated and a new bitmap will be generated.

Using 3D properties provides most of the benefits of manually setting the `cacheAsBitmapMatrix` property. The one exception is that setting a 3D object's `visible` property to `false` will invalidate its cached bitmap.

Working with GPU Blend

Some of the largest performance gains are once again to be had when using AIR 2.0's GPU-Blend rendering mode.

If you have been using Flash Professional CS5 and developing on an older iOS device, then the examples from the *Rotating an object* and *Zooming an object* recipes in *Chapter 5* may have performed poorly. Setting the `cacheAsBitmap` and `cacheAsBitmapMatrix` properties will ensure the movie clip used in each example is stored and transformed directly on the GPU.

If performance was an issue, then revisit these recipes and add the following two lines of code to the constructor within each FLA's document class:

```
bubble.cacheAsBitmap = true;
bubble.cacheAsBitmapMatrix = new Matrix();
```

Also, remember to import the `Matrix` class:

```
import flash.geom.Matrix;
```

It is also worth noting that it is not just vector graphics that benefit from Cache as Bitmap Matrix when using GPU Blend. Cache as Bitmap Matrix will also accelerate the rendering of bitmaps that have two-dimensional transformations applied to them. However, the opposite is true for GPU Vector, where Cache as Bitmap Matrix will actually harm performance when using bitmaps.

See also

▶ *Rotating an object, Chapter 5*

▶ *Zooming an object, Chapter 5*

Accessing bitmaps with ActionScript

The GPU found on iOS devices is optimized for rendering bitmaps rather than the complex vector shapes that can be produced using Flash. This makes bitmaps the preferred graphics option when building high performance apps. While bitmaps can be stored in the library and simply dragged to a timeline during development, they can also be directly manipulated at runtime using ActionScript.

This recipe will show you how to add a bitmap to the display list at runtime.

Getting ready

From the book's accompanying code bundle, open `chapter6\recipe6\recipe.fla` into Flash Professional.

Sitting in the library is a bitmap named **monkey.png**. We will write code to add this bitmap to the display list.

How to do it...

We will split this recipe into two parts. First we will export the bitmap for ActionScript usage, before actually writing some ActionScript to display it at runtime.

Exporting the bitmap

Let us start by exporting the bitmap's data for ActionScript usage.

1. Within the library, right-click on **monkey.png** and select **Properties** from the context menu.

2. From the **Bitmap Properties** dialog box, set the **Compression** field to **Lossless (PNG/GIF)**. If you are using Flash Professional CS5.5, then ensure that the **Options** tab is selected first.

3. Now check the **Export for ActionScript** checkbox and change the text within the **Class** field to `MonkeyBitmapData`. If you are using Flash Professional CS5.5, then this should be performed from the panel's **ActionScript** tab.

   A warning panel will appear containing the following text:

   A definition for this class could not be found in the classpath, so one will be automatically generated in the SWF file upon export.

   This is the expected behavior. Click on **OK**.

4. Save the FLA.

Displaying the bitmap using ActionScript

With the bitmap's data now accessible to ActionScript, let us go ahead and write some code to display it.

1. Create a document class and name it `Main`.

2. Add the following import statement:

```
import flash.display.Bitmap;
import flash.display.MovieClip;
```

3. Within the constructor add a line of ActionScript to create an instance of the bitmap data sitting in the library:

```
public function Main() {
    var bitmapData:MonkeyBitmapData = new MonkeyBitmapData();
}
```

4. Now, create a `Bitmap` object that uses the bitmap data:

```
public function Main() {
    var bitmapData:MonkeyBitmapData = new MonkeyBitmapData();
    var bitmap:Bitmap = new Bitmap(bitmapData);
}
```

5. Finally, position the bitmap and add it to the display list:

```
public function Main() {
    var bitmapData:MonkeyBitmapData = new MonkeyBitmapData();
    var bitmap:Bitmap = new Bitmap(bitmapData);
    bitmap.x = 23;
    bitmap.y = 57;
    addChild(bitmap);
}
```

6. Save the class as `Main.as`.

7. Save your FLA and test using ADL. The bitmap image stored in the library will be displayed on screen.

8. Publish the FLA and deploy it to your device.

How it works...

In order to access an image within the library, you need to explicitly export the image's bitmap data for ActionScript usage. We did this by assigning the bitmap a unique class name of `MonkeyBitmapData` from the **Bitmap Properties** dialog box. By using this class name, it is then possible to create an instance of that bitmap data using ActionScript.

Once the bitmap data was obtained, we simply created a `Bitmap` display object and passed it a reference to the bitmap data. Displaying it was then a simple case of setting the bitmap's `x` and `y` properties before adding it to the display list.

It should be noted that the class you linked the bitmap to is automatically generated when the SWF is published—there is no need to write code as it is done for you. When generated, it will inherit from `flash.display.BitmapData` allowing you to treat any instances of it as a `BitmapData` object.

Every bitmap you export for ActionScript will be included directly within your app's binary, which will increase both its initial load time and memory footprint. Be careful as there is no way to free these bitmaps from memory once you are finished with them—an app that supports both standard and Retina graphics for example, could easily exhaust memory using this technique. However, with the bitmap data stored directly within the app's binary, access to that data will be fast.

For more information regarding bitmaps, perform a search for `flash.display.Bitmap` and `flash.display.BitmapData` within Adobe Community Help.

There's more...

There are performance gains to be had when using bitmaps. The following information will help you take full advantage of GPU acceleration when working directly with them.

Managing image sizes

If you are using GPU rendering and working with bitmap images, then there are some optimizations you can perform to maximize performance.

The GPU allocates memory using powers of 2 for each of a bitmap's dimensions. For example, a 31x15 bitmap will be allocated the same amount of memory as a 32x16 bitmap, while a 33x17 bitmap will consume the same memory as a 64x32 bitmap. The size of each bitmap also impacts rendering performance, as memory copies take longer for larger bitmaps.

Use bitmaps with dimensions that are close to a power of 2 but not larger. The dimensions don't have to be exact powers of 2, as Flash will pad the bitmaps for you.

Size restrictions

There is a size restriction imposed by the GPU. The actual size depends on the iOS hardware you are using. For older devices, your display objects cannot exceed 1024x1024 pixels in size. The more recent devices allow display objects with a maximum of 2048x2048 pixels in size. The following table summarizes this:

	iPhone		iPod touch		iPad
	original and 3G	3GS and 4/4S	1st and 2nd gen	3rd and 4th gen	1 and 2
1024x1024	✓		✓		
2048x2048		✓		✓	✓

If you need to work with a display object that is larger than the size permitted by the GPU, then consider using Cache as Bitmap Matrix to cache a smaller representation of it.

Storing bitmap data on the GPU

When utilizing GPU rendering, any `BitmapData` that you export for ActionScript will be stored directly in GPU memory as a texture when instantiated. This is the case for both Flash Professional CS5's GPU-Blend mode and CS5.5's GPU-Vector mode, providing the fastest possible rendering path for both.

There is no need to explicitly set a `Bitmap` object's `cacheAsBitmap` and `cacheAsBitmapMatrix` properties, as the bitmap data used by it will already be GPU-accelerated. In fact, doing so will only serve to create a duplicate copy of the data that is already on the GPU, which would be a waste of memory.

While display objects that have bitmap caching applied to them become textures, `BitmapData` objects _are_ textures on the GPU. This distinction is important and has implications when managing memory. When working with multiple `Bitmap` instances, each bitmap can be made to point to the exact same `BitmapData` object, meaning only one texture is required on the GPU and shared by all. Applying bitmap caching to multiple instances of the same display object, however, uploads an individual texture for each, consuming more memory.

See also

▸ _Linking classes to movie-clip symbols, Chapter 3_

▸ _Using Cache as Bitmap Matrix_

▸ _Loading bitmaps at runtime_

Loading bitmaps at runtime

It is a common practice to minimize an app's up-front load time and memory footprint by loading graphics resources on demand. When making use of bitmaps, it is possible to store them outside of your app's binary and use ActionScript to load them at runtime when required.

Let us see how this is done.

Getting ready

An FLA has been provided as a starting point.

From the book's accompanying code bundle, open `chapter6\recipe7\recipe.fla` into Flash Professional. Its AIR for iOS settings have been applied and a dynamic text field has been added at the bottom of the stage.

Additionally, `chapter6\recipe7\monkey.png` has been provided, which is the bitmap we will load at runtime.

How to do it...

This recipe is split into two parts. First, we will bundle the bitmap with the app, then we will write some ActionScript to load it.

Bundling the bitmap

Perform the following steps to bundle the bitmap with the app.

1. Open the **AIR for iOS Settings** panel and ensure that the panel's **General** tab is selected.

2. At the bottom of the panel is the **Included files** list. Click on the **+** symbol above the list and select **monkey.png** from your FLA's root folder. Click on **Open** to select the file. You should now see **monkey.png** in the **Included files** list.

3. Click on **OK** to close the **AIR for iOS Settings** panel.

Loading the bitmap at runtime

Now, let us write the ActionScript required to load the bitmap and display it.

1. Create a document class and name it `Main`.

2. Add the following import statements:

```
import flash.display.MovieClip;
import flash.display.Bitmap;
import flash.display.Loader;
import flash.events.Event;
import flash.net.URLRequest;
```

3. Within the constructor, create an instance of the `Loader` class; listen for `Event.COMPLETE` being dispatched when the bitmap has loaded; and initiate the load:

```
public function Main() {
    var loader:Loader = new Loader();
    loader.contentLoaderInfo.addEventListener(Event.COMPLETE,
        bitmapLoaded);
    loader.load(new URLRequest("monkey.png"));
}
```

4. Finally, add a handler for `Event.COMPLETE`.

```
private function bitmapLoaded(e:Event):void {
    var b:Bitmap = e.target.content as Bitmap;
    b.x = 23;
    b.y = 57;
    addChild(b);

    msgField.text = "loaded";
}
```

The `bitmapLoaded()` handler will add the loaded bitmap to the stage. The bitmap is obtained from the handler's event parameter, positioned then added to the display list.

5. Save the class; when prompted name the file `Main.as`.

6. Save the FLA and test using ADL to ensure there are no compiler errors. The bitmap should load and be positioned on screen. Additionally, the text field should be populated with the word **loaded** indicating success.

7. Finally, publish your app for iOS and deploy it to a device.

How it works...

Resources can be bundled with an app by adding them to the **Included files** list from the AIR for iOS Settings panel. You can either add files individually or include the contents of a folder. For this recipe, we simply selected the `monkey.png` file, ensuring it would be bundled with the IPA.

Your app's start-up time won't be affected by this as bundled resources aren't part of its binary. Instead, during installation, they will be copied to the same directory as the app, allowing the app to load them from the device's file system at runtime.

To actually load the bitmap, an instance of the `Loader` class was used and a call to its `load()` method was made. Load operations are asynchronous—loading from the device's file system can take time—meaning we had to listen for `Event.COMPLETE` being dispatched before attempting to access the bitmap.

With `monkey.png` being bundled into the same folder as the app itself, a relative file path was passed to `load()` rather than an absolute path:

```
loader.load(new URLRequest("monkey.png"));
```

Once the bitmap has loaded, the `COMPLETE` event's handler is called and the bitmap is displayed on screen.

To actually obtain the bitmap, simply extract the loaded content from the `Event` object and cast it to a `Bitmap`. The following line of code does that:

```
var b:Bitmap = e.target.content as Bitmap;
```

You are then free to manipulate the bitmap and add it to the display list.

Loading bitmaps at runtime rather than including them directly within your FLA's library will reduce the overall size of an app's binary, which will lead to improved start-up times. Additionally, in contrast to resources embedded directly within the app's binary, you will be able to manage your app's memory usage by freeing those bitmaps once you are done with them. While bitmaps directly included within the app will be immediately available, you will actually need to wait for bitmaps from the file system to load.

The `Loader` class loads content asynchronously. This is convenient as it prevents the execution of your application from being blocked while resources are being loaded.

You can obtain more detail regarding the classes used in this recipe from Adobe Community Help. Specifically, take a look at `flash.display.Loader`, `flash.display.Bitmap`, and `flash.display.BitmapData`.

There's more...

Before moving on, let us cover a few more points related to bitmap data.

Handling load errors

When loading bitmaps, you should also listen for `IOErrorEvent.IO_ERROR`, which is dispatched when a load operation fails. This will most commonly happen when a file path is incorrect or the resource that you are trying to load is missing.

Accessing the bitmap's data

You can easily access the bitmap's data through the `Bitmap.bitmapData` property. The following code snippet illustrates this:

```
private function bitmapLoaded(e:Event):void {
   var b:Bitmap = e.target.content as Bitmap;
   var bd:BitmapData = b.bitmapData;
}
```

It is also possible to point the `bitmapData` property to a different `BitmapData` object, changing the bitmap's appearance. This is extremely useful for creating animations programmatically and can be used to fully utilize hardware acceleration on the GPU.

Disposing of bitmap data

While you typically rely on the garbage collector to free memory, you can force AIR, at runtime, to immediately release the bitmap data memory occupied by a `BitmapData` object. This is done by calling `BitmapData.dispose()` and is shown in the following code snippet:

```
private function bitmapLoaded(e:Event):void {
   var b:Bitmap = e.target.content as Bitmap;
   var bd:BitmapData = b.bitmapData;
   bd.dispose();
}
```

The `BitmapData` object itself isn't released, just its bitmap data. The memory consumed by the actual `BitmapData` object is eventually released by the garbage collector.

When you no longer have a use for a bitmap, remember to dispose of its data. This will free memory, allowing you to load other bitmaps that couldn't otherwise be loaded and stored. You should, however, be careful when freeing bitmap data memory. Memory management can consume precious CPU cycles and hinder the performance of your application. You should attempt to free memory at convenient opportunities when the performance of your app isn't critical.

See also

- *Working with external SWFs, Chapter 4*
- *Accessing bitmaps with ActionScript*
- *Working with sprite sheets*

Working with sprite sheets

When working with multiple bitmap resources, you may want to consider using a sprite sheet. A **sprite sheet** is a single bitmap that holds a collection of individual images. Typically, the sheet is separated into a grid with each image occupying identically sized slots.

Once a sprite sheet is loaded into memory, the bitmap data for its individual images can be extracted and stored separately. This allows the data for each image to be accessed quickly by the application.

Let us see how this is done.

Getting ready

From the book's accompanying code bundle, open `chapter6\recipe8\recipe.fla`. The majority of the FLA's AIR for iOS settings have been applied as a starting point.

Additionally, a bitmap named `sprite-sheet.png` has been provided within the same folder as the FLA. Take a look at the bitmap in an image editor such as Adobe Photoshop. It contains a collection of images that we will extract and store in memory.

How to do it...

Start by bundling the bitmap with your app.

1. To do this, open the **AIR for iOS Settings** panel and ensure that the panel's **General** tab is selected. Click on the **+** symbol above the **Included files** list and select `sprite-sheet.png` from the FLA's root folder. Finally, click on **OK** to close the **AIR for iOS Settings** panel.

Now, let us write some ActionScript to load the sprite sheet before cutting it into individual bitmaps.

2. Create a document class and name it `Main`.

3. Add the following import statements:

```
import flash.display.Bitmap;
import flash.display.BitmapData;
import flash.display.Loader;
import flash.display.MovieClip;
import flash.events.Event;
import flash.geom.Point;
import flash.geom.Rectangle;
import flash.net.URLRequest;
```

4. The sprite sheet contains four images aligned in a 2x2 grid. Each image is 192x256 pixels in size. Store this information within your class by adding the following constants:

```
public class Main extends MovieClip {

    static private const GRID_W:uint = 2;
    static private const GRID_H:uint = 2;

    static private const FRAME_W:uint = 192;
    static private const FRAME_H:uint = 256;
```

5. Add a member variable of type `Array` that will be used to store the bitmap data for each of the images once they have been extracted from the sprite sheet:

```
private var bitmaps:Array = [];
```

6. Let us also add a member variable of type `Bitmap`, which will be used to verify that the bitmaps have been extracted by displaying one of them on screen:

```
private var monkey:Bitmap = new Bitmap();
```

7. Within the constructor, use the `Loader` class to load the sprite sheet:

```
public function Main() {
    var loader:Loader = new Loader();
    loader.contentLoaderInfo.addEventListener(Event.COMPLETE,
      bitmapLoaded);
    loader.load(new URLRequest("sprite-sheet.png"));
}
```

8. Write the handler that will be called when the sprite sheet has loaded. The handler itself will call two methods—sliceSpriteSheet() and createMonkey(). The first will extract the bitmap data from the sprite sheet, while the second will create and display a bitmap object that will use the bitmap data from one of the extracted images:

```
private function bitmapLoaded(e:Event):void {
  sliceSpriteSheet(e.target.content.bitmapData);
  createMonkey();
}
```

9. Now, add the method that actually extracts the bitmap data for each of the sprite sheet's images:

```
private function sliceSpriteSheet(sheet:BitmapData):void {
  for(var y:uint = 0; y < GRID_H; y++)
  {
    for(var x:uint = 0; x < GRID_W; x++)
    {
      var bd:BitmapData = new BitmapData(
        FRAME_W, FRAME_H, true);
      var srcRect:Rectangle = new Rectangle(
        (x * FRAME_W), (y * FRAME_H), FRAME_W, FRAME_H);
      bd.copyPixels(sheet, srcRect, new Point(0,0));
      bitmaps.push(bd);
    }
  }
  sheet.dispose();
}
```

10. Finally, add the method that creates a bitmap that uses the bitmap data from the first image cut from the sprite sheet:

```
private function createMonkey():void {
  monkey = new Bitmap(bitmaps[0]);
  monkey.x = 64;
  monkey.y = 112;

  addChild(monkey);
}
```

11. Save your document class as Main.as.

12. Save your FLA and test it using ADL.

    The SWF will load the sprite sheet, extract the data for all four images, then display the first of those images on screen.

13. Once satisfied, publish for iOS and deploy the app to a device for testing.

How it works...

The bulk of this recipe's work is performed within the `sliceSpriteSheet()` method. Using a nested `for` loop, it traverses the sheet's bitmap data, copying the data for each of the images into their own `BitmapData` objects. Each of these `BitmapData` objects is added to the `bitmaps` array for use later.

Once the data has been extracted, the sprite sheet's own bitmap data is released from memory. The sprite sheet itself is no longer required as the bitmap data for each of its images is now stored individually within the `bitmaps` array and can be easily accessed from there.

Think of the `bitmaps` array as a library, with each index position representing a different image. If you are using GPU-rendering mode, then the data for each image will be stored as a texture in video memory providing hardware acceleration when rendering.

Using any of these images is as easy as creating a `Bitmap` object and pointing its `bitmapData` property to one of the `BitmapData` objects stored within the `bitmaps` array. Alternatively, you can pass one of the `BitmapData` references into the `Bitmap` object's constructor. Within the `createMonkey()` method, we simply created a `Bitmap` object that used the first image (index position 0) stored within the `bitmaps` array. Although, we could just as easily have used the bitmap data from one of the other three images.

As with the sprite sheet, you can call `dispose()` on any of the `BitmapData` objects stored within the `bitmaps` array in order to release them from memory. It is important that you do this when any of the `BitmapData` objects are no longer required.

Sprite sheets have many advantages. When working with multiple bitmap images that are loaded at runtime, a sprite sheet requires only a single load request. This is significantly faster than loading individual bitmaps from the file system. Also, in addition to using identically sized slots for each bitmap, it is possible to tightly pack arbitrary-sized bitmaps into a sprite sheet. Doing so can lead to savings when holding the sprite sheet in memory compared to storing each individual bitmap.

The use of sprite sheets is the de facto standard for working with bitmaps in many development environments and frameworks. For example, native iOS and Android frameworks such as Cocos2D, Sparrow, and Corona take advantage of sprite sheets. Both the Starling and ND2D ActionScript 3.0 frameworks, which are built on top of Stage 3D, also rely on sprite sheets when using their hardware-accelerated 2D graphics APIs.

Finally, don't confuse sprite sheets with Flash's `Sprite` class. Any of Flash's display objects that support bitmaps can be used to render content from within a sprite sheet, not just the `Sprite` class.

You can obtain more detail regarding the classes used in this recipe from Adobe Community Help. Specifically, take a look at `flash.display.Loader`, `flash.display.Bitmap`, and `flash.display.BitmapData`. Spend some time looking at `BitmapData.copyPixels()` which is used to copy data from the sprite sheet into each individual `BitmapData` object.

There's more...

Following are a few more things to consider when working with sprite sheets.

Creating sprite sheets

There are many great tools for creating sprite sheets. Take a look at TexturePacker, which is freely available for both Mac OS X and Microsoft Windows at `www.texturepacker.com`.

Comparing performance and memory consumption

Extracting and storing the bitmap data for each individual image provides the fastest access to that data when it is eventually required by your app. However, cutting the sprite sheet into individual `BitmapData` objects may come at the cost of memory, especially when rendering directly on the GPU.

The GPU allocates memory using powers of 2 for each of a bitmap's dimensions. When creating a sprite sheet, you can use this knowledge to your advantage, packing and arranging images into the sheet until its dimensions are exact powers of 2. However, this may not be the case for the individual images contained within the sheet, and can lead to significant memory overheads once the bitmap data for all the images has been extracted.

Consider carefully your artwork when creating bitmap images. If performance is of the utmost importance, then you may need to accept these memory overheads. Otherwise consider an alternative approach—perhaps keeping the sprite sheet in memory and extracting only the data that you need at a particular moment in time. This of course will be slower than extracting all the image data up-front but is a viable option, which is often used by professional developers.

See also

- ▶ *Working with external SWFs, Chapter 4*
- ▶ *Accessing bitmaps with ActionScript*
- ▶ *Loading bitmaps at runtime*
- ▶ *Performing bitmap animation with ActionScript*

Performing bitmap animation with ActionScript

It might be the obvious choice for most situations, but the timeline isn't the only way to perform frame-by-frame animation. With a collection of `BitmapData` objects stored in memory, it is perfectly possible to apply animations to `Bitmap` objects using ActionScript.

We will see how to do that in this recipe.

Getting ready

You can continue to work with the code you wrote during the *Working with sprite sheets* recipe. Alternatively, open `chapter6\recipe9\recipe.fla` from the book's accompanying code bundle and work from there. You will also find the FLA's document class and a sprite sheet in the same folder. The sprite sheet has already been added to the **Included files** list in the FLA's **AIR for iOS Settings** panel.

How to do it...

We will perform the animation by cycling through each of the bitmaps cut from the sprite sheet.

1. Open the FLA's document class.

2. Add a constant that stores the number of frames within the animation:

   ```
   static private const MAX_FRAMES:uint = GRID_W * GRID_H;
   ```

3. We will also need a member variable that keeps track of the current frame being shown:

   ```
   private var frame:uint = 0;
   ```

4. Within the `bitmapLoaded()` method, listen for `Event.ENTER_FRAME`. Its event handler will act as the app's main loop:

   ```
   private function bitmapLoaded(e:Event):void {
     sliceSpriteSheet(e.target.content.bitmapData);
     createMonkey();
     addEventListener(Event.ENTER_FRAME, update);
   }
   ```

5. Now, let us add the method for the main loop. On each call, it will point the `monkey` bitmap to a different `BitmapData` object, essentially causing the bitmap to animate:

   ```
   private function update(e:Event):void {
     monkey.bitmapData = bitmaps[frame];
     if(++frame == MAX_FRAMES)
     {
       frame = 0;
     }
   }
   ```

6. Save your document class and your FLA.

7. Test the FLA in ADL. You should now see the `monkey` bitmap animating by cycling through a series of images.

8. Publish your app and test it on a device.

How it works...

Once you have a collection of `BitmapData` objects, it doesn't take too much effort to perform animation using them.

The `frame` member variable was used as an index position into the `bitmaps` array in order to retrieve the next `BitmapData` object for the animation. You can see this in the following code snippet, where the `bitmapData` property is updated to point to a new `BitmapData` object:

```
monkey.bitmapData = bitmaps[frame];
```

Some additional logic was also added to ensure that the animation looped back round to the first frame again. This was taken care of by comparing the value of `frame` against the `MAX_FRAMES` constant and setting `frame` back to 0 when both values matched.

It may seem like a considerable amount of work for a task that can be performed relatively quickly using a timeline animation. However, even the simplest timeline animations struggle for performance on older iOS devices. This is especially true when using GPU Blend, where each frame needs to be copied from the CPU to the GPU whenever the playhead's position changes.

Programmatic animation using ActionScript, however, can be incredibly fast, with GPU Blend benefitting especially from it. Remember, `BitmapData` objects are stored directly in video memory as textures and, therefore, don't suffer the same rendering bottlenecks experienced by timeline animations.

If you are using Flash Professional CS5, then this may be the only real option if you want to maximize the performance of your animations. Utilizing GPU-Blend mode and performing bitmap animations using ActionScript can increase performance anywhere between five and ten times that of a timeline-based approach. For a comparison, publish `recipe-bitmaps.fla` from the *Comparing vector and bitmap graphics* recipe. The performance difference between it and this recipe's example FLA should be considerable when running on a device.

There's more...

Following are a few final points regarding sprite sheets and animation.

Animation sequences

You may find that the existing animation runs too quickly and be tempted to reduce the FLA's frame rate to correct this. A better approach is to hold each bitmap for a few frames before moving to the next. This provides more control over your animations without reducing the SWF's frame rate.

We can achieve this by creating an array that holds a sequence of frame indexes for your animation. Each element within the array represents one frame of animation. Therefore, we can slow the animation by storing duplicate copies of each frame index. Take a look at the following sequence:

[0, 0, 0, 0, 1, 1, 1, 1, 2, 2, 2, 2, 3, 3, 3, 3]

Each integer represents a frame index, with 0 being the first bitmap of the animation and 3 being the last. Therefore, this sequence holds the animation on each of the bitmaps for four screen redraws before moving to the next. Let us implement this in your code.

First, add a constant that holds the animation sequence:

```
static private const SEQUENCE:Array =
    [0, 0, 0, 0, 1, 1, 1, 1, 2, 2, 2, 2, 3, 3, 3, 3];
```

Finally, replace the update() method with this new version, which cycles through the frame indexes listed in the sequence:

```
private function update(e:Event):void {
   monkey.bitmapData = bitmaps[SEQUENCE[frame]];
   if(++frame == SEQUENCE.length)
   {
      frame = 0;
   }
}
```

Save your document class and test the new version of your FLA.

While this example uses a frame-based approach to animation, there is really nothing stopping you from writing your own ActionScript animation library that can be time-based.

Loading resources at runtime

Another reason for employing bitmap-based animation with ActionScript is for runtime loading of resources. If you can't fit all your resources into memory at once or simply want to reduce the initial load time of your app, then you should consider this above timeline-based animations.

Remember, it is not currently possible to instantiate any library symbols within external SWFs that you have loaded into your AIR for iOS app. Therefore, as an alternative, you may want to load sprite sheets at runtime, extract the images from them, and then use ActionScript to perform the animations required by your app's display objects.

Stage 3D

Perhaps the most compelling reason for using sprite sheets is Adobe's Stage 3D API. Stage 3D (previously codenamed Molehill) provides advanced 2D and 3D hardware acceleration on GPU hardware. Its API is intentionally low-level in order to maximize performance but you can use various ActionScript 3.0 frameworks built on top of Stage 3D that are still capable of results far exceeding Flash's traditional display list.

Two such APIs aimed at 2D graphics are Starling and ND2D, which make heavy use of sprite sheets. Flash's traditional display list cannot be used with these frameworks. Instead, everything must be performed programmatically using ActionScript and the graphics elements provided by each.

At the time of writing, Stage 3D isn't yet available for mobile. However, Adobe is actively working to bring it to AIR for iOS. If you would like to take advantage of Stage 3D when it becomes available, then you should consider using sprite sheets in your current projects. This should make the process of porting them to Stage 3D relatively straightforward.

You can find out more about Stage 3D from Adobe Developer Connection at `www.adobe.com/devnet/flashplayer/stage3d.html`. Links to both Starling and ND2D can be found there too.

See also

- ▶ *Using an update loop, Chapter 3*
- ▶ *Working with external SWFs, Chapter 4*
- ▶ *Working with sprite sheets*

7
Working with Text and the Virtual Keyboard

In this chapter, we will cover:

- ▸ Using device fonts within text fields
- ▸ Using embedded fonts within text fields
- ▸ Providing text entry
- ▸ Capturing text input
- ▸ Configurable panning with virtual keyboard activation
- ▸ Updating dynamic text fields
- ▸ Using native iOS text controls

Introduction

With the omission of physical buttons the iPhone has changed forever how many of us will enter text. Gone are the fixed keypad configurations of previous phones; replaced instead by a touch-screen keyboard that adapts its keys and layout for different applications. In addition, iOS comes with a comprehensive library of fonts and impressive text rendering capabilities, allowing user input to be shown in crisp detail.

In this chapter, you will explore Flash's support for the native iOS virtual keyboard and learn how to work with text.

Using device fonts within text fields

A comprehensive list of fonts is installed on iOS devices and is available for use directly within your AIR for iOS app.

This recipe will take you through the steps required to create a text field that uses a device font.

Getting ready

From the book's accompanying code bundle, open `chapter7\recipe1\recipe.fla` into Flash Professional. The FLA's stage is empty but its AIR for iOS settings have already been applied, saving you the time and effort when you build and deploy it to a device.

How to do it...

Perform the following steps to take advantage of a device font:

1. Using the **Text Tool** (**T**), draw a text field on the stage.

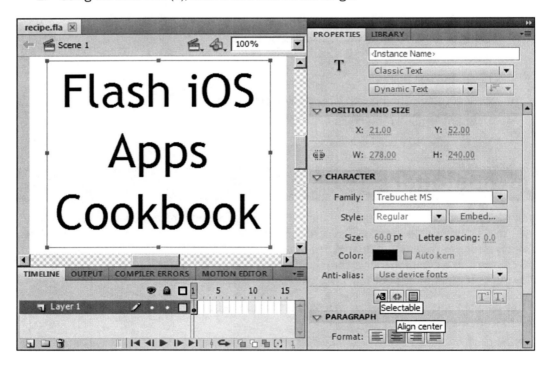

2. Enter **Flash iOS Apps Cookbook** into the text field.

3. From the **Properties** panel, ensure that **Classic Text** and **Dynamic Text** are selected from the two top-most drop-down boxes.

4. Position the text field at (21,52). Set its width and height to 278 and 240 respectively.

5. Expand the **CHARACTER** section within the Properties panel. Set the **Family** drop-down to **Trebuchet MS**, the **Size** to **60.0** pt, and change the font color to black. Also, select **Use device fonts** for the **Anti-alias** field and ensure that the **Selectable** icon directly underneath is not selected. All these settings are shown in the preceding screenshot.

6. Finally, expand the **PARAGRAPH** section. Select **Align center** for the **Format** field and **Multiline** from the **Behavior** field's drop-down box.

7. Save your FLA.

8. Publish the FLA and install the IPA on your device.

How it works...

Although Flash can embed fonts directly within your SWF, iOS provides its own, which can be used instead. These are known as **device fonts** and using them carries a number of advantages:

▸ The final size of your app will be reduced as there will be no need for Flash to include any of the font's glyphs directly within your SWF

▸ It will guarantee that the font renders identically to other iOS apps that use it

▸ Device fonts render to the screen faster than fonts embedded by Flash

Device fonts have a few drawbacks too, which might dictate whether or not you can use them in your project:

▸ Alpha transparency can't be applied directly to your text

▸ Embedded fonts will not render if the text field has been rotated

If you select a font that is available on the device, then ensure that **Use device fonts** is selected from the **Anti-alias** field. The fonts must also be installed on your development computer or you won't be able to select them from Flash Professional.

Flash can't stop you from selecting a font that is not actually installed on your device—there is no way for it to tell. If a font you selected isn't available, then all text fields that require its use will default to **_sans**.

Device fonts can be used with all three classic text types: static, dynamic, and input text.

There's more...

Choosing the correct fonts for your application is important. First you need to know which fonts are actually available.

Device fonts on iOS

Not being able to tell from Flash Professional's IDE which fonts are actually embedded on your device can be problematic. Fortunately, there are several apps that list the fonts installed on a device and let you preview them at various point sizes. Most will also let you enter and preview your own text.

Two apps worth taking a look at are **Fast Fonts** and **Fonts**. Both are free and can be downloaded from iTunes or the App Store.

Be careful, the number of installed fonts varies across devices and versions of iOS. For example, on iOS 4.3, 40 font families are installed on iPhone whereas iPad has 57. Check the availability of a font across all devices you wish to target before using it.

The following are a few device fonts that are commonly used:

  ▸ Serif: Times New Roman, Georgia, and _serif
  ▸ Sans-serif: Helvetica, Arial, Verdana, Trebuchet, Tahoma, and _sans
  ▸ Fixed-width: Courier, Courier New, and _typewriter

For a complete list of the fonts supported on the most recent version of iOS, take a look at the iOS Fonts website at `http://iosfonts.com`.

Enumerating the available device fonts

It is possible to determine the fonts that are installed on a device. The following is a simple code example:

```
var f:Font;
var fonts:Array = Font.enumerateFonts(true);
for(var i:int = 0; i < fonts.length; i++)
{
  f = fonts[i];
  trace(f.fontName + "," + f.fontStyle + "," + f.fontType);
}
```

By passing `true` to the static `Font.enumerateFonts()` method, you can retrieve an array of `Font` instances that represent the device's embedded fonts. Simply query an instance's `fontName`, `fontStyle`, and `fontType` properties to find out more about the font it represents.

Also, you will need to import `flash.text.Font` before using the `Font` class. To find out more about each property, perform a search for the `Font` class within Adobe Community Help.

Pixel density

The pixel density of your iOS device is likely to be higher than that of a typical monitor. Font sizes that look adequate when working within Flash Professional could potentially be too small when viewed on an actual device. This is particularly true when targeting the iPhone 4/4S's Retina display. An app such as Fast Fonts will help you select a suitable size directly from your device. Try not to use a point size lower than 14.

TLF text

Flash Professional CS5 introduced a new text engine called **Text Layout Framework** (**TLF**). While TLF provides superior text layout features compared to the previous classic text engine, it is not recommended that you use it when targeting iOS due to the framework's heavy performance constraints. TLF text will not be covered in this book.

See also

  ▶ _Using embedded fonts within text fields_

Using embedded fonts within text fields

It is likely that you will eventually want to make use of a font that isn't installed on your device. When this is the case, you can embed the font allowing it to be rendered correctly within your app.

Let us see how this is done.

Getting ready

Launch Flash Professional and open `chapter7\recipe2\recipe.fla` from the book's accompanying code bundle. The FLA's stage is empty but its AIR for iOS settings have already been applied letting you easily publish once you are ready.

How to do it...

The Impact font isn't installed on iOS devices. Let us create a text field that makes use of it by embedding the font directly within your app.

1. Select the **Text Tool** (**T**) and draw a text field on the stage.

2. Enter **Flash iOS Apps Cookbook** into the text field.

3. From the **Properties** panel, select **Classic Text** and **Dynamic Text** from the two top-most drop-down boxes.

4. Position the text field at (21,52). Set its width and height to 278 and 240 respectively.

5. Expand the **CHARACTER** section within the Properties panel. Set the **Family** field to **Impact**, the **Size** to **60.0** pt, and change the font color to black. Also, ensure that the **Selectable** icon is not selected.

6. Staying within the **CHARACTER** section, set the **Anti-alias** field to **Anti-alias for readability**. A **Font Embedding Warning** dialog box may appear stating that you need to select the fonts and characters to embed. If it does, then click on its **Embed** button to open the **Font Embedding** panel. If it doesn't, then simply click on the **Embed** button next to the **Style** field to open the panel as shown in the following screenshot:

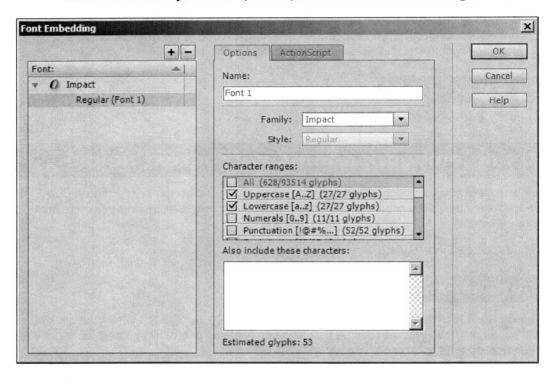

7. From the **Font Embedding** panel, check the **Uppercase [A..Z]** and **Lowercase [a..z]** checkboxes within the **Character ranges** list. Click on the **OK** button to close the panel.

8. Now expand the **PARAGRAPH** section within the **Properties** panel. Select **Align center** for the **Format** field and **Multiline** from the **Behavior** field's drop-down box.

9. Save your FLA.

10. Publish the FLA and install the IPA on your device.

How it works...

Any font installed on your computer can be embedded within your SWF. This will allow the font to be rendered correctly within your app, even if it is not available directly from your device.

You can manage the fonts you would like to embed from the Font Embedding panel, which is launched by clicking on the **Embed** button on the Properties panel. From here you can also set the range of characters that you wish to include for a particular font. It is important you select only the characters that are required as your app's file size will increase with the number of character glyphs you add. Additionally, you can export fonts for ActionScript usage from this panel too.

Embedded fonts can be used with all classic text field types. However, when using a static text field, you have no control over the range of characters that get embedded into your SWF. Instead, Flash simply includes the characters that appear within the field.

When using embedded fonts, make sure the text field's **Anti-alias** option is set to anything other than **Use device fonts**. Setting it to **Use device fonts** won't actually embed the font and will instead assume that the font comes installed with the device.

Only embed a font if it isn't available on the device and there isn't a suitable alternative device font that you can use. Embedded fonts increase the size of your app and in most cases don't render as quickly as device fonts.

There's more...

You should carefully manage the fonts you embed and try to keep your app's file size as small as possible.

Size considerations

Embedding a font is useful when that font isn't available directly from the device. However, embedded fonts can impact the final size of your app.

You can generate a size report from Flash, which provides a breakdown of all the assets within your SWF and how much of the SWF's file size they consume. This report will also include size information for each of your embedded fonts. Simply move to the **Publish Settings** panel and check the **Generate Size Report** checkbox. Flash CS5 users should click on the **Flash** tab within the **Publish Settings** panel first.

When you publish the FLA, a size report will be generated and displayed in the **Output** panel. Within the report is a section where you can see a list of the embedded fonts and their character sets. The number of bytes used by each font is also shown.

The following is the result taken from the size report for this recipe's FLA:

```
Font Name    Bytes        Characters
---------    ----------   ----------
Impact       6606         ABCDEFGHIJKLMNOPQRSTUVWXYZabcdefghijk
                          lmnopqrstuvwxyz
```

As you can see, approximately 7 KB is required to hold this font's character set.

Move back to the Font Embedding panel and include all the font's glyphs by checking the first checkbox within the **Character ranges** list.

Re-publish the FLA and take a look at the new size report. The font now consumes almost 47 KB!

 It is important that you include only fonts that are required and that you keep each font's character set to the absolute minimum. Your app's final file size can quickly escalate due to poor management of embedded fonts.

See also

▶ *Using device fonts within text fields*

Providing text entry

All iOS devices forego a physical keyboard in favor of a virtual touch-screen equivalent. AIR provides virtual keyboard support, allowing a user to enter text within an input text field.

Let us see how this is done.

Getting ready

An FLA has been provided as a starting point for this recipe.

From the book's accompanying code bundle, open `chapter7\recipe3\recipe.fla` into Flash Professional.

Three static text fields are already sitting on the stage and will act as labels. We will add three input text fields to the stage, associating one with each of the labels.

How to do it...

Perform the following steps to create the three input text fields:

1. Create a new layer on the timeline by selecting **Insert | Timeline | Layer**.
2. Select the **Text Tool** (**T**) from the Tools panel.
3. On the newly created layer, draw a text field adjacent to the **Forename** text field as shown in the following screenshot:

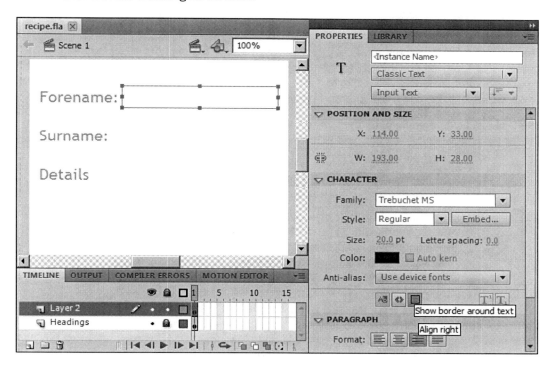

4. From the **Properties** panel, select **Classic Text** and **Input Text** from the two top-most drop-down boxes.
5. Expand the Properties panel's **CHARACTER** section. Set the **Family** drop-down to **Trebuchet MS**, the **Size** to **20.0** pt, and the text color to black. Also, set the **Anti-alias** field to **Use device fonts** and select the **Show border around text** icon.
6. Position the text field at (114,33) and set its size to 193x28.
7. Expand the **PARAGRAPH** section. Set the **Format** by selecting the **Align right** icon, and select **Single line** from the **Behavior** drop-down box.
8. Create a second input text field similar to the first. Position this one next to the **Surname** label at (114,83) and set its **Format** field to **Align center**.

9. Finally draw a third input text field directly below the **Details** label. Position it at (11,174) and set its size to 298x154. Within the **PARAGRAPH** section, select the **Align left** icon for the **Format** field and select **Multiline** from the **Behavior** drop-down box.

10. Save your FLA.

11. Publish the FLA and install the IPA on your device.

12. Run the app and enter text into each of the fields.

How it works...

The virtual keyboard will automatically appear when a user touches any input text field. Many of the same features provided by native iOS applications are also available directly from your input text fields, including predictive text and a button to clear the field. Apps running on iOS 4 or above will also benefit from copy and paste support.

The first two fields are single-line and, if text has been entered, will provide a clear button on the far-right. However, if the text field is too narrow, the button won't be shown.

When you have finished entering text into a single-line text field, you can dismiss the virtual keyboard by tapping the **Done** key or by tapping outside the text field.

 If you built your app using Flash Professional CS5, then you will notice that the alignment settings for the **Forename** and **Surname** fields are ignored when entering text. When using the AIR 2.0 SDK, input text fields in iOS only support left alignment. It is, therefore, recommended that you don't select alternative alignments when working with CS5.

When editing the **Details** field, which is multiline, the virtual keyboard doesn't provide a **Done** key. Instead a **return** key is found in its place, allowing the user to jump to the next line. To dismiss the virtual keyboard when editing a multiline input text field, the user must tap anywhere outside the field. Unfortunately this is not standard practice for iOS apps and may confuse users. Also, make sure you include an area outside the text field that the user can tap. If the field is too large, then it may be impossible for the user to dismiss the keyboard.

The position of input text fields is important. If the field you wish to edit sits within the area used by the virtual keyboard, then AIR will adjust the position of the stage at runtime. You can see this by attempting to edit the **Details** input text field. The stage will be panned, ensuring that the field isn't obscured. Both the **Forename** and **Surname** input fields, however, are pushed out of view to make room for **Details**.

 When designing your application, take into consideration the area used by the keyboard and the effects of editing a text field that sits within this area.

You should also ensure that the height of your multiline text fields does not exceed the height remaining after the virtual keyboard has been raised as text field scrolling is not directly provided.

[🔆 To improve performance and render quality, use device fonts over embedded fonts within your input text fields.]

There's more...

Activation of the virtual keyboard and its many text editing features comes free of charge. But what if you want a little more control?

Keyboard types

Whereas those developing native apps using the iOS SDK can configure the type of keyboard that appears, AIR does not currently provide such control when working with input text fields. You are limited to two very similar layouts—one for single-line input fields and another for multiline.

If the virtual keyboard does not meet your requirements, then consider using the native iOS text controls provided by AIR 3.0. Doing so will provide you with access to additional keyboard configurations. Refer to the *Using native iOS text controls* recipe at the end of this chapter for more detail.

Launching the virtual keyboard programmatically

The virtual keyboard is launched automatically when a user taps on an input text field. However, there may be times when you need to launch the keyboard programmatically using ActionScript.

In AIR 2.6 and above, you can force the virtual keyboard to appear by setting a text field's `needsSoftKeyboard` property to `true` and then calling its `requestSoftKeyboard()` method. The following code is an example that launches the virtual keyboard by setting focus on a text field with an instance name of `forename`.

```
forename.needsSoftKeyboard = true;
var success:Boolean = forename.requestSoftKeyboard();
```

The `requestSoftKeyboard()` method returns a Boolean value indicating whether or not the virtual keyboard was successfully raised.

If you are using Flash Professional CS5 and AIR 2.0, then you can force the virtual keyboard to appear by using the `Stage` class' `focus` property. The following code is an example using a text field with an instance name of `forename`:

```
stage.focus = forename;
```

Remember you can retrieve a reference to the stage from any `DisplayObject` including your document class. The `DisplayObject` class provides a `stage` property that you can access.

See also

▶ *Capturing text input*

▶ *Configurable panning with virtual keyboard activation*

▶ *Using native iOS text controls*

Capturing text input

You can obtain text stored within any non-static text field. This is particularly useful for input text fields where an app may want to immediately respond to the user's input or collect the information for use later.

This recipe will show you how to capture user input.

Getting ready

From the book's accompanying code bundle, open `chapter7\recipe4\recipe.fla` into Flash Professional.

An input text field named `submit` is sitting on the stage. Beneath it is a dynamic text field named `echo`.

We will write some ActionScript to grab any text that the user enters into the `submit` field and display it within the `echo` field.

How to do it...

Perform the following steps:

1. Create a document class named `Main`.

2. Within the class, listen for `FocusEvent.FOCUS_OUT` being dispatched from the `submit` input field. You will also need to add an import statement for the `FocusEvent` class:

```
package {

    import flash.display.MovieClip;
    import flash.events.FocusEvent;
```

```
public class Main extends MovieClip {

    public function Main() {
        submit.addEventListener(FocusEvent.FOCUS_OUT,
            focusLost);
    }
}
}
```

3. Now, add a handler for the FOCUS_OUT event:

```
private function focusLost(e:FocusEvent):void {
    echo.text = e.target.text;
}
```

4. Save the class and when prompted name the file Main.as.

5. Finally save and compile the FLA. Test the app on your device.

Any text you enter into the input text field will be echoed to the dynamic text field below it. This will happen whenever you tap outside the input field.

How it works...

Both dynamic and input fields provide a text property that can be used to get or set their current text. However, before we can obtain the submit field's text, we need to know when the user has actually finished typing. We can tell this by listening for the FOCUS_OUT event, which is dispatched by an input text field in response to the following user actions:

- ▸ The user touches the screen anywhere outside the text field's bounds
- ▸ The user taps the virtual keyboard's **Done** key

Within this recipe's code, the focusLost() handler responds to the submit field's FOCUS_OUT event. It sets the text within the echo field to that of the submit field. The following is the handler's code again:

```
private function focusLost(e:FocusEvent):void {
    echo.text = e.target.text;
}
```

The submit field is actually accessed through the FocusEvent parameter's target property. We can do this because the FOCUS_OUT event was dispatched from the submit field making it the event's target. Alternatively, we could have ignored the actual FocusEvent parameter and accessed the submit field directly by using the following code snippet:

```
private function focusLost(e:FocusEvent):void {
    echo.text = submit.text;
}
```

As the recipe has shown, the mechanics of retrieving and setting text within fields is trivial. When capturing a user's text input, however, you first need to make sure the user has finished typing.

For more information perform a search for `flash.text.TextField` and `flash.events.FocusEvent` within Adobe Community Help.

There's more...

Before we move on, the following is some additional information.

Listening for focus

As well as `FocusEvent.FOCUS_OUT`, you can also listen for the `FOCUS_IN` event, which lets you know when a user has tapped on an input text field. This is ideal if you need to carry out any preparation before the user starts entering text. For example, you may want to clear a field's current text before the user starts typing. Let us go ahead and implement this.

Within your document class' constructor, listen for the `FOCUS_IN` event:

```
submit.addEventListener(FocusEvent.FOCUS_IN, clearField);
```

Now add a handler for the event, which simply clears the text field:

```
private function clearField(e:FocusEvent):void {
  e.target.text = "";
}
```

Save the class and test the latest version of the app on your device.

See also

▶ *Providing text entry*

Configurable panning with virtual keyboard activation

The virtual keyboard appears automatically when a user touches an input text field. If the text field sits within the region used by the keyboard, then the stage will automatically pan to prevent the text field from being obscured. However, it is possible to switch off this default behavior and modify the layout yourself in response to the keyboard being activated.

The steps covered here are applicable only to those using Flash Professional CS5.5 and AIR 2.6 or above.

Getting ready

An FLA has been provided as a starting point.

From the book's accompanying code bundle, open `chapter7\recipe5\recipe.fla` into Flash Professional.

Centered on the stage is an input text field named `field`. We will write some ActionScript to reposition this text field when the virtual keyboard is activated.

How to do it...

First, you will need to switch off automatic panning from the application descriptor file.

1. Select **File | Open** from Flash Professional CS5.5. From the file browser, select `recipe-app.xml`, which can be found within the same folder as your FLA.

2. Add the following line to the descriptor file's XML:

```
<initialWindow>
  <content>recipe.swf</content>
  <systemChrome>standard</systemChrome>
  <transparent>false</transparent>
  <visible>true</visible>
  <fullScreen>true</fullScreen>
  <aspectRatio>portrait</aspectRatio>
  <renderMode>gpu</renderMode>
  <autoOrients>false</autoOrients>
  <softKeyboardBehavior>none</softKeyboardBehavior>
</initialWindow>
```

3. Save the file.

4. Now, create a document class for your FLA and name it `Main`.

5. Add the following import statements:

```
import flash.display.MovieClip;
import flash.events.SoftKeyboardEvent;
import flash.geom.Rectangle;
```

6. Within the constructor, listen for the virtual keyboard being activated and deactivated:

```
public function Main() {
  stage.addEventListener(
    SoftKeyboardEvent.SOFT_KEYBOARD_ACTIVATE, activate);

  stage.addEventListener(
    SoftKeyboardEvent.SOFT_KEYBOARD_DEACTIVATE, deactivate);
}
```

7. Add a handler for the `SOFT_KEYBOARD_ACTIVATE` event. It will be called when the virtual keyboard has been activated and will position the input text field outside of the keyboard's bounds:

```
private function activate(e:SoftKeyboardEvent):void {
  var keysRect:Rectangle = stage.softKeyboardRect;
  if(field.y + field.height > keysRect.top)
  {
    offset = field.y + field.height - keysRect.top;
    field.y -= offset;
  }
  else
  {
    offset = 0;
  }
}
```

8. The `activate()` handler calculates the number of pixels the text field needs to be moved by vertically in order to be positioned outside the keyboard's bounding area. This value is stored within a member variable named `offset`. Declare the `offset` member variable within your class:

```
public class Main extends MovieClip {

  private var offset:Number;

  public function Main() {
```

9. Finally, we need to place the text field back in its original position when the keyboard is removed. The handler for the `SOFT_KEYBOARD_DEACTIVATE` event will use the `offset` member variable to take care of this:

```
private function deactivate(e:SoftKeyboardEvent):void {
  field.y += offset;
}
```

10. Save the class and when prompted, name the file `Main.as`. Also save your FLA.

11. Publish the app and test it on your device.

When you select the input text field, the virtual keyboard will be shown and the field will be repositioned directly above it. Tapping outside the field will place it back in its original position after the keyboard has left the screen.

How it works...

Normally the stage is automatically panned if the virtual keyboard obscures the input text field that has focus. However, we disabled this default behavior by setting the softKeyboardBehavior element in the application descriptor file to none:

```
<softKeyboardBehavior>none</softKeyboardBehavior>
```

 The term **Soft Keyboard** refers to a software keyboard, which is AIR's generic term for the virtual keyboard used by iOS.

With automatic panning switched off, we can simply change the application's layout whenever the user taps on an input text field, and change it back when the user has finished typing.

In order to do this, we listened for the following two events being dispatched from the stage:

- SoftKeyboardEvent.SOFT_KEYBOARD_ACTIVATE
- SoftKeyboardEvent.SOFT_KEYBOARD_DEACTIVATE

The SOFT_KEYBOARD_ACTIVATE event is fired when the virtual keyboard appears on screen. It is in response to this event that we reposition the input text field. When the user taps outside an input text field or presses the **Done** key, the virtual keyboard is dismissed and SOFT_KEYBOARD_DEACTIVATE is dispatched. When we capture this event, we place the input text field back in its original position.

Although it is perfectly acceptable to hard-code the positions of the text field for these two events, our example code goes a little further and dynamically shifts the text field away from the area occupied by the keyboard, before shifting it back once the keyboard is dismissed.

It does this by first checking to see if the input text field is within the keyboard's bounding region. If so it positions the text field above the keyboard by calculating how far it needs to be offset by. The following is the code again:

```
private function activate(e:SoftKeyboardEvent):void {
  var keysRect:Rectangle = stage.softKeyboardRect;
  if(field.y + field.height > keysRect.top)
  {
    offset = field.y + field.height - keysRect.top;
    field.y -= offset;
  }
  else
  {
    offset = 0;
  }
}
```

The virtual keyboard's bounding region is retrieved from `Stage.softKeyboardRect` and represents the area of the stage that is covered by the virtual keyboard. Be careful when using this property as it will return a size of zero when the keyboard is not visible. Also notice that the offset is stored within our `offset` member variable and will be set to zero if the text field doesn't fall within the keyboard's bounds.

Finally, when the virtual keyboard is dismissed, we use the value of the `offset` member variable to shift the text field back:

```
private function deactivate(e:SoftKeyboardEvent):void {
    field.y += offset;
}
```

For more information, perform a search for `flash.events.SoftKeyboardEvent` and `Stage.softKeyboardRect` within Adobe Community Help.

There's more...

You may find the following information of interest.

Related object

The `SoftKeyboardEvent` class provides the `relatedObject` property, which holds the `InteractiveObject` that previously had focus. This is useful when listening for `SoftKeyboardEvent.DEACTIVATE` as you will be able to determine which input text field the user was last editing.

Updating dynamic text fields

Rendering text is expensive and can reduce the overall performance of your app. This is particularly noticeable on older devices such as the first and second-generation iPhone and iPod touch where every CPU cycle counts. Minimize the amount of text you update and the frequency with which these updates take place.

Let us look at ways to do this.

Getting ready

An FLA has been provided at `chapter7\recipe6\recipe.fla` within the book's accompanying code bundle.

You will find two text fields sitting on the stage. The first is static and contains the text **Elapsed Time:**. The second is dynamic, contains a zero and has an instance name of `timerField`.

We will write some ActionScript to continuously update the `timerField` with the number of seconds that have elapsed since the app was launched.

How to do it...

Let us go ahead and do this by performing the following steps:

1. Create a document class and named it `Main`.

2. We will require two member variables. One to store the time the app was launched and another to store the number of seconds that have elapsed. Let us also initialize both variables within the class' constructor:

```
package {

  import flash.display.MovieClip;

  public class Main extends MovieClip {

    private var startTime:Date;
    private var elapsed:uint;

    public function Main() {
      startTime = new Date();
      elapsed = 0;
    }
  }
}
```

3. We will use a loop to calculate the number of seconds that have elapsed and update the `timerField` with that value. The loop will be called on every frame redraw.

   First, add a listener for `Event.ENTER_FRAME` and also add an import statement for the `Event` class:

```
package {

  import flash.display.MovieClip;
  import flash.events.Event;

  public class Main extends MovieClip {

    private var startTime:Date;
    private var elapsed:uint;

    public function Main() {
      startTime = new Date();
      elapsed = 0;
      addEventListener(Event.ENTER_FRAME, update);
    }
  }
}
```

4. Now, add the event handler that will act as the update loop:

```
private function update(e:Event):void {
  var currTime:Date = new Date();
  var prevElapsed:uint = elapsed;
  elapsed = (currTime.getTime()-startTime.getTime()) / 1000;
  if(elapsed != prevElapsed)
  {
    timerField.text = String(elapsed);
  }
}
```

5. Save the class and when prompted, name the file `Main.as`. Save the FLA.

6. Compile the app and deploy it to your device.

When you test the app, you should see the dynamic text field continuously update with the number of seconds that have elapsed.

How it works...

Although the `update()` handler is called on every ENTER_FRAME, we only set the elapsed time within the text field when it has actually changed. A common mistake is to repeatedly write an identical string to a text field, which is unnecessary and will degrade performance. We guard against this with the following `if` statement:

```
if(elapsed != prevElapsed)
{
  timerField.text = String(elapsed);
}
```

Basically the text field only gets updated if the number of seconds that have elapsed differs from the value used in the previous call to the loop. For this recipe, it means the text field only gets updated once every second rather than 24 times per second (the FLA's frame rate). This is a significant saving.

As well as reducing the frequency with which a text field is updated, we can also improve performance by only setting the characters that need to change. The two text fields within this recipe could easily have been represented by a single field. If we had taken this approach, then the code to update the field would have looked like this:

```
timerField.text = "Elapsed Time: " + elapsed;
```

Of course this is wasteful, as the string **Elapsed Time:** would be written to the text field every time. Displaying and updating just the time within its own separate text field helped further improve the performance of this recipe's app.

Although these suggestions may seem obvious, they are often overlooked by developers used to targeting the Flash and AIR desktop runtimes. Every saving counts when developing for iOS and this is equally true for text, which can have a large performance impact, even for small amounts of text.

There's more...

The following may help you obtain further performance gains.

Device fonts

This recipe used embedded fonts. However, an additional saving can be made by using the fonts that come installed directly on iOS devices. This will not only reduce the size of your SWF but will also increase performance as device fonts render to the screen faster than embedded fonts. Also, before embedding a font, check to see if it is available on the device.

Appending text

Appending a string to the end of a text field is another common task that can be expensive. It is often done using the concatenation assignment operator (+=) and is shown in the following simple example:

```
textField.text = "Hello ";
textField.text += "Christopher";
```

The `TextField` class, however, provides `appendText()` which performs this operation many times faster:

```
textField.text = "Hello ";
textField.appendText("Christopher");
```

If you are appending text, then use this method instead of the concatenation assignment operator.

Replacing text fields with bitmaps

Where performance is critical, use bitmaps to represent text.

As an example, consider a game where the user's score is constantly being updated. Using a dynamic text field can hurt performance. Instead, write some ActionScript to display and arrange bitmap representations of each number. Although it will require more effort to code, using bitmaps will typically outperform fonts, which are constructed from complex vector shapes.

Cache as Bitmap

A text field can be cached as a bitmap, preventing it from being re-rendered under certain circumstances, and providing a performance boost. Caching of text fields cannot be applied from the Flash IDE and instead must be done using ActionScript. Use the `cacheAsBitmap` and `cacheAsBitmapMatrix` properties, which are available to the `TextField` class. Bitmap caching cannot be directly applied to a static text field.

For more information, refer to the *Using Cache As Bitmap* and *Using Cache As Bitmap Matrix* recipes from *Chapter 6*.

See also

- ▶ *Using an update loop, Chapter 3*
- ▶ *Using device fonts within text fields*
- ▶ *Using embedded fonts within text fields*

Using native iOS text controls

AIR 3.0 introduced the `StageText` class, which provides access to iOS's native text-input controls and the ability to customize the virtual keyboard.

Let us see how to create a native text input field and specify the type of virtual keyboard that is launched when performing text entry.

The steps covered here are applicable only to those using AIR 3.0 and above. If you are using Flash Professional CS5, then you will be unable to attempt this recipe as it only supports AIR 2.0.

Getting ready

An FLA has been provided as a starting point. From the book's accompanying code bundle, open `chapter7\recipe7\recipe.fla` into Flash Professional CS5.5.

Sitting on the stage is a background bitmap image. We will write some ActionScript to overlay a native text input field, which when tapped will launch a virtual keyboard configured for entering a person's name.

How to do it...

We will make heavy use of the classes found in the `flash.text` package by performing the following steps:

1. Create a document class and name it `Main`.

2. Add the following import statements to the class:

```
import flash.display.MovieClip;
import flash.events.FocusEvent;
import flash.geom.Rectangle;
import flash.text.ReturnKeyLabel;
import flash.text.SoftKeyboardType;
import flash.text.StageText;
import flash.text.TextFormatAlign;
import flash.text.engine.FontWeight;
```

3. Declare a `StageText` member variable:

```
private var nativeText:StageText;
```

4. Now within the constructor, create and initialize a native text input field. As part of initialization, we will ensure that it contains text prompting the user to enter their name:

```
public function Main() {
  nativeText = new StageText();
  nativeText.stage = stage;
  nativeText.viewPort = new Rectangle(30, 28, 420, 116);
  nativeText.fontFamily = "ChalkboardSE-Bold";
  nativeText.fontSize = 50;
  nativeText.color = 0xB88858;
  nativeText.fontWeight = FontWeight.BOLD;
  nativeText.textAlign = TextFormatAlign.CENTER;
  nativeText.text = "enter name";
  nativeText.maxChars = 11;
  nativeText.softKeyboardType = SoftKeyboardType.CONTACT;
  nativeText.returnKeyLabel = ReturnKeyLabel.DONE;
}
```

5. In addition, listen for the text field receiving focus when the user touches it by adding the highlighted code:

```
  nativeText.returnKeyLabel = ReturnKeyLabel.DONE;
  nativeText.addEventListener(FocusEvent.FOCUS_IN, focusIn);
}
```

6. When it receives focus, we will remove the field's default text, allowing the user to enter their name without first having to delete characters. The following code snippet is the event handler for this:

```
private function focusIn(e:FocusEvent):void {
  if(nativeText.text == "enter name")
  {
    nativeText.text = "";
  }
}
```

7. Save the class and when prompted name the file `Main.as`.

8. Move back to your FLA and save it. Now publish the app and test it on your device.

Tap the **enter name** text field and use the virtual keyboard to input text. Press the **Done** key to commit your changes.

How it works...

The `StageText` class allows native iOS text input fields to be added to an application. Unlike Flash's Classic and TLF text field types, `StageText` provides the same user interaction behaviors found on iOS such as magnification, text selection, auto-capitalization, auto-correction, and virtual keyboard customization.

However, while Classic and TLF text fields can be added using the IDE's Tools panel, each `StageText` instance must be added, positioned, and sized programmatically. This is shown in the following code snippet:

```
nativeText = new StageText();
nativeText.stage = stage;
nativeText.viewPort = new Rectangle(30, 28, 420, 116);
```

In this code snippet, the `stage` property is used to add a text field—`StageText` objects can't be added to the display list and instead must be attached directly to the stage. The text field's position and size are specified by passing a `Rectangle` object to its `viewPort` property. Additionally, all `StageText` instances will appear above content in the display list and their depths cannot be ordered. It is, therefore, advisable that you avoid overlapping native text fields.

The `fontFamily` property is used to dictate the device font to use—embedded Flash fonts can't be used. When specifying a device font, ensure that it is available on all iOS devices you wish to target.

The current text shown within the native text field can be set using the `text` property, and if the field permits user input, then the number of characters can be restricted with `maxChars`.

Finally, the type of keyboard that is to be used when entering text is set using the `softKeyboardType` property. The keyboard can be further configured by using `returnKeyLabel` to specify the label used for its return key:

```
nativeText.softKeyboardType = SoftKeyboardType.CONTACT;
nativeText.returnKeyLabel = ReturnKeyLabel.DONE;
```

Constants provided by the `SoftKeyboardType` class are used to specify the keyboard type, while the `ReturnKeyLabel` class represents the various different labels that can be used for the return key. This code specifies a keyboard configured for name entry with its return label set to **Done**.

If the field's `editable` property is set to `true` (it is by default), then a virtual keyboard will appear when the user touches it.

For more information, perform a search for `flash.text.StageText` within Adobe Community Help.

There's more...

Before we leave this chapter, here is some additional detail regarding native text input fields and the virtual keyboard.

Virtual keyboard types

The supported virtual keyboard types are specified as public constants within the `flash.text.SoftKeyboardType` class and are listed as follows for your convenience:

- ▶ CONTACT: Designed for entering a person's name or phone number
- ▶ DEFAULT: The default keyboard configuration
- ▶ EMAIL: This configuration is suited to the entry of email addresses
- ▶ NUMBER: A numeric keypad
- ▶ PUNCTUATION: Designed for text entry that includes punctuation
- ▶ URL: Optimized for URL entry

Return key label types

The `flash.text.ReturnKeyLabel` class provides the following constants, which can be used to set the virtual keyboard's return key: DEFAULT, DONE, GO, NEXT, and SEARCH.

Enumerating device fonts

It is possible to enumerate a device's available fonts by passing `true` to the `flash.text.Font.enumarateFonts()` static method. This will let you know, which strings you can select from when setting a native text input field's `fontFamily` property.

Events

The following events may be dispatched when interacting with a `StageText` instance:

- ▶ `FocusEvent.FOCUS_IN`: The native text input field has received focus
- ▶ `FocusEvent:FOCUS_OUT`: The native text input field has lost focus
- ▶ `KeyboardEvent.KEY_DOWN`: A virtual key has been pressed
- ▶ `KeyboardEvent.KEY_UP`: A virtual key as been released
- ▶ `SoftKeyboardEvent.SOFT_KEYBOARD_ACTIVATING`: The virtual keyboard is being activated and is currently moving into view
- ▶ `SoftKeyboardEvent.SOFT_KEYBOARD_ACTIVATE`: The virtual keyboard has been activated and can now be interacted with `SoftKeyboardEvent.SOFT_KEYBOARD_ACTIVATE`
- ▶ `SoftKeyboardEvent.SOFT_KEYBOARD_DEACTIVATE`: The virtual keyboard has been deactivated

Auto-correction and auto-capitalization

You can enable iOS's auto-correction and auto-capitalization features by setting your `StageText` object's `autoCorrect` and `autoCapitalize` properties to `true`.

See also

- ▶ *Using device fonts within text fields*
- ▶ *Configurable panning with virtual keyboard activation*

8
Screen Resolution and Orientation Changes

In this chapter, we will cover:

- ▸ Targeting a device
- ▸ Targeting the Retina display
- ▸ Supporting multiple resolutions
- ▸ Setting the default aspect ratio
- ▸ Enabling auto-orientation
- ▸ Listening for orientation changes
- ▸ Responding to orientation changes

Introduction

The inclusion of an accelerometer allowed the original iPhone to detect changes in its physical orientation; reflowing its on-screen content to suit the user's preference for either portrait or landscape viewing. Offering this, however, meant that an application had to be designed and coded for two screen aspect ratios—one for the portrait and another for landscape.

As the iOS family has grown, so too has the number of screen resolutions that must be supported. With the launch of the iPad and the introduction of Retina display devices, there are now three separate resolutions. If you also take into consideration the two aspect ratios, then screen layout management for your application can become daunting.

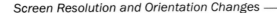

This chapter provides recipes that will help you render content properly on any iOS device, regardless of its screen resolution and physical orientation.

Targeting a device

The iOS family consists of three devices: iPhone, iPod touch, and iPad. When developing for iOS, you must state the devices that you are specifically targeting. Your choice will dictate how your app is run by each of the three.

This recipe will take you through the necessary steps required to create an app that targets the entire family.

Getting ready

An FLA has been provided as a starting point for this recipe. Open `chapter8\recipe1\ recipe.fla` from the book's accompanying code bundle.

Sitting on the stage is a dynamic text field with an instance name of `output`. We will use this text field to report which device your app is currently being run on.

For the avoidance of doubt, this recipe will not take advantage of the Retina display resolution of the iPhone 4/4S and fourth-generation iPod touch. If you would like to provide Retina support, then refer to this chapter's *Targeting the Retina display* recipe.

How to do it...

We will specify the target devices from the AIR for iOS Settings panel and then write some ActionScript to report which device the app is currently running on.

Setting the target devices

Let us start by setting the target devices:

1. Open the AIR for iOS Settings panel by selecting **File | AIR for iOS Settings** from Flash Professional.

2. Ensure that the **General** tab is selected.

3. Select **iPhone and iPad** from the **Device** field.

4. If you are using Flash Professional CS5.5, then also set the **Resolution** field to **Standard**.

5. Click on **OK** to close the panel.

Detecting the current device

Now, let us move onto the ActionScript required for this recipe:

1. Create a document class; name it `Main`.

2. Add the following three import statements to the class:

```
import flash.display.MovieClip;
import flash.display.StageAlign;
import flash.display.StageScaleMode;
import flash.system.Capabilities;
```

3. Within the constructor, set a scale mode and alignment for the stage:

```
public function Main() {
    stage.scaleMode = StageScaleMode.NO_SCALE;
    stage.align = StageAlign.TOP_LEFT;
}
```

4. Using the `Capabilities` class, determine which device the app is running on:

```
public function Main() {
    stage.scaleMode = StageScaleMode.NO_SCALE;
    stage.align = StageAlign.TOP_LEFT;

    if(Capabilities.screenResolutionX == 320)
    {
        output.text = "iPhone / iPod touch";
    }
    else if(Capabilities.screenResolutionX == 768)
    {
        output.text = "iPad";
    }
}
```

5. Save the document class within the same folder as your FLA and name it `Main.as`. Also save the FLA.

6. Publish and test the app on your device. Install it on multiple devices if you have access to more than one.

When you run it on an iPhone or iPod touch, the following text will be output to the screen:

iPhone / iPod touch

Those testing on an iPad will see the following:

iPad

How it works...

You specify the devices you wish to target by setting the **Device** field within the AIR for iOS Settings panel. The following three options are available to you:

- ▶ **iPhone**
- ▶ **iPad**
- ▶ **iPhone and iPad**

The iPod touch is not listed because it is treated as an iPhone—both devices share the same aspect ratio and resolution.

Selecting **iPhone** restricts your screen size to that of the iPhone and the iPod touch. Your app will still run on the iPad but it won't attempt to take advantage of the iPad's increased resolution. Instead, the iPad will run the app using the iPhone's standard 320x480 resolution. Users can either run the app at its normal size or use pixel-doubling to cover almost the entire screen.

Selecting **iPad** does take advantage of the iPad's entire 768x1024 resolution but restricts your app to that device.

If you are writing an app that can run across all three devices by adapting to the different screen sizes then select **iPhone and iPad**. This is more commonly known as a universal app and is the type of application we have opted for in this recipe.

Apple acknowledges the difficulty of writing for multiple devices and screen resolutions. To ease development, they provide the following two options when targeting the entire iOS family:

- ▶ Write two separate apps—one for iPad and another for iPhone/iPod touch
- ▶ Write a universal app that adapts to each device's screen size

Of course it is not mandatory that you support all three devices. For example, it is perfectly acceptable to write an app that only targets the iPad.

It is possible to determine the device your app is running on by querying the device's screen resolution. Both the iPhone and iPod touch have a horizontal resolution of 320 pixels, while the iPad's is 768 pixels wide. Therefore, we only need to query the static `Capabilities.screenResolutionX` property to determine the device type rather than also examining the vertical resolution with `Capabilities.screenResolutionY`.

You may be tempted to use `Stage.stageWidth` instead, but remember that with the stage dimensions fixed, the same width will be returned across all device types for this recipe.

You can obtain more information regarding `flash.system.Capabilities`, `flash.display.StageScaleMode` and `flash.display.StageAlign` from Adobe Community Help.

There's more...

It is also worth considering the following information when targeting multiple devices.

Application launch image

When targeting multiple device types, remember to include a launch image for each supported resolution. Alternative launch images can also be provided for different orientations if you choose to support them. For more detail, refer to the *Including an application launch image* recipe from *Chapter 3*.

Including icons

Remember to include the appropriate icon artwork required by each device type you wish to support. Refer to the *Including icons* recipe from *Chapter 3* for more detail.

Landscape aspect ratio

The `screenResolutionX` and `screenResolutionY` properties are always returned as if the device is being held in its portrait orientation. For example, an iPad app that has a default landscape orientation will still return a horizontal resolution of 768 pixels and a vertical resolution of 1024 pixels.

See also

- ▶ *AIR for iOS general settings, Chapter 2*
- ▶ *Targeting the Retina display*
- ▶ *Setting the default aspect ratio*

Targeting the Retina display

The iPhone 4 introduced the world to the Retina display. It packs four times the number of pixels into the same screen found on earlier models, providing the sharpest images yet seen on a mobile device.

Those using Flash Professional CS5.5 and at least AIR 2.6 can use the full 640x960 resolution provided by Retina display iPhones and iPod touches.

Getting ready

From the book's accompanying code samples, open `chapter8\recipe2\recipe.fla` into Flash Professional CS5.5.

This FLA has been provided as a starting point and has a dynamic text field named `output` sitting on the stage. We will use this text field to report whether or not the app is being run on a Retina display device.

While this recipe's example app will run on an iPad, it won't target its 768x1024 screen resolution. Instead, it will simulate a standard resolution iPhone/iPod touch.

How to do it...

Retina display support is specified from the AIR for iOS Settings panel. We will also write a basic document class to determine whether the app is actually running on a Retina device or not.

Setting Retina display support

Let us start by enabling support for the Retina display's screen resolution:

1. Open the AIR for iOS Settings panel by selecting **File | AIR for iOS Settings**.
2. Ensure the **General** tab is selected.
3. Set the **Resolution** field to **High**.
4. Also, for this recipe, ensure that the **Device** field is set to **iPhone**.
5. Click on the **OK** button to close the panel.

Detecting a Retina display device

With the AIR for iOS settings taken care of, we can turn our attention to the ActionScript required to determine if the app is being run on a Retina display device:

1. Create a document class and name it `Main`.
2. Add the following three import statements to the class:

```
import flash.display.MovieClip;
import flash.display.StageAlign;
import flash.display.StageScaleMode;
import flash.system.Capabilities;
```

3. Set the stage's scale mode and alignment properties:

```
public function Main() {
   stage.scaleMode = StageScaleMode.NO_SCALE;
   stage.align = StageAlign.TOP_LEFT;
}
```

4. Query the device's screen resolution to determine whether or not it has a Retina display:

```
public function Main() {
  stage.scaleMode = StageScaleMode.NO_SCALE;
  stage.align = StageAlign.TOP_LEFT;

  if(Capabilities.screenResolutionX == 320)
  {
    output.text = "Standard Resolution";
  }
  else if(Capabilities.screenResolutionX == 640)
  {
    output.text = "Retina Resolution";
  }
}
```

5. Save the class file as `Main.as` within the same folder as the FLA. Also save the FLA.

6. Publish and deploy the IPA to your device. If you have a Retina and a standard display device available, then install the app on both.

When you run the app on a Retina display iPhone or iPod touch, the following text will be output to the screen:

Retina Resolution

For standard display devices, you will see the following:

Standard Resolution

How it works...

Although the aspect ratio has been maintained, there are now two screen resolutions that you can target when developing for iPhone and iPod touch:

▶ Standard: 320x480

▶ Retina: 640x960

The Retina display resolution is found in post third-generation iPhone and iPod touches. All previous models use the standard display resolution.

If you choose to support the Retina display, then your app must also provide support for the standard display. Apple does not permit you to submit separate IPAs for each supported resolution. You can, however, opt to support just the standard display and the app will be pixel-doubled by iOS to fit Retina display screens.

To specify the resolutions your app will support, set the **Resolution** field within the AIR for iOS Settings panel. The following two options are available:

- ▸ **Standard**
- ▸ **High**

Select **High** if you are providing support for both the Retina and standard displays. Otherwise select **Standard**.

When targeting multiple screen resolutions, it is important you set the stage's scale mode and alignment.

Setting the scale mode to NO_SCALE prevents the stage's content from being scaled to fit the Retina screen's resolution. Instead, your content will maintain its defined size. Setting the stage alignment to TOP_LEFT forces all content to be positioned relative to the top left-hand corner.

While scaling may sound desirable, it really isn't advisable for applications that use bitmap images, which become pixelated when scaled. Instead, you should write logic within your app to swap between standard and Retina resolution versions of any bitmaps and also handle the layout and positioning of content yourself.

In addition, your FLA's stage size should match that of the standard resolution display—320x480 pixels. When running on a Retina display device and with the stage's scale mode set to NO_SCALE, the stage's dimensions will be reported as being twice what you set within Flash Professional. This will allow you to take advantage of the higher resolution.

It is possible to determine the screen resolution your app is using by querying the static screenResolutionX and screenResolutionY properties that belong to the Capabilities class. For this recipe, we simply checked screenResolutionX as this was enough to determine whether the standard or Retina screen resolution was being used.

You can obtain more information regarding flash.system.Capabilities, flash. display.StageScaleMode, and flash.display.StageAlign from Adobe Community Help.

There's more...

There are several other considerations when utilizing the Retina display.

Retina home screen icon

When supporting the Retina display, you must provide a home screen icon of size 114x114. Detailed instructions are available from the *Including icons* recipe in *Chapter 3*.

Retina application launch image

You can include with your IPA an additional launch image that takes advantage of the Retina display's higher resolution. For more details, refer to the *Including an application launch image* recipe from *Chapter 3*.

Vector-only apps

If your application uses only vector content, then you can simply let AIR take care of scaling for you. This will allow you to write an app targeting the standard 320x480 pixel display, which will also take advantage of the higher resolution Retina display.

To enable this, set the stage's scale mode and alignment to the following:

```
stage.scaleMode = StageScaleMode.SHOW_ALL;
stage.align = StageAlign.TOP_LEFT;
```

Also, remember to set the **Resolution** field from the AIR for iOS Settings panel to **High**.

Don't confuse this with pixel doubling that's employed by iOS. Your app's vector content will actually be scaled, rather than each pixel being doubled in size. Essentially there will be a noticeable improvement in image fidelity on Retina devices.

Of course, you can still use bitmaps but unlike the vector content, pixelation will be obvious when they are scaled up.

iPad display

Both the iPad 1 and 2 support a single screen resolution of 768x1024. When targeting the iPad or the non-Retina display iPhone and iPod touch, set the **Resolution** field to **Standard**.

See also

- ▸ *AIR for iOS general settings, Chapter 2*
- ▸ *Targeting a device*
- ▸ *Supporting multiple resolutions*

Supporting multiple resolutions

The launch of the iPad led to developers having to support two different physical screen sizes and resolutions. This was exacerbated by the introduction of the Retina display for iPhone and iPod touch, where screen resolutions were no longer guaranteed to be identical across the same device type.

When targeting multiple device types and models, it is important that your app can adapt its layout to different screen resolutions.

Let us walk through a simple example that creates a universal app that supports the various portrait resolutions used by the iPhone, iPod touch, and iPad.

Getting ready

An FLA containing graphics has been provided in the book's accompanying code bundle for you to work from.

Open `chapter8\recipe3\recipe.fla` into Flash Professional.

Within the FLA's library, you will find three PNGs—one for each screen resolution we intend to support. Each has also been linked for ActionScript usage allowing it to be easily added to the screen at runtime. The following table summarizes this:

	Bitmap name	AS linkage
Standard display 320x480	rocket-standard.png	RocketStandardBitmapData
Retina display 640x960	rocket-retina.png	RocketRetinaBitmapData
iPad display 768x1024	rocket-ipad.png	RocketIPadBitmapData

When running on a standard display iPhone or iPod touch, **rocket-standard.png** will be shown on screen. For Retina display screens, the app will use **rocket-retina.png**. Finally, **rocket-ipad. png** will be shown if an iPad's screen resolution is detected.

If you are using Flash Professional CS5 for this recipe, then your app will be unable to take advantage of the higher resolution provided by Retina display devices. Retina display support is only available from AIR 2.6 onwards.

How to do it...

We will split this recipe into two parts. First, from the AIR for iOS Settings panel, we will declare support for all device resolutions. Secondly, we will write the code required to display the correct bitmap for each supported resolution.

Setting supported devices and resolutions

Let us start by targeting all available device resolutions:

1. Open the AIR for iOS Settings panel by selecting **File | AIR for iOS Settings**.
2. Ensure the **General** tab is selected.
3. Set the **Device** field to **iPhone and iPad**.

4. If you are using Flash Professional CS5.5, then also set the **Resolution** field to **High**.

   These settings are required if you wish a single app to support all devices in the iOS family and take advantage of the higher resolution provided by Retina display devices.

5. Click on the **OK** button to close the panel.

Displaying the correct bitmap

Now, we will write some ActionScript to adapt to each of the expected screen resolutions:

1. Create a document class and name it `Main`.

2. Add import statements for the required classes:

```
import flash.display.MovieClip;
import flash.display.Bitmap;
import flash.display.StageAlign;
import flash.display.StageScaleMode;
import flash.system.Capabilities;
```

3. Within the constructor, set the stage's scale mode and alignment properties:

```
public function Main() {
   stage.scaleMode = StageScaleMode.NO_SCALE;
   stage.align = StageAlign.TOP_LEFT;
}
```

4. Staying within the constructor, call a method to create the correct bitmap for the current device's screen resolution:

```
public function Main() {
   stage.scaleMode = StageScaleMode.NO_SCALE;
   stage.align = StageAlign.TOP_LEFT;

   var b:Bitmap = createRocketBitmap();
   addChild(b);
}
```

5. Now, write the method which instantiates and returns the bitmap:

```
private function createRocketBitmap():Bitmap {
   var b:Bitmap;
   if(Capabilities.screenResolutionX == 320)
   {
     b = new Bitmap(new RocketStandardBitmapData());
   }
   else if(Capabilities.screenResolutionX == 640)
   {
     b = new Bitmap(new RocketRetinaBitmapData());
```

```
      }
      else if(Capabilities.screenResolutionX == 768)
      {
        b = new Bitmap(new RocketIPadBitmapData());
      }
      return b;
    }
```

6. Save the class file as `Main.as`. Also move back to your FLA and save it too.

7. Publish the FLA and test your app on a range of iOS devices.

How it works...

This recipe's example determines the screen resolution being used and displays a bitmap image that has been prepared for that resolution.

The following portrait resolutions are supported:

- iPad
    - 768x1024

- iPhone and iPod touch
    - 320x480: Standard
    - 640x960: Retina

From the AIR for iOS Settings panel, you must explicitly state that you intend to create a universal app that supports all three devices and their screen resolutions. This is done by setting the **Device** field to **iPhone and iPad** and the **Resolution** field to **High**.

When targeting multiple screen resolutions, it is important that you set the stage's scale mode and alignment.

Setting the stage's scale mode to `NO_SCALE` ensures that your content maintains its defined size across multiple screen resolutions. This leaves you in full control of the sizing and layout of your content. It also ensures that any bitmaps being used aren't scaled at runtime, which will prevent them from becoming pixelated. Setting the stage alignment to `TOP_LEFT` forces all content to be positioned relative to the top left-hand corner, making positioning easier to work with.

The actual code that creates the correct bitmap simply examines the static `Capabilities. screenResolutionX` property to determine which of the three expected screen resolutions the app currently has to cater for. Once a decision is made, the correct bitmap from the library is instantiated and added to the display list at its default position of (0,0).

While the stage and timeline are still an option for the layout of content, you may find yourself relying more heavily on ActionScript for more complex projects.

You can obtain more information from Adobe Community Help. Perform a search for the following classes: `flash.system.Capabilities`, `flash.display.StageScaleMode`, and `flash.display.StageAlign`.

There's more...

Our example was somewhat trivial. Unfortunately, adapting a real-world application to multiple screen resolutions can be difficult.

Default stage size

When its scale mode is set to `NO_SCALE`, the stage's default size is of little importance to a universal app. For example, this recipe's FLA uses a stage size of 320x480, which obviously falls far short of the iPad's 768x1024 resolution. This, however, does not restrict the app's display list to the stage's default dimensions—the app is still able to target the full screen resolution of the device it is running on.

Try not to rely on the default stage size when performing layout management across multiple resolutions. The same is also true when determining what device your app is currently running on. Instead use `Capabilities.screenResolutionX` and `Capabilities.screenResolutionY`.

Model-View-Controller architecture

Although outside the scope of this book, you should consider using the Model-View-Controller (MVC) design pattern to manage layout across each supported screen resolution.

MVC consists of three elements: a single Model that contains the application's data and state management logic; at least one View, which presents the application's on-screen state; and at least one Controller, which handles user interaction.

Typically, a View is paired with a Controller, and you will write a View-Controller pair for each screen resolution you wish to support. The Controller acts as an intermediary between its own View and the Model.

There are many ActionScript MVC frameworks available, such as PureMVC and Robotlegs. You can visit the PureMVC home page at `http://puremvc.org`, while Robotlegs can be downloaded from `www.robotlegs.org`.

 Apple encourages the use of MVC when writing apps for iOS.

Dynamic sizing and layout

When working with multiple screen resolutions and pixel densities, you may consider developing your app to dynamically re-size and lay out its content. Although this can be a complex approach, it will future-proof your app, allowing it to fit additional screens that may one day become available. However, for a limited number of screens, you may find MVC more feasible.

For more detail, take a look at the "Writing multi-screen AIR apps" article on the Adobe AIR Developer Center: `www.adobe.com/devnet/air/flex/articles/writing_multiscreen_air_apps.html`.

Supporting iPad separately

The aspect ratio of the iPad's screen differs from that of the iPhone and the iPod touch. This can make the development of a single app that works across all three devices awkward as the app will need to tailor its UI at runtime for three different resolutions. In addition, for bitmap-heavy applications, storing three sets of graphics will consume a significant portion of memory.

To alleviate the complexities of supporting three devices within a single app, you can write your iPad version separately. The App Store will accept an iPad-specific version of your app and another that supports both the iPhone and iPod touch. Simply specify your target device from the AIR for iOS Settings panel.

See also

- ▸ *AIR for iOS general settings, Chapter 2*
- ▸ *Accessing bitmaps with ActionScript, Chapter 6*
- ▸ *Resizing bitmaps, Chapter 4*

Setting the default aspect ratio

Devices, such as the iPhone, can be freely rotated in real space. This is convenient as it provides two aspect ratios that can be worked with—portrait and landscape.

Let us see how to select a default aspect ratio.

Getting ready

Using Flash Professional, open `chapter8\recipe4\recipe.fla` from the book's accompanying code bundle.

The library contains a bitmap image of a fire truck that has been designed for a landscape resolution of 480x320 pixels.

How to do it...

We will begin by locking the FLA to a landscape aspect ratio:

1. Using the **Selection Tool (V)**, click anywhere on the stage. From the **Properties** panel, change the stage's aspect ratio from **portrait** to **landscape**. To do this, simply set its width to **480** and the height to **320**.

2. Although the stage size implies it, the AIR for iOS settings also need to be changed to reflect our choice of aspect ratio. Select **File | AIR for iOS Settings** from the drop-down menu.

3. Ensure the **General** tab is selected.

4. Select **Landscape** from the **Aspect ratio** drop-down box.

5. Click on **OK** to close the panel.

6. Finally, drag the bitmap image from the library onto the stage and position it at the top-left corner of the screen.

7. Save your FLA and publish it.

8. Install the app on your device and launch it.

In order to correctly view the fire truck image, you will be forced to turn your device on its side, matching the device's physical orientation with that of the stage.

How it works...

You can have your application start in one of two aspect ratios: Portrait or Landscape. This is done from the **General** tab within the AIR for iOS Settings panel. Simply make a selection from the **Aspect ratio** drop-down box.

In addition, you will need to set the stage to match that of your chosen aspect ratio. This will allow you to properly lay out any content when designing your app.

 When you create a new AIR for iOS document, a portrait aspect ratio is set by default.

There's more...

There is an additional option available when setting the default aspect ratio from Flash Professional CS5.5.

Auto aspect ratio

From AIR 2.6 onwards, your app can be instructed to select, when launched, the aspect ratio that matches the device's current orientation. To accommodate this, a third option named **Auto** is provided from the **Aspect Ratio** drop-down box.

This feature can only be enabled in conjunction with auto-orientation, which is covered in the next recipe.

See also

 ▸ *AIR for iOS general settings, Chapter 2*
 ▸ *Enabling auto-orientation*

Enabling auto-orientation

The user can change the device's orientation in real space at any moment and will likely expect the on-screen content to reflect this. AIR for iOS can detect these changes and automatically rotate the stage to match the device's new physical orientation.

This recipe will show you how to enable auto-orientation.

Getting ready

If you have completed the *Setting the default aspect ratio* recipe, then you can continue to work from its FLA. Alternatively, from the book's accompanying source code, open `chapter8\recipe5\recipe.fla` into Flash Professional and work from there.

In either case, you will find a bitmap image of a fire truck sitting on the stage. The stage itself is sized to fit a landscape aspect ratio and the FLA's AIR for iOS settings reflect this.

How to do it...

Enable auto-orientation by performing the following steps:

1. Open the AIR for iOS Settings panel by selecting **File | AIR for iOS Settings**.
2. Ensure the **General** tab is selected.
3. Set the **Aspect ratio** drop-down box to **Portrait**.
4. Check on the **Auto orientation** checkbox.
5. Click on the **OK** button to close the panel.
6. Save your FLA and publish it.
7. Deploy the app to your device and launch it.

As the device's physical orientation changes, the stage will be automatically rotated to match the change.

How it works...

When auto-orientation is enabled, the stage will attempt to match the device's current orientation each time it is rotated. Four orientations are supported on iOS:

- Default: The default portrait orientation for iOS devices
- Rotated left: Rotated 90 degrees clockwise
- Rotated right: Rotated 90 degrees counter-clockwise
- Upside down: Rotated 180 degrees

Auto-orientation is convenient as it prevents you from having to manually rotate objects on the display list yourself. Instead, this task will be performed on your behalf.

During auto-orientation, the stage's scale mode and its current alignment setting will be adhered to.

Also, if you decide to support both portrait and landscape aspect ratios, then Apple recommends that your app be launched in portrait mode.

There's more...

It is likely that you will want some control over how the content on the stage is handled during auto-orientation.

Checking for orientation support

Although Flash provides support for device orientation changes across all iOS devices, when writing cross-platform code, you may want to confirm support by checking that the stage's `supportsOrientationChange` property returns `true`.

Programmatically setting auto-orientation

In addition to using the AIR for iOS Settings panel, you can activate and deactivate auto-orientation programmatically by setting the `Stage.autoOrients` property. The property's initial value is derived from the value of the **Auto Orientation** field from the AIR for iOS Settings panel.

The following ActionScript activates auto-orientation:

```
stage.autoOrients = true;
```

Stage scale mode

You can specify how the stage is scaled when the device's physical orientation changes. This is achieved by setting the `Stage.scaleMode` property to one of four constants provided by the `flash.display.StageScaleMode` class.

The default mode is `StageScaleMode.SHOW_ALL` and ensures that the entire stage is made visible within the screen while maintaining its aspect ratio. If you don't want resizing of the stage's content to take place during changes in orientation, then set the scale mode to `NO_SCALE`. This specifies that the size of the content on the stage is to be fixed.

More information regarding scale modes can be obtained from Adobe Community Help.

Stage alignment

How the stage content is aligned when the device's physical orientation changes can also be specified. Simply set the `Stage.align` property to one of the constants defined by `flash.display.StageAlign`.

The stage's content will align to the center of the screen by default, however, there are eight constants that can be used to align the stage's content around the edges of the screen. For example, the following ActionScript will align the stage to the top left:

```
stage.align = StageAlign.TOP_LEFT;
```

More information regarding stage alignment can be found on Adobe Community Help.

See also

- ▶ *AIR for iOS general settings, Chapter 2*
- ▶ *Listening for orientation changes*

Listening for orientation changes

The accelerometer present in iOS devices can detect changes in physical orientation. AIR provides APIs for detecting these changes and determining the device's actual orientation in real space.

Let us see how this is done.

Getting ready

Start by opening `chapter8\recipe6\recipe.fla` from the book's accompanying code bundle.

A dynamic text field named `output` can be found on the stage. We will use this text field to report any orientation changes experienced by the device.

How to do it...

Perform the following steps to listen for changes in orientation:

1. Select **File | AIR for iOS Settings** from Flash Professional's drop-down menu.

2. From the **General** tab, check on the **Auto orientation** checkbox; then click on the panel's **OK** button.

3. Create a document class and name it `Main`.

4. Add the following import statements:

```
import flash.display.MovieClip;
import flash.display.StageAlign;
import flash.display.StageScaleMode;
import flash.events.StageOrientationEvent;
```

5. Within the constructor, set up the stage, and listen for the ORIENTATION_CHANGING and ORIENTATION_CHANGE events being dispatched:

```
public function Main() {
  stage.align = StageAlign.TOP_LEFT;
  stage.scaleMode = StageScaleMode.NO_SCALE;
  stage.addEventListener(
    StageOrientationEvent.ORIENTATION_CHANGING,
    orientationChanging);
  stage.addEventListener(
    StageOrientationEvent.ORIENTATION_CHANGE,
    orientationChanged);

  output.text = "Rotate the device.";
}
```

6. Write a handler for the ORIENTATION_CHANGING event:

```
private function orientationChanging(e:StageOrientationEvent):void
{
  output.text = "Orientation Changing\n";
  output.appendText(
    "Current orientation: " + e.beforeOrientation + "\n");
  output.appendText(
    "Target orientation: " + e.afterOrientation + "\n\n");
}
```

7. Finally, add a handler for the `ORIENTATION_CHANGE` event:

```
private function orientationChanged(e:StageOrientationEvent):void
{
  output.appendText("Orientation Changed\n");
  output.appendText(
    "Previous orientation: " + e.beforeOrientation + "\n");
  output.appendText(
    "Current orientation: " + e.afterOrientation + "\n\n");
}
```

8. Save the class and name it `Main.as` when prompted. Also, save your FLA.

9. Publish the app and test it on your device.

Experiment by rotating the device. As changes in orientation are detected they will be reported on-screen.

How it works...

Changes in orientation can be detected by listening for the following two events from the stage:

- `StageOrientationEvent.ORIENTATION_CHANGING`
- `StageOrientationEvent.ORIENTATION_CHANGE`

The `ORIENTATION_CHANGING` event is dispatched as the device's accelerometer detects that an orientation change is taking place and before auto-orientation's default behavior occurs. The `ORIENTATION_CHANGE` event is dispatched after any default behavior has taken place.

Your app receives the `ORIENTATION_CHANGING` and `ORIENTATION_CHANGE` events only if auto-orientation is enabled from the AIR for iOS Settings panel or through ActionScript.

You can retrieve information regarding the change in orientation by querying the event's `beforeOrientation` and `afterOrientation` properties. Both properties are read-only and will be set to one of the following constants from `flash.display.StageOrientation`:

- `DEFAULT`: The default portrait orientation for iOS devices.
- `ROTATED_LEFT`: Rotated 90 degrees clockwise.
- `ROTATED_RIGHT`: Rotated 90 degrees counter-clockwise.
- `UPSIDE_DOWN`: Rotated 180 degrees.

When handling an `ORIENTATION_CHANGING` event, `beforeOrientation` will hold the device's current orientation while `afterOrientation` will specify the target orientation that the device is being rotated towards.

For the `ORIENTATION_CHANGE` event, use `beforeOrientation` to find out the device's previous orientation and `afterOrientation` to determine the current orientation.

You can see both these properties being used within our document class' `orientationChanging()` and `orientationChanged()` event handlers. Their values are obtained and written to the `output` text field.

There's more...

It is also possible to determine the device's orientation without using event listeners.

Determining device orientation

You can also determine the device's physical orientation by accessing the `deviceOrientation` property of the `Stage` class. This property is read-only and will return one of the constants defined in the `StageOrientation` class.

In addition to the four constants that we have already covered, `deviceOrientation` can also return `StageOrientation.UNKNOWN`. The `deviceOrientation` property does not contain the starting orientation of the device and is, therefore, set to `UNKNOWN` until the first change in physical orientation takes place.

See also

- *AIR for iOS general settings, Chapter 2*
- *Responding to orientation changes*
- *Enabling auto-orientation*

Responding to orientation changes

It is likely that you will want to update your app's on-screen content to reflect a change in the device's physical orientation. While auto-orientation in conjunction with the stage's default alignment and scale mode will attempt this on your behalf, you may want to handle the layout yourself.

This recipe will show you how to do that.

Getting ready

An FLA has been provided as a starting point. From the book's accompanying code bundle, open `chapter8\recipe7\recipe.fla` within Flash Professional.

You will find two movie clips sitting on the stage. The first movie clip is an image of an arrow pointing upwards and has been created to fit the screen's dimensions using a portrait orientation. The second shows the same arrow but this time the image's dimensions fit the screen's landscape orientations.

Both movie clips are positioned at the top-left corner of the stage and have instance names of `portrait` and `landscape` respectively.

We will write some code to ensure that the user sees an arrow pointing upwards no matter which of the four possible physical orientations they rotate the device to. We will do this by showing the appropriate movie clip for the current device orientation.

The stage dimensions are set for an initial portrait aspect ratio and this is already reflected in the AIR for iOS settings.

How to do it...

We will make a quick change to the AIR for iOS settings before moving onto the ActionScript:

1. Select **File | AIR for iOS Settings** from Flash Professional's drop-down menu.

2. From the **General** tab, check the **Auto orientation** checkbox; then click on the panel's **OK** button.

3. Create a document class and name it `Main`.

4. Add the following import statements to the class:

```
import flash.display.MovieClip;
import flash.display.StageAlign;
import flash.display.StageScaleMode;
import flash.display.StageOrientation;
import flash.events.StageOrientationEvent;
```

5. Within the constructor, set up the stage and listen for the ORIENTATION_CHANGING event:

```
public function Main() {
  stage.align = StageAlign.TOP_LEFT;
  stage.scaleMode = StageScaleMode.NO_SCALE;
  stage.addEventListener(
    StageOrientationEvent.ORIENTATION_CHANGING,
    orientationChanging);

  landscape.visible = false;
}
```

6. Finally, add a handler for the `ORIENTATION_CHANGING` event:

```
private function orientationChanging(e:StageOrientationEvent):void
{
  if(
    e.afterOrientation == StageOrientation.DEFAULT ||
    e.afterOrientation == StageOrientation.UPSIDE_DOWN
  )
  {
    portrait.visible = true;
    landscape.visible = false;
  }
  else if(
    e.afterOrientation == StageOrientation.ROTATED_LEFT ||
    e.afterOrientation == StageOrientation.ROTATED_RIGHT
  )
  {
    portrait.visible = false;
    landscape.visible = true;
  }
}
```

7. Save the class file as `Main.as`. Also move to your FLA and save it too.

8. Publish the FLA and deploy the IPA to your device.

9. Test the app by rotating your device. The screen will update to reflect any change in orientation.

How it works...

Rather than letting the stage's current on-screen content automatically resize when the device's orientation changes, we instead opted to display a different view.

The first step towards accomplishing this is to set the stage's scale mode and alignment.

Setting the scale mode to `NO_SCALE` prevents your content from being scaled to fit any changes in stage size. This ensures that the `portrait` and `landscape` movie clips maintain their defined sizes during orientation changes.

Setting the alignment to `TOP_LEFT` forces all content to be positioned relative to the top-left corner of the screen. Essentially both our movie clips, which are positioned at (0,0) on the stage will always start from the screen's top-left corner no matter what orientation the device is in.

The next step is to make the appropriate movie clip visible in response to a change in orientation. This is done by handling the `ORIENTATION_CHANGING` event and selecting a movie clip depending on the value of the `afterOrientation` property.

If the device is being rotated to one of the two portrait orientations (DEFAULT or UPSIDE_ DOWN), then the `portrait` movie clip is made visible and `landscape` is hidden. For either of the two landscape orientations (ROTATED_LEFT or ROTATED_RIGHT) the `landscape` movie clip is shown and `portrait` is hidden from view.

You may be wondering why we only have two movie clips for four possible orientations. Won't `portrait` and `landscape` appear upside-down for the UPSIDE_DOWN and ROTATED_LEFT orientations? Well they are for a brief moment, but remember that one of the benefits of auto-orientation is that it rotates your on-screen content ensuring that it is shown the right way up. Without auto-orientation, you would have to rotate all the items on the display list manually.

There's more...

Here are some more details to help complete your knowledge of screen orientation.

The stage color

Your choice of stage color is important as areas outside the stage's dimensions will be visible while auto-orientation is taking place. Select a stage color that will compliment your content. For example, this recipe used black as it matched the background color of both movie clips.

Change the stage color to white and re-deploy the app to your device. During orientation changes, you will now be able to see just how much area is actually visible.

Stage orientation

Although they often match, the actual orientation of the device in real space is independent of the content viewed on screen. For example, the user could be holding the device in landscape orientation while the app's content is still being rendered in portrait.

While the `Stage.deviceOrientation` property is available to determine the device's physical orientation, you can use the `Stage.orientation` property to retrieve the current orientation of the stage in relation to the device.

It is also possible to change the stage's orientation independently of the device's. This is achieved by calling `Stage.setOrientation()` and passing to it one of the constants defined in the `flash.display.StageOrientation` class. You can respond to this orientation change by listening for and responding to the ORIENTATION_CHANGING and ORIENTATION_CHANGE events.

Preventing auto-orientation

Auto-orientation takes place immediately after the ORIENTATION_CHANGING event but before ORIENTATION_CHANGE is dispatched. It is, therefore, possible to prevent auto-orientation for a particular orientation (or all of them) by calling `preventDefault()` on the ORIENTATION_CHANGING event's object.

For example, the following modification to our `orientationChanging()` handler will prevent the stage being orientated when the device is rotated to either of the two landscape orientations:

```
private function orientationChanging(e:StageOrientationEvent):void {
  if(
    e.afterOrientation == StageOrientation.ROTATED_LEFT ||
    e.afterOrientation == StageOrientation.ROTATED_RIGHT
  )
  {
    e.preventDefault();
  }
}
```

You can also use `preventDefault()` to block auto-orientation in order to completely manage the rotation and positioning of the stage's content yourself.

See also

▸ *AIR for iOS general settings, Chapter 2*

▸ *Listening for orientation changes*

▸ *Enabling auto-orientation*

9
Geolocation and Accelerometer APIs

In this chapter, we will cover:

- ▸ Determining your current location
- ▸ Determining your speed and heading
- ▸ Checking for geolocation access
- ▸ Responding to accelerometer changes
- ▸ Detecting a shake

Introduction

The iOS family makes use of many onboard sensors including the three-axis accelerometer, digital compass, camera, microphone, and global positioning system (GPS). Their inclusion has created a world of opportunity for developers, and has resulted in a slew of innovative, creative, and fun apps that have contributed to the overwhelming success of the App Store.

This chapter will focus on two of the most popular sensors—the accelerometer and GPS; both of which are supported by AIR for iOS.

The accelerometer measures g-force, enabling the detection of physical orientation, motion, and vibration. While originally seen by many as a gimmick, its uses have become increasingly more sophisticated as the platform has evolved. From games to remote controls, paint packages to sound generation, the accelerometer has become the input method of choice for many apps.

Devices such as the iPhone are also location-aware; its GPS receiver is able to determine its position anywhere in the world. Movement can be tracked, the current speed can be obtained, and even the direction the device is facing can be determined. In addition to mapping, location services are finding their way into all kinds of areas ranging from photography to messaging clients.

AIR provides APIs that allow access to both the accelerometer and location data collected by the device's sensors. Support for the accelerometer is provided by the `flash.sensors.Accelerometer` class, while `flash.sensors.Geolocation` is used when writing location-aware apps.

Determining your current location

The iOS family of devices are location-aware, allowing your approximate geographic position to be determined. How this is achieved depends on the hardware present in the device. For example, the original iPhone, all models of the iPod touch, and Wi-Fi-only iPads use Wi-Fi network triangulation to provide location information. The remaining devices can more accurately calculate their position using an on-board GPS chip or cell-phone tower triangulation.

The AIR SDK provides a layer of abstraction that allows you to extract location information in a hardware-independent manner, meaning you can access the information on any iOS device using the same code.

This recipe will take you through the steps required to determine your current location.

Getting ready

An FLA has been provided as a starting point for this recipe.

From Flash Professional, open `chapter9\recipe1\recipe.fla` from the book's accompanying code bundle.

You will find six dynamic text fields positioned on the stage. We will populate each of them with location data obtained from the device.

How to do it...

Perform the following steps to listen for and display geolocation data:

1. Create a document class and name it `Main`.
2. Import the following classes and add a member variable of type `Geolocation`:

   ```
   package {

       import flash.display.MovieClip;
   ```

```
import flash.events.GeolocationEvent;
import flash.sensors.Geolocation;

public class Main extends MovieClip {

   private var geo:Geolocation;

   public function Main() {
      // constructor code
   }
 }
}
```

3. Within the class' constructor, instantiate a `Geolocation` object and listen for updates from it:

```
public function Main() {
   if(Geolocation.isSupported)
   {
      geo = new Geolocation();
      geo.setRequestedUpdateInterval(1000);
      geo.addEventListener(GeolocationEvent.UPDATE, geoUpdated);
   }
}
```

4. Now, write an event handler that will obtain the updated geolocation data and populate the dynamic text fields with it:

```
private function geoUpdated(e:GeolocationEvent):void {
   latitudeField.text = e.latitude.toString();
   longitudeField.text = e.longitude.toString();
   altitudeField.text = e.altitude.toString();
   hAccuracyField.text = e.horizontalAccuracy.toString();
   vAccuracyField.text = e.verticalAccuracy.toString();
   timestampField.text = e.timestamp.toString();
}
```

5. Save the class file as `Main.as` within the same folder as the FLA. Move back to the FLA and save it too.

6. Publish and test the app on your device.

7. When launched for the first time, a native iOS dialog will appear with the following prompt:

"c9 r1" Would Like to Use Your Current Location

Tap the **OK** button to grant your app access to the device's location data.

 Devices running iOS 4 or above will remember your choice, while devices running older versions of iOS will prompt you each time the app is launched.

The location data will be shown on screen and periodically updated. Take your device on the move and you will see changes in the data as your geographical location changes.

How it works...

AIR provides the `Geolocation` class in the `flash.sensors` package, allowing the location data to be retrieved from your device. To access the data, create a `Geolocation` instance and listen for it dispatching `GeolocationEvent.UPDATE` events.

We did this within our document class' constructor, using the `geo` member variable to hold a reference to the object:

```
geo = new Geolocation();
geo.setRequestedUpdateInterval(1000);
geo.addEventListener(GeolocationEvent.UPDATE, geoUpdated);
```

The frequency with which location data is retrieved can be set by calling the `Geolocation.setRequestedUpdateInterval()` method. You can see this in the earlier code where we requested an update interval of 1000 milliseconds. This only acts as a hint to the device, meaning the actual time between updates may be greater or smaller than your request. Omitting this call will result in the device using a default update interval. The default interval can be anything ranging from milliseconds to seconds depending on the device's hardware capabilities.

Each `UPDATE` event dispatches a `GeolocationEvent` object, which contains properties describing your current location. Our `geoUpdated()` method handles this event by outputting several of the properties to the dynamic text fields sitting on the stage:

```
private function geoUpdated(e:GeolocationEvent):void {
   latitudeField.text = e.latitude.toString();
   longitudeField.text = e.longitude.toString();
   altitudeField.text = e.altitude.toString();
   hAccuracyField.text = e.horizontalAccuracy.toString();
   vAccuracyField.text = e.verticalAccuracy.toString();
   timestampField.text = e.timestamp.toString();
}
```

The following information was output:

- ▸ Latitude and longitude
- ▸ Altitude
- ▸ Horizontal and vertical accuracy
- ▸ Timestamp

The latitude and longitude positions are used to identify your geographical location. Your altitude is also obtained and is measured in meters. As you move with the device, these values will update to reflect your new location.

The accuracy of the location data is also shown and depends on the hardware capabilities of the device. Both the horizontal and vertical accuracy are measured in meters.

Finally, a timestamp is associated with every `GeolocationEvent` object that is dispatched, allowing you to determine the actual time interval between each. The timestamp specifies the milliseconds that have passed since the app was launched.

Some older devices that do not include a GPS unit only dispatch `UPDATE` events occasionally. Initially, one or two `UPDATE` events are dispatched, with additional events only being dispatched when location information changes noticeably.

Also note the use of the static `Geolocation.isSupported` property within the constructor. Although this will currently return `true` for all iOS devices, it cannot be guaranteed for future devices. Checking for geolocation support is also advisable when writing cross-platform code.

For more information, perform a search for `flash.sensors.Geolocation` and `flash.events.GeolocationEvent` within Adobe Community Help.

There's more...

The amount of information made available and the accuracy of that information depends on the capabilities of the device.

Accuracy

The accuracy of the location data depends on the method employed by the device to calculate your position. Typically, iOS devices with an on-board GPS chip will have a benefit over those that rely on Wi-Fi triangulation.

For example, running this recipe's app on an iPhone 4, which contains a GPS unit, results in a horizontal accuracy of around 10 meters. The same app running on a third-generation iPod touch and relying on a Wi-Fi network, reports a horizontal accuracy of around 100 meters. Quite a difference!

Altitude support

The current altitude can only be obtained from GPS-enabled devices. On devices without a GPS unit, the `GeolocationEvent.verticalAccuracy` property will return `-1` and `GeolocationEvent.altitude` will return `0`. A vertical accuracy of `-1` indicates that altitude cannot be detected.

You should be aware of, and code for these restrictions when developing apps that provide location-based services. Do not make assumptions about a device's capabilities.

If your application relies on the presence of GPS hardware, then it is possible to state this within your application descriptor file. Doing so will prevent users without the necessary hardware from downloading your app from the App Store.

For more information, take a look at the *Declaring device capabilities* recipe from *Chapter 13*.

Mapping your location

The most obvious use for the retrieval of geolocation data is mapping. Typically, an app will obtain a geographic location and display a map of its surrounding area. There are several ways to achieve this, but launching and passing location data to the device's native maps application is possibly the easiest solution. Take a look at *Launching the Maps application* from *Chapter 13* to see how this is done.

If you would prefer an ActionScript solution, then there is the UMap ActionScript 3.0 API, which integrates with map data from a wide range of providers including Bing, Google, and Yahoo!. You can sign up and download the API from `www.umapper.com`. Also tutorials are available at `www.afcomponents.com/tutorials/umap_as3`.

Calculating distance between geolocations

When the geographic coordinates of two separate locations are known, it is possible to determine the distance between them. AIR does not provide an API for this but an AS3 solution can be found on the Adobe Developer Connection website at: `http://cookbooks.adobe.com/index.cfm?event=showdetails&postId=5701`.

The UMap ActionScript 3.0 API can also be used to calculate distances. Refer to `www.umapper.com`.

Geocoding

Mapping providers, such as Google and Yahoo!, provide geocoding and reverse-geocoding web services. Geocoding is the process of finding the latitude and longitude of an address, whereas reverse-geocoding converts a latitude-longitude pair into a readable address.

You can make HTTP requests from your AIR for iOS application to any of these services. As an example, take a look at the Yahoo! PlaceFinder web service at `http://developer.yahoo.com/geo/placefinder`.

Alternatively, the UMap ActionScript 3.0 API integrates with many of these services to provide geocoding functionality directly within your Flash projects. Refer to the uMapper website.

Gyroscope support

Another popular sensor is the gyroscope, which is found in more recent iOS devices. While the AIR SDK does not directly support gyroscope access, Adobe has made available a native extension for AIR 3.0, which provides a `Gyroscope` ActionScript class.

A download link and usage examples can be found on the Adobe Developer Connection site at `www.adobe.com/devnet/air/native-extensions-for-air/extensions/gyroscope.html`.

See also

▸ *Determining your speed and heading*

▸ *Launching the Maps application, Chapter 13*

Determining your speed and heading

The availability of an on-board GPS unit makes it possible to determine your speed and heading. In this recipe, we will write a simple app that uses the `Geolocation` class to obtain and use this information. In addition, we will add compass functionality by utilizing the user's current heading.

Getting ready

You will need a GPS-enabled iOS device. The iPhone has featured an on-board GPS unit since the release of the 3G. GPS hardware can also be found in all cellular network-enabled iPads.

From Flash Professional, open `chapter9\recipe2\recipe.fla` from the book's accompanying code bundle.

Sitting on the stage are three dynamic text fields. The first two (`speed1Field` and `speed2Field`) will be used to display the current speed in meters per second and miles per hour respectively. We will write the device's current heading into the third—`headingField`.

Also, a movie clip named `compass` has been positioned near the bottom of the stage and represents a compass with north, south, east, and west clearly marked on it. We will update the rotation of this clip in response to heading changes to ensure that it always points towards true north.

How to do it...

To obtain the device's speed and heading, carry out the following steps:

1. Create a document class and name it `Main`.

2. Add the necessary import statements, a constant, and a member variable of type `Geolocation`:

```
package {

    import flash.display.MovieClip;
    import flash.events.GeolocationEvent;
    import flash.sensors.Geolocation;

    public class Main extends MovieClip {

        private const CONVERSION_FACTOR:Number = 2.237;
        private var geo:Geolocation;

        public function Main() {
          // constructor code
        }
    }
}
```

3. Within the constructor, instantiate a `Geolocation` object and listen for updates:

```
public function Main() {
    if(Geolocation.isSupported)
    {
        geo = new Geolocation();
        geo.setRequestedUpdateInterval(50);
        geo.addEventListener(GeolocationEvent.UPDATE, geoUpdated);
    }
}
```

4. We will need an event listener for the `Geolocation` object's `UPDATE` event. This is where we will obtain and display the current speed and heading, and also update the `compass` movie clip to ensure it points towards true north. Add the following method:

```
private function geoUpdated(e:GeolocationEvent):void {
    var metersPerSecond:Number = e.speed;
    var milesPerHour:uint = getMilesPerHour(metersPerSecond);
    speed1Field.text = String(metersPerSecond);
    speed2Field.text = String(milesPerHour);
```

```
    var heading:Number = e.heading;
    compass.rotation = 360 - heading;
    headingField.text = String(heading);
}
```

5. Finally, add this support method to convert meters per second to miles per hour:

```
private function getMilesPerHour(metersPerSecond:Number):uint
{
    return metersPerSecond * CONVERSION_FACTOR;
}
```

6. Save the class file as `Main.as`. Move back to the FLA and save it too.

7. Compile the FLA and deploy the IPA to your device.

8. Launch the app. When prompted, grant your app access to the GPS unit.

Hold the device in front of you and start turning on the spot. The **heading (degrees)** field will update to show the direction you are facing. The `compass` movie clip will also update, showing you where true north is in relation to your current heading.

Take your device outside and start walking, or better still, start running. On average every 50 milliseconds you will see the top two text fields update and show your current speed, measured in both meters per second and miles per hour.

How it works...

In this recipe, we created a `Geolocation` object and listened for it dispatching UPDATE events. An update interval of 50 milliseconds was specified in an attempt to receive the speed and heading information frequently.

Both the speed and heading information are obtained from the `GeolocationEvent` object, which is dispatched on each UPDATE event. The event is captured and handled by our `geoUpdated()` handler, which displays the speed and heading information from the accelerometer.

The current speed is measured in meters per second and is obtained by querying the `GeolocationEvent.speed` property. Our handler also converts the speed to miles per hour before displaying each value within the appropriate text field. The following code does this:

```
var metersPerSecond:Number = e.speed;
var milesPerHour:uint = getMilesPerHour(metersPerSecond);
speed1Field.text = String(metersPerSecond);
speed2Field.text = String(milesPerHour);
```

The heading, which represents the direction of movement (with respect to true north) in degrees, is retrieved from the `GeolocationEvent.heading` property. The value is used to set the `rotation` property of the `compass` movie clip and is also written to the `headingField` text field:

```
var heading:Number = e.heading;
compass.rotation = 360 - heading;
headingField.text = String(heading);
```

The remaining method is `getMilesPerHour()` and is used within `geoUpdated()` to convert the current speed from meters per second into miles per hour. Notice the use of the `CONVERSION_FACTOR` constant that was declared within your document class:

```
private function getMilesPerHour(metersPerSecond:Number):uint
{
   return metersPerSecond * CONVERSION_FACTOR;
}
```

Although the speed and heading obtained from the GPS unit will suffice for most applications, the accuracy can vary across devices. Your surroundings can also have an affect; moving through streets with tall buildings or under tree coverage can impair the readings.

You can find more information regarding `flash.sensors.Geolocation` and `flash.events.GeolocationEvent` within Adobe Community Help.

There's more...

The following information provides some additional detail.

Determining support

Your current speed and heading can only be determined by devices that possess a GPS receiver.

Although you can install this recipe's app on any iOS device, you won't receive valid readings from any model of iPod touch, the original iPhone, or W-Fi-only iPads. Instead the `GeolocationEvent.speed` property will return -1 and `GeolocationEvent.heading` will return NaN.

If your application relies on the presence of GPS hardware, then it is possible to state this within the application descriptor file. Doing so will prevent users without the necessary hardware from downloading your app from the App Store.

For more information, take a look at the *Declaring device capabilities* recipe from *Chapter 13*.

Simulating the GPS receiver

During the development lifecycle it is not feasible to continually test your app in a live environment. Instead you will probably want to record live data from your device and re-use it during testing. There are various apps available that will log data from the sensors on your device.

One such app is xSensor, which can be downloaded from iTunes or the App Store and is free. Its data sensor log is limited to 5KB but this restriction can be lifted by purchasing xSensor Pro.

Preventing screen idle

Many of this chapter's apps don't require you to touch the screen that often. Therefore you will be likely to experience the backlight dimming or the screen locking while testing them. This can be inconvenient and can be prevented by disabling screen locking. For more details, see the _Preventing screen idle_ recipe in _Chapter 3_.

See also

- ▶ _Determining your current location_
- ▶ _Checking for geolocation access_

Checking for geolocation access

Applications that make use of a device's location data must be granted permission by the user. The user is prompted when an app attempts to access location data for the first time. Devices running iOS 4 or above will remember this choice, whereas older versions of iOS will request access each time the app is launched. In addition, access privileges can be changed at any time from the device's settings.

It is important that your app can detect the availability of geolocation data, and also respond to permission changes at runtime. Let us see how this is done.

Getting ready

An FLA has been provided as a starting point.

From the book's accompanying code bundle, open `chapter9\recipe3\recipe.fla` into Flash Professional.

A dynamic text field with an instance name of `output` has been added to the stage.

We will write an app that listens for the availability of the geolocation data and reports any changes to the `output` text field.

How to do it...

Carry out the following steps:

1. Create a document class and name it `Main`.

2. Add the following import statements and a member variable of type `Geolocation`:

```
package {

    import flash.display.MovieClip;
    import flash.events.GeolocationEvent;
    import flash.events.StatusEvent;
    import flash.sensors.Geolocation;

    public class Main extends MovieClip {

        private var geo:Geolocation;

        public function Main() {
            // constructor code
        }
    }
}
```

3. Within the constructor, create a `Geolocation` object and listen for it dispatching `GeolocationEvent.UPDATE` and `StatusEvent.STATUS`:

```
public function Main() {
    output.text = "Obtaining location...";
    if (Geolocation.isSupported)
    {
        geo = new Geolocation();
        geo.setRequestedUpdateInterval(1000);
        geo.addEventListener(GeolocationEvent.UPDATE, geoUpdated);
        geo.addEventListener(StatusEvent.STATUS, statusUpdated);
    }
    else
    {
        output.text = "Geolocation is not supported.";
    }
}
```

4.   Finally, add a handler for each event:

```
private function geoUpdated(e:GeolocationEvent):void {
  output.text = "Location received.";
}

private function statusUpdated(e:StatusEvent):void {
  if(e.code == "Geolocation.Muted")
  {
    output.text = "Geolocation access denied.";
  }
}
```

5.   Save the class file as `Main.as`.

6.   Save the FLA and publish it. Install the IPA and launch it on your device.

     A native iOS dialog will appear with the following prompt:

     "c9 r3" Would Like to Use Your Current Location

7.   Tap the **Don't Allow** button to deny the app access to the device's location data.

     The following text will appear on-screen:

     Obtaining location...

     And will quickly be replaced with:

     Geolocation access denied.

8.   Now re-launch the app. If you are using iOS 4 or above, your previous setting will be remembered and access to the geolocation data will once again be denied. If you are using an earlier version of iOS, then you will be prompted to grant access each time.

 To re-launch an app in iOS 4 or above, you will first need to kill it using the fast app switcher. Refer to the *Exiting gracefully from an app* recipe in *Chapter 3*, for details on how to do this.

On devices running iOS 4 or above, an app's access privileges can be changed from the device's settings. Let us do this for our app.

9. Exit from the app by pressing the Home button. From the device's settings, move to **Location Services**. You will be presented with a list of apps that have attempted to access location data. Scroll down until you find **c9 r3**. Tap the button next to it to allow access to it.

10. Now move back to the home screen and launch this recipe's app again.

    This time you will see the following text:

    Obtaining location...

    And it will quickly be replaced with:

    Location received.

How it works...

When the user prevents an AIR for iOS app from accessing location data, `GeolocationEvent.UPDATE` events cease and `StatusEvent.STATUS` is dispatched from the `Geolocation` object. It is therefore possible to determine when access to location data has been revoked by simply listening for the `STATUS` event:

```
geo = new Geolocation();
geo.setRequestedUpdateInterval(1000);
geo.addEventListener(GeolocationEvent.UPDATE, geoUpdated);
geo.addEventListener(StatusEvent.STATUS, statusUpdated);
```

A final check is performed within the `statusUpdated()` handler:

```
private function statusUpdated(e:StatusEvent):void {
  if(e.code == "Geolocation.Muted")
  {
    output.text = "Geolocation access denied.";
  }
}
```

In this method, we query the `StatusEvent` object's `code` property. If it has a string value of `Geolocation.Muted`, then we know that access to the geolocation data is no longer available.

Finally, although it wasn't used in this recipe's example, you can also access the `Geolocation.muted` property to determine if geolocation data is available. When a newly installed app is launched for the first time, `muted` will be set to `true` until the user grants permission from the native iOS dialog.

More information regarding `flash.events.StatusEvent` can be found in Adobe Community Help.

See also

▸ *Determining your current location*

Responding to accelerometer changes

The accelerometer provides access to data that represents the device's location or movement along a three-dimensional axis. When motion is detected, it is returned as data, which can be accessed by ActionScript.

This recipe will show you how to take advantage of the accelerometer found in iOS devices.

Getting ready

An FLA has been provided as a starting point.

Open `chapter9\recipe4\recipe.fla` from the book's accompanying code bundle into Flash Professional.

You will find five dynamic text fields positioned on the stage. Below them is a movie clip with an instance name of `arrow`. We will populate each text field with data retrieved from the device's accelerometer and rotate the movie clip to reflect physical changes in the device's orientation.

Also notice the stage's dimensions are set to 480x320. For this recipe, landscape orientation will be used.

How to do it...

Perform these steps to listen for and respond to accelerometer changes:

1. Create a document class and name it `Main`.

2. Add the following two import statements and a member variable of type `Accelerometer`:

```
package {

    import flash.display.MovieClip;
    import flash.events.AccelerometerEvent;
    import flash.sensors.Accelerometer;

    public class Main extends MovieClip {

        private var acc:Accelerometer;

        public function Main() {
            // constructor code
        }
    }
}
```

3. Within the constructor, instantiate an `Accelerometer` object and listen for updates from it:

```
public function Main() {
    if(Accelerometer.isSupported)
    {
        acc = new Accelerometer();
        acc.setRequestedUpdateInterval(50);
```

```
    acc.addEventListener(AccelerometerEvent.UPDATE,
        accUpdated);
  }
}
```

4. Finish by writing an event handler that will obtain and use the updated accelerometer data:

```
private function accUpdated(e:AccelerometerEvent):void {
  var radians:Number = Math.atan2(e.accelerationY,
    e.accelerationX);
  var degrees:Number = (radians * (180 / Math.PI)) - 90;
  arrow.rotation = -degrees;

  accXField.text = e.accelerationX.toString();
  accYField.text = e.accelerationY.toString();
  accZField.text = e.accelerationZ.toString();
  timeField.text = e.timestamp.toString();
  rotField.text = degrees.toString();
}
```

5. Save the class file as `Main.as`.

6. Also, save your FLA and then publish it. Install the app to your device and launch it.

As the device's motion sensor detects activity, the text fields will update. Holding the device in front of yourself and tilting it clockwise and counter-clockwise will update the rotation of the `arrow` movie clip, ensuring that it always points upwards.

How it works...

We accessed the accelerometer's data by creating an instance of the `Accelerometer` class and listening for it dispatching the `AccelerometerEvent.UPDATE` event:

```
acc = new Accelerometer();
acc.setRequestedUpdateInterval(50);
acc.addEventListener(AccelerometerEvent.UPDATE, accUpdated);
```

The frequency with which UPDATE events are received can be set by calling the `Accelerometer.setRequestedUpdateInterval()` method. You can see this in the earlier code where we requested an update every 50 milliseconds. This only acts as a hint to the device, meaning the actual time between updates may be greater or smaller than your request. Omitting this call will result in the device using a default update interval. The default interval can be anything ranging from milliseconds to seconds depending on the device's hardware capabilities.

The UPDATE event is an AccelerometerEvent object and provides access to the following properties:

- accelerationX—Acceleration along the x-axis. When the device is upright, the x-axis runs from left to right. Acceleration is positive if the device is moved to the right.

- accelerationY—Acceleration along the y-axis. When the device is upright, the y-axis runs from bottom to top. Acceleration is positive if the device is moved upwards.

- accelerationZ—Acceleration along the z-axis. The acceleration is positive if the device is moved so that its face points upwards. Acceleration is negative if it faces towards the ground.

- timestamp—The number of milliseconds that have elapsed since the app was launched.

 Acceleration is measured in "g" with 1g being the standard acceleration due to gravity, which is approximately 9.8 meters per second squared.

We obtain these properties within the accUpdated() handler and write them to our dynamic text fields:

```
accXField.text = e.accelerationX.toString();
accYField.text = e.accelerationY.toString();
accZField.text = e.accelerationZ.toString();
timeField.text = e.timestamp.toString();
```

Additionally, the accelerometerX and accelerometerY properties are used to calculate the angle at which the device is being held (with the screen facing you). This is used to update the rotation of the arrow movie clip. The following is the code that does this:

```
var radians:Number = Math.atan2(e.accelerationY,
  e.accelerationX);
var degrees:Number = (radians * (180 / Math.PI)) - 90;
arrow.rotation = -degrees;
```

Knowing the angle, at which the device is being tilted, is useful for many applications. In particular games, where tilting the device may be used to move a character along a platform or simulate the movement of a steering wheel.

Finally, within the constructor, note the use of the static read-only property Accelerometer. isSupported to check for the availability of an accelerometer. The accelerometer is supported on all existing iOS devices but isn't guaranteed for future devices. It is therefore a good practice to check for support and is also beneficial when writing cross-platform code.

There's more...

The following is some more information regarding the accelerometer and how to work with its data.

Orientation and the accelerometer axes

The accelerometer axes are re-oriented with the device's display rather than the physical orientation of the device itself. In other words, when auto-orientation is active, the y-axis will be vertical when the display's content is being viewed in a normal up-right position. This is true for both apps that default to a portrait aspect-ratio and apps that default to a landscape aspect-ratio. If however, auto-orientation is not active, then the accelerometer axes will not be re-oriented when the device is rotated.

Determining device orientation

Data from the accelerometer is affected by gravity and can be useful to determine the device's current orientation. The following are the values to check for:

- `accelerationX` > 0.5—Rotated 90 degrees counter clockwise
- `accelerationX` < -0.5—Rotated 90 degrees clockwise
- `accelerationY` > 0.5—Normal upright position
- `accelerationY` < -0.5—Upside down
- `accelerationZ` > 0.5—Face up
- `accelerationZ` < -0.5—Face down

This provides an alternative to determining orientation by listening for `StageOrientationEvent` objects being dispatched from the stage. In addition, using the acceleration data makes it possible to determine whether the device's screen display is facing upwards or towards the ground.

Applying a low-pass filter

Data from the accelerometer is affected by both the effect of gravity and sudden changes in motion. If you are using this data to detect the device's orientation, then you should isolate the gravity component from the data by applying a low-pass filter.

This can be achieved by smoothing out the data over time. To do this, start by creating a filtering factor and three member variables to store the previous value for each axis:

```
private const FACTOR:Number = 0.1;
private var accX:Number = 0;
private var accY:Number = 0;
private var accZ:Number = 0;
```

Now in response to each `AccelerometerEvent.UPDATE`, apply a low-pass filter to keep only the gravity component from each axis:

```
accX = (e.accelerationX * FACTOR) + (accX * (1 - FACTOR));
accY = (e.accelerationY * FACTOR) + (accY * (1 - FACTOR));
accZ = (e.accelerationZ * FACTOR) + (accZ * (1 - FACTOR));
```

Essentially this code generates a value for each axis that uses 10 percent of its current data and 90 percent of the previously filtered data. This will ensure that data responds slowly to sudden and short-lived changes in motion.

Applying a high-pass filter

Many types of applications use accelerometer data to detect sudden changes in motion. A high-pass filter can be used to isolate the portion of the data that is caused by sudden changes in motion.

Similar to the implementation of a low-pass filter, use a filtering factor plus three member variables to store the previous value for each axis. Then in response to each `AccelerometerEvent.UPDATE`, apply the filter:

```
accX = e.accelerationX - ((e.accelerationX * FACTOR) +
   (accX * (1 - FACTOR)));
accY = e.accelerationY - ((e.accelerationY * FACTOR) +
   (accY * (1 - FACTOR)));
accZ = e.accelerationZ - ((e.accelerationZ * FACTOR) +
   (accZ * (1 - FACTOR)));
```

In this example, a low-pass filter value is calculated for each axis and subtracted from the current value. Doing so keeps the sudden changes in motion while removing the gravity component.

The "muted" property

The `Accelerometer` class has a static read-only property named `muted`. It is used to determine if a user has granted the app permission to access accelerometer data. This property isn't required for iOS as there is no way, at present, to deny an app access to the accelerometer.

See also

▸ *Setting the default aspect ratio, Chapter 8*

▸ *Enabling auto-orientation, Chapter 8*

▸ *Responding to orientation changes, Chapter 8*

Detecting a shake

A common use of the accelerometer is to detect a shake and this has become a popular method of interaction in games and applications. For example, many of the apps that come with iOS allow the user to perform an undo by shaking the device.

This recipe will show you how to determine if the user is shaking their device by examining the data coming from the accelerometer.

Getting ready

From the book's accompanying code bundle, open `chapter9\recipe5\recipe.fla` into Flash Professional.

You will find a movie clip named `shake` sitting in the center of the stage. Its timeline consists of two key-frames.

We will write some ActionScript that will move the clip in response to changes along the device's three axes. When the motion is pronounced, we will indicate to the user that a shake has been detected by jumping to the movie clip's second frame.

The stage uses a landscape aspect ratio for this recipe.

How to do it...

Perform the following steps to detect a shake:

1. Create a document class and name it `Main`.
2. Import the classes required to work with the accelerometer and add the following member variables:

```
package {

    import flash.display.MovieClip;
    import flash.events.AccelerometerEvent;
    import flash.sensors.Accelerometer;

    public class Main extends MovieClip {

        private const THRESHOLD:Number = 0.8;

        private var acc:Accelerometer;
        private var prevX:Number;
        private var prevY:Number;
        private var prevZ:Number;
```

```
        private var startX:Number;
        private var startY:Number;

        public function Main() {
          // constructor code
        }
      }
    }
```

3. Initialize the member variables and the shake movie clip. Also, instantiate an Accelerometer object and listen for it dispatching UPDATE events:

```
public function Main() {
  prevX = prevY = prevZ = 0;

  shake.gotoAndStop(1);
  startX = shake.x;
  startY = shake.y;

  if(Accelerometer.isSupported)
  {
    acc = new Accelerometer();
    acc.setRequestedUpdateInterval(50);
    acc.addEventListener(AccelerometerEvent.UPDATE,
      accUpdated);
  }
}
```

4. Add a handler for the UPDATE event:

```
private function accUpdated(e:AccelerometerEvent):void {
  var changeX:Number = prevX - e.accelerationX;
  var changeY:Number = prevY - e.accelerationY;
  var changeZ:Number = prevZ - e.accelerationZ;

  prevX = e.accelerationX;
  prevY = e.accelerationY;
  prevZ = e.accelerationZ;

  shake.x = startX + (changeX * 100);
  shake.y = startY + (changeY * 100);
  shake.z = (changeZ * 100);

  if(Math.abs(changeX) > THRESHOLD ||
     Math.abs(changeY) > THRESHOLD ||
     Math.abs(changeZ) > THRESHOLD)
  {
```

```
        shake.gotoAndStop(2);
    }
    else
    {
        shake.gotoAndStop(1);
    }
}
```

5. Save the class file and when prompted name it `Main.as`.

6. Now save the FLA and publish it. Test the app on your device.

Gently shaking the device will displace the movie clip from the center of the screen. A more violent motion will also change its appearance indicating that a sufficiently large shake has been detected.

How it works...

This example compares the current acceleration data with the previous to see if a sufficiently large change has occurred.

The previous acceleration data is stored within the `prevX`, `prevY`, and `prevZ` member variables and is compared against the current data to determine the change for each axis:

```
var changeX:Number = prevX - e.accelerationX;
var changeY:Number = prevY - e.accelerationY;
var changeZ:Number = prevZ - e.accelerationZ;

prevX = e.accelerationX;
prevY = e.accelerationY;
prevZ = e.accelerationZ;
```

If the change in any one of the three axes is large enough, then it is safe to assume that the device is being shaken. This information is fed back to the user by moving to the second frame of the `shake` movie clip. The following is the code that does this:

```
if(Math.abs(changeX) > THRESHOLD ||
   Math.abs(changeY) > THRESHOLD ||
   Math.abs(changeZ) > THRESHOLD)
{
    shake.gotoAndStop(2);
}
else
{
    shake.gotoAndStop(1);
}
```

The `THRESHOLD` constant simply dictates the amount of change that needs to take place in any of the axes for the motion to be deemed a shake. Lowering this value will reduce the effort required by the user to trigger a shake, while increasing it will make it more difficult.

To provide greater visual feedback, we also update the x, y, and z positions of the `shake` movie clip in response to changes from the accelerometer. The more violent the shaking motion, the more the clip is displaced from its original starting position:

```
shake.x = startX + (changeX * 100);
shake.y = startY + (changeY * 100);
shake.z = (changeZ * 100);
```

The `startX` and `startY` member variables used are initialized within the constructor and are set to the `shake` movie clip's original position.

The majority of the work in this example is performed within the `accUpdated()` event handler, which is called each time `AccelerometerEvent.UPDATE` is dispatched from the `Accelerometer` object. To ensure the app is responsive, a call is made to the `setRequestedUpdateInterval()` method requesting frequent updates.

There's more...

Let us look at some options to further improve this recipe's example.

Checking multiple axes

We checked for a large enough change in only one of the axes before deciding that the user was shaking the device. Another approach is to wait for a significant change in two of the three axes. The code for this would look as follows:

```
var changeX:Number = Math.abs(e.accelerationX);
var changeY:Number = Math.abs(e.accelerationY);
var changeZ:Number = Math.abs(e.accelerationZ);
if((changeX > THRESHOLD && changeY > THRESHOLD) ||
   (changeX > THRESHOLD && changeZ > THRESHOLD) ||
   (changeY > THRESHOLD && changeZ > THRESHOLD))
{
   // Shake detected.
}
```

For multiple axes you may want to reduce the `THRESHOLD` value slightly to compensate for the fact that the user must make a more exaggerated motion to initiate a shake.

Smoothing accelerometer data

You may have noticed that even when holding the device still, the `shake` movie clip shudders slightly. Accelerometers aren't perfectly accurate and the data returned will contain some noise.

This noise can be reduced by applying a high-pass filter to your data over time and is detailed in the _Responding to accelerometer changes_ recipe. Try experimenting with the filtering factor and the threshold constant until you find values that give you a result you are happy with.

See also

- ▶ _Responding to accelerometer changes_

10
Camera and Microphone Support

In this chapter, we will cover:

- ▸ Saving to the camera roll
- ▸ Reading from the camera roll
- ▸ Capturing with the default camera app
- ▸ Working with the built-in cameras
- ▸ Recording microphone audio
- ▸ Playing recorded audio

Introduction

The camera and microphone are possibly the two most popular sensors built into iOS devices. In fact, iPhone owners rely on the microphone on a daily basis when making calls. Those who use Apple's FaceTime depend on both the microphone and the camera to keep in touch. And of course, everyone has taken a photo or shot a video from time-to-time.

Developers are finding increasingly sophisticated uses for both sensors that extend far beyond the functionality provided by Apple's pre-installed applications. Image and voice recognition, augmented reality, language translation, and voice distortion are just a handful.

Adobe introduced camera and microphone support in AIR 2.6, allowing Flash developers to take advantage of both sensors within their apps. While you can work through all of this chapter's recipes using Flash Professional CS5.5, those with Flash Professional CS5 will be limited to the first recipe, *Saving to the camera roll*.

Saving to the camera roll

Many iOS applications allow the user to save an image to the camera roll. Drawing tools and avatar creators are popular examples, where the user can easily show off their creation to friends and family from the device's native photo gallery.

This recipe will show you how to save a snapshot of the stage to the device's camera roll.

Getting ready

From the book's accompanying code bundle, open `chapter10\recipe1\recipe.fla` into Flash Professional.

You will find two bitmaps and a movie clip sitting on the stage. The bitmaps have been composited to produce a background image, which we will save to the camera roll. The movie clip represents a button and will initiate the save when pressed.

The button movie clip has an instance name of `saveBtn` and its library symbol is linked to a class named `Button`. This class was introduced in the *Handling user interaction* recipe from *Chapter 4*.

Okay, let us write some code.

How to do it...

We will make use of AIR's `CameraRoll` class for this recipe.

1. Create a document class and name it `Main`.
2. Add the following import statements and a member variable of type `CameraRoll`:

```
package {

    import flash.display.BitmapData;
    import flash.display.MovieClip;
    import flash.events.Event;
    import flash.events.MouseEvent;
    import flash.media.CameraRoll;

    public class Main extends MovieClip {

        private var cameraRoll:CameraRoll;

        public function Main() {
            // constructor code
        }
    }
}
```

3. Within the constructor, create a `CameraRoll` object and listen for it dispatching `Event.COMPLETE`. Also listen for `MouseEvent.MOUSE_UP` being dispatched from the `saveBtn` movie clip:

```
public function Main() {
  cameraRoll = new CameraRoll();
  cameraRoll.addEventListener(Event.COMPLETE, saved);

  saveBtn.addEventListener(MouseEvent.MOUSE_UP, pressed);
}
```

4. When the save button is pressed, we will add a bitmap image of the stage to the camera roll. To prevent the button appearing in the captured bitmap image, we will hide it from view first. Add a `pressed()` event handler:

```
private function pressed(e:MouseEvent):void {
  saveBtn.visible = false;

  var bitmapData:BitmapData = new BitmapData(
    stage.stageWidth, stage.stageHeight, false);
  bitmapData.draw(stage);

  if(CameraRoll.supportsAddBitmapData)
  {
    cameraRoll.addBitmapData(bitmapData);
  }
}
```

5. Once the bitmap has been successfully added to the camera roll, we will make the button visible again. Write a `saved()` event handler for this:

```
private function saved(e:Event):void {
  saveBtn.visible = true;
}
```

6. Save the class, and when prompted name the file `Main.as`.

7. Move back to your FLA.

8. Publish the app and deploy it to your device.

9. Launch the app and press the **SAVE** button. Go to the Photos app where you will see your image saved to the camera roll as shown in the following screenshot:

How it works...

The CameraRoll class allows access to the device's photo library and belongs to the flash. media package.

Calling the CameraRoll.addBitmapData() method will save a specified bitmap to the device. Upon a successful save, Event.COMPLETE is dispatched.

For this recipe, we created and passed a BitmapData object to the addBitmapData() method. The BitmapData object contained a bitmap representation of the stage, which was created by calling the BitmapData.draw() method and passing the stage property to it.

The static CameraRoll.supportsAddBitmapData property was also used. It determines whether or not saving bitmap data to the device's camera roll is supported for your target platform. Although this property returns true for all iOS devices, it is wise to check if you are writing cross-platform code.

There's more...

The following information will be of use to you when saving to the camera roll.

Handling a failed save

Don't assume that a bitmap will always successfully save to the camera roll. For example, the device may not have the required storage space available.

When a bitmap cannot be added, the `CameraRoll` object will dispatch `ErrorEvent.ERROR`. Querying the `ErrorEvent` object's `text` property retrieves a message associated with the error.

Your code should listen for this event and handle any failed attempts at adding bitmap data. Perform a search for `flash.media.CameraRoll` within Adobe Community Help for a full list of possible errors.

Saving specific display objects

Although we grabbed the entire stage for this recipe, you can create a bitmap image of any display object and add it to the camera roll. Simply create a `BitmapData` object and call its `draw()` method, passing your target display object as an argument. The `BitmapData` object's dimensions should be made to match that of your display object.

Video and the camera roll

At present, the AIR SDK does not provide support for adding video content to the camera roll.

See also

  ▸   *Reading from the camera roll*

Reading from the camera roll

Depending on the version of the AIR SDK you are using, it is possible to load an image from the device's camera roll. AIR for iOS facilitates this by launching the native Photos application and allowing the user to select an image. The image can then be loaded and added to your display list.

Let us see how to write a simple app that loads an image selected from the camera roll.

The steps covered here are applicable only to those using Flash Professional CS5.5. The AIR 2.0 SDK used by Flash Professional CS5 does not feature an API for loading images from the camera roll.

Getting ready

An FLA has been provided as a starting point for this recipe. From the book's accompanying code bundle, open `chapter10\recipe2\recipe.fla` into Flash Professional CS5.5.

A movie clip with an instance name of `browseBtn` can be found on the stage. The clip's library symbol is linked to a class named `Button`, which was introduced in the *Handling user interaction* recipe from *Chapter 4*.

Let us write some code to let the user browse for, and load an image from the camera roll after pressing the `browseBtn` movie clip.

How to do it...

We will make use of several classes, including `CameraRoll`, `Loader`, and `MediaPromise`.

1. Create a document class and name it `Main`.

2. Import the required classes and add two member variables—one of type CameraRoll and the other of type `Loader`:

```
package {

    import flash.display.Loader;
    import flash.display.MovieClip;
    import flash.events.Event;
    import flash.events.MediaEvent;
    import flash.events.MouseEvent;
    import flash.media.CameraRoll;
    import flash.media.MediaPromise;

    public class Main extends MovieClip {

        private var cameraRoll:CameraRoll;
        private var loader:Loader;

        public function Main() {
            // constructor code
        }
    }
}
```

3. Instantiate a `CameraRoll` object and listen for it dispatching `MediaEvent.SELECT` and `Event.CANCEL`. Also, listen for the `browseBtn` movie clip being pressed:

```
public function Main() {
    cameraRoll = new CameraRoll();
    cameraRoll.addEventListener(MediaEvent.SELECT,
        photoSelected);
    cameraRoll.addEventListener(Event.CANCEL, cancelled);

    browseBtn.addEventListener(MouseEvent.MOUSE_UP,
        buttonPressed);
}
```

4. When the `browseBtn` movie clip is pressed, we will hide it from view and also launch the native Photos application. Add the following method to handle this:

```
private function buttonPressed(e:MouseEvent):void {
    browseBtn.visible = false;
    if (CameraRoll.supportsBrowseForImage)
    {
        cameraRoll.browseForImage();
    }
}
```

5. We will make the `browseBtn` movie clip visible again if the user cancels from the Photos application:

```
private function cancelled(e:Event):void {
  browseBtn.visible = true;
}
```

6. If the user makes a selection, then we will create a `Loader` object and start loading the photo. Add the `photoSelected()` method to handle this:

```
private function photoSelected(e:MediaEvent):void {
  var photoPromise:MediaPromise = e.data;

  loader = new Loader();
  loader.contentLoaderInfo.addEventListener(Event.COMPLETE,
    photoLoaded);
  loader.loadFilePromise(photoPromise);
}
```

7. Finally, write the `photoLoaded()` event handler, which will be called when the photo's image has successfully loaded. This method will re-size and orientate the image before adding it to the display list:

```
private function photoLoaded(e:Event):void {
  var mc:Loader = e.currentTarget.loader as Loader;
  var scale:Number;
  if(mc.width > mc.height)
  {
    scale = stage.stageHeight / mc.width;
    mc.scaleX = scale;
    mc.scaleY = scale;
    mc.x = stage.stageWidth;
    mc.rotation = 90;
    addChild(mc);
  }
  else
  {
    scale = stage.stageWidth / mc.width;
    mc.scaleX = scale;
    mc.scaleY = scale;
    addChild(mc);
  }
}
```

8. Save the class and name the file `Main.as` when prompted.

9. Also, move back to your FLA and save it too.

10. Publish the FLA and deploy the resultant `.ipa` file to your device.

11. Launch the app, tap the **BROWSE** button, and then select an image from the camera roll. Your app will load and display the image.

How it works...

The `flash.media.CameraRoll` class allows access to the device's photo library.

Its `browseForImage()` method opens the native Photos application, allowing the user to select an image from the device's camera roll. At this point, your application will lose focus and will wait in the background.

When a selection is made by the user, your application will regain focus and the `CameraRoll` object will dispatch `MediaEvent.SELECT`. If however, the user cancels out of the Photos app, then `Event.CANCEL` is dispatched instead.

In this recipe, the `browseForImage()` method is called in response to the user pressing the **BROWSE** button. However, just before the call is made, the static `CameraRoll.supportsBrowseForImage` property is checked. This determines whether or not browsing for an image is supported by your target platform. Although the property returns `true` for all iOS devices, it is useful when targeting multiple platforms.

Once the user has selected an image, the `photoSelected()` event handler is called and a `MediaEvent` object is passed to it. From the `MediaEvent` object, we retrieve information regarding the selected image by querying its `data` property. This returns a `MediaPromise` object, which we pass to a `Loader` object's `loadFilePromise()` method to actually load the image. Once complete, the `Loader` object will dispatch `Event.COMPLETE`.

The `photoLoaded()` handler captures the `Loader` object's `COMPLETE` event and displays the actual image on screen. Images saved to the camera roll can be of a much higher resolution than the stage's dimensions and can be either portrait or landscape orientation. The `photoLoaded()` method scales the image to fit the stage and if it has a landscape aspect ratio, rotates it by 90 degrees.

 The `MediaPromise` class also provides a `file` property, which can be used to obtain a URL to the selected camera roll image. While this property will be valid for certain platforms, such as Android, it will always return `null` on iOS. When writing cross-platform code, use `Loader.loadFilePromise()` rather than attempting to obtain and pass a URL to `Loader.load()`.

You can obtain more information regarding `flash.media.CameraRoll` and `flash.media.MediaPromise` from Adobe Community Help.

There's more...

When saving photos to a device, iOS embeds additional metadata with the image. Depending on the application you are writing, the following information may be useful.

Parsing Exif data

Photos taken on iOS devices adhere to the **Exchangeable image file** (**Exif**) format and can contain thumbnail data and tags of additional information. These tags can describe anything ranging from the GPS coordinates associated with the image to its orientation.

Although the AIR SDK does not directly provide support for these tags, there are some third-party parsers available. Take a look at `http://code.shichiseki.jp/as3/ExifInfo` and `www.mxml.it/index.php/2010/01/04/reading-exif-data-with-actionscript-30`. Additionally, the Exif specification can be found at `www.exif.org/exif2-2.pdf`.

See also

▶ *Saving to the camera roll*

Capturing with the default camera app

Most iOS devices have a built-in camera. More recent models have two—one mounted on the rear and another on the front. Users can capture photos and shoot video using the camera app that comes pre-installed. Third-party applications can also utilize the camera with many applications simply launching the default camera app for this purpose. Once the user has finished with the camera, the third-party app is able to access the photo or video that was taken.

AIR 2.6 and above provides the `CameraUI` class, making it possible to launch and use the default camera app. This recipe will show you how to do this from Flash Professional CS5.5. AIR 2.0 and Flash CS5 do not provide camera support.

Getting ready

You will need a device that features a camera. The fourth-generation iPod touch, iPad 2, and all models of iPhone have cameras.

From the book's accompanying code bundle, open `chapter10\recipe3\recipe.fla` into Flash Professional CS5.5.

You will find a movie clip named `captureBtn` and a dynamic text field named `output` positioned on the stage. The button clip's library symbol is linked to a class named `Button`, which was introduced in the *Handling user interaction* recipe from *Chapter 4*.

We will create a simple app that launches the default camera app when the button is pressed, allowing the user to capture a photo.

How to do it...

Let us write the ActionScript required to do this.

1. Create a document class and name it `Main`.

2. Import the various classes required for this recipe and create a member variable of type `CameraUI`:

```
package {

    import flash.display.MovieClip;
    import flash.events.Event;
    import flash.events.MediaEvent;
    import flash.events.MouseEvent;
    import flash.media.CameraUI;
    import flash.media.MediaPromise;
    import flash.media.MediaType;

    public class Main extends MovieClip {

      private var camera:CameraUI;

      public function Main() {
        // constructor code
      }
    }
}
```

3. Within the constructor, instantiate a `CameraUI` object and listen for it dispatching `MediaEvent.COMPLETE` and `Event.CANCEL`. Also, listen for the user pressing the `captureBtn` movie clip:

```
public function Main() {
  camera = new CameraUI();
  camera.addEventListener(MediaEvent.COMPLETE, captured);
  camera.addEventListener(Event.CANCEL, cancelled);

  captureBtn.addEventListener(MouseEvent.MOUSE_UP, pressed);
}
```

4. When the button is pressed, we will launch the camera app allowing the user to take a photo. Add a `pressed()` event handler for this:

```
private function pressed(e:MouseEvent):void {
  if (CameraUI.isSupported)
  {
    camera.launch(MediaType.IMAGE);
  }
}
```

5. When the user returns from the camera app, we will check that the photo was successfully obtained and write confirmation to the `output` text field. Handle this by adding a `captured()` method to your class:

```
private function captured(e:MediaEvent):void {
  var mediaPromise:MediaPromise = e.data;
  if (mediaPromise != null)
  {
    output.text = "Photo captured.";
  }
}
```

6. The user can cancel from the default camera app, discarding any photo that they may have taken. Add an event handler for this, stating within the `output` text field that the operation was cancelled:

```
private function cancelled(e:Event):void {
  output.text = "Cancelled.";
}
```

7. Save the class and name the file `Main.as` when prompted.

8. Move back to your FLA and save it too.

9. Publish the app and launch it once you have deployed the IPA to your device.

10. Tap the **CAPTURE** button to launch the default camera app. Take a photo and press the **Use** button. A message will be displayed confirming that the photo was successfully captured and is now accessible by your app.

How it works...

The `flash.media.CameraUI` class allows access to the default camera app. Calling its `launch()` method will open the camera app and allow the user to capture either an image or video. At this point, your application will lose focus and will wait in the background. Once the user has finished, your application will regain focus and the `CameraUI` object will dispatch `MediaEvent.COMPLETE`. If the user cancels out of the camera app, then `Event.CANCEL` will be dispatched instead.

When calling `launch()`, you must pass a constant defined by `flash.media.MediaType`, specifying whether you wish to take a photo or shoot video. For this recipe, we passed `MediaType.IMAGE`.

The captured media is accessed using the `data` property of the `COMPLETE` event's `MediaEvent` object. This property is an instance of the `MediaPromise` class and can be used to load the image or even access its data.

Notice the use of the static `isSupported` property within the `pressed()` event handler. It determines whether or not access to the default camera app is supported by the device that is currently running your app.

You can obtain more information regarding `flash.media.CameraUI` and `flash.media.MediaPromise` from Adobe Community Help.

There's more...

The following information will help complete your understanding.

Handling errors

A `CameraUI` object will dispatch an error if the default camera app is already in use. You can capture this event by listening for `flash.events.ErrorEvent.ERROR`. Query the `ErrorEvent` object's `errorID` and `text` properties to discover more about the error.

Displaying the captured image

We didn't go so far as to actually load and display the photo that was taken with the default camera app. This can be achieved by creating a `Loader` object and passing the photo's `MediaPromise` object to the loader's `loadFilePromise()` method. Refer to the previous recipe, *Reading from the camera roll*, for more detail.

Saving the captured image to the camera roll

Unlike some other mobile operating systems, the captured photo isn't actually stored by iOS in the camera roll. If you want the photo to appear in the camera roll, you will need to manually add it yourself. This is done by using a `Loader` object to load your `MediaPromise` object's binary data, then writing its bitmap data to the camera roll using a `CameraRoll` instance.

Refer to the *Reading from the camera roll* and the *Saving to the camera roll* recipes from earlier in this chapter.

Capturing video

While we captured a photo using the default camera app, a simple code change is all that is required to shoot video instead. You can see this in the following code snippet where `MediaType.VIDEO` is passed to the `CameraUI` object's `launch()` method:

```
camera.launch(MediaType.VIDEO);
```

It is not possible for the user to change between photo and camera mode while using the default camera app launched from AIR. You can only use the camera app for capturing a single media type at any one time.

Take a look at the *Playing local H.264 video* recipe from *Chapter 12* to see how to playback your captured video.

Reading the captured data

It is also possible to directly access the binary data that represents the image or video captured from the camera. This is useful for applications that perhaps need to write the media directly to the device's file system, upload the data to a server, or to simply parse or alter the data in some way. The `MediaPromise` object provides an `open()` method that can be used to access the data. You can then read it into a `ByteArray` object.

To do this within this recipe's example, add the following member variables:

```
private var dataSource:IDataInput;
private var eventSource:IEventDispatcher;
```

Add the following code snippet at the end of the `captured()` event handler:

```
dataSource = mediaPromise.open();
eventSource = dataSource as IEventDispatcher;
eventSource.addEventListener(Event.COMPLETE, dataCaptured);
```

Now write an event handler to copy the data into a `ByteArray` object:

```
private function dataCaptured(e:Event):void {
  var mediaBytes:ByteArray = new ByteArray();
  dataSource.readBytes(mediaBytes);
}
```

Also include the following import statements:

```
import flash.events.IEventDispatcher;
import flash.utils.ByteArray;
import flash.utils.IDataInput;
```

You will now have access to the media's binary data within the `dataCaptured()` method.

See also

- ▸ *Saving to the camera roll*
- ▸ *Reading from the camera roll*
- ▸ *Working with the built-in cameras*

Working with the built-in cameras

While launching and using the default camera app provides the user with the native camera experience that they are familiar with, it may not be appropriate for all types of applications. In addition to `CameraUI`, AIR also provides the `Camera` class, which receives the video data captured by the device's on-board camera, allowing it to be directly displayed within your app.

In this recipe, you will learn how to receive a video stream from the camera and display it within your app using Flash Professional CS5.5. The `Camera` class is not supported by Flash CS5 and AIR 2.0 for iOS.

Getting ready

You will need a device that features a camera. The fourth generation iPod touch, iPad 2, and all models of iPhone have cameras.

From the book's accompanying code bundle, open `chapter10\recipe4\recipe.fla` into Flash Professional CS5.5.

A landscape aspect ratio has been set for the stage and this has also been reflected within the FLA's AIR for iOS settings.

How to do it...

Follow these steps to receive video from the camera and display it on the stage:

1. Create a document class and name it `Main`.
2. Declare two member variables—one of type `Camera` and the other of type `Video`:

```
package {

    import flash.display.MovieClip;
    import flash.media.Camera;
    import flash.media.Video;

    public class Main extends MovieClip {

        private var camera:Camera;
```

```
    private var video:Video;

    public function Main() {
      // constructor code
    }
  }
}
```

3. Within the constructor, obtain a reference to the device's default camera and attach it to a `Video` object. Also, add the `Video` object to the stage allowing the video data to be viewed by the user:

```
public function Main() {
  if(Camera.names.length > 0)
  {
    camera = Camera.getCamera();
    camera.setMode(stage.stageWidth, stage.stageHeight,
      stage.frameRate);

    video = new Video(camera.width, camera.height);
    video.attachCamera(camera);

    addChild(video);
  }
}
```

4. Save the class as `Main.as`. Also move back to your FLA and save it too.

5. Publish the FLA and test it on your device.

6. Hold the device in landscape orientation. Video from the rear-facing camera will be rendered to the screen.

How it works...

The `flash.media.Camera` class is a singleton, meaning only one instance of it can exist. To guarantee this, the class has no public constructor. Instead, access to the camera is obtained by calling the `Camera` class' `getCamera()` static method, which returns the `Camera` instance for you to work with.

Once the `Camera` instance is obtained, the capture mode to be used by the camera can be specified. This is done by calling `setMode()` and passing to it a width, height, and target frame rate. For this recipe, we passed the stage's dimensions and frame rate. If the specified requirements cannot be met by the camera, then it will use a mode which is the closest match.

In order to display the live video being streamed from the camera, it must be attached to a `Video` object. The `flash.media.Video` class inherits `DisplayObject` allowing any `Video` object to be added to the display list. First the `Video` object is created and a width and height for it are passed to its constructor—we set its dimensions to match those used by the camera. Then a call to `attachCamera()` is made, providing the `Video` object with access to the `Camera` object's video stream. Finally, the `Video` object is added to the display list by calling `addChild()`.

Before attempting to connect to a camera, you should first check that one is available. The `Camera.names` static property returns an array of available cameras. We checked at the beginning of the document class' constructor that the array's length was greater than 0 before proceeding. Alternatively, check for `null` being returned by `Camera.getCamera()`.

For more information regarding camera support, perform a search for `flash.media.Camera` and `flash.media.Video` within Adobe Community Help.

There's more...

Let us look at some additional options when capturing live video from the camera.

Portrait mode

On iOS, a `Camera` object captures video in landscape orientation. If your application uses a portrait aspect ratio, then you will need to swap the camera's capture dimensions and also rotate and re-position the `Video` object. To do this, make the following changes to this recipe's constructor:

```
camera = Camera.getCamera();
camera.setMode(stage.stageHeight, stage.stageWidth,
    stage.frameRate);

video = new Video(camera.width, camera.height);
video.attachCamera(camera);
video.rotation = 90;
video.x += stage.stageWidth;
```

Remember to change the stage's dimensions and update the AIR for iOS settings to use a portrait aspect ratio. There is a performance hit when capturing portrait video due to the rotation applied to the `Video` object. Where possible, try to use landscape for applications that use the camera.

Selecting a camera

The `Camera.getCamera()` static method connects to the rear-facing camera by default. For devices that support more than one, you can specify a camera by passing a string representing the zero-based index position within the array specified by `Camera.names`. For example, the following code uses the iPhone 4/4S's front-facing camera:

```
camera = Camera.getCamera("1");
```

It is important that you pass a string rather than an integer when making this call.

Only one camera can be active at any one time on iOS. If you connect to a second camera, then the previous camera's connection will be dropped.

Grabbing a bitmap image

It is possible to capture a bitmap image from the camera's live video stream. The following code extracts the bitmap data from the video's current frame and stores it within a `Bitmap` object:

```
var bd:BitmapData = new BitmapData(video.width, video.height,
    false);
bd.draw(video);
var b:Bitmap = new Bitmap(bd);
```

As you can see, the `BitmapData` object's dimensions are made to match those of the video. The current frame is then drawn into the `BitmapData` object, which is used to create the actual bitmap.

Live streaming

For this recipe, we simply used the camera's video stream locally on the device. However, by using the `NetConnection` and `NetStream` classes, it is possible to transmit the video stream to a Flash Media Server, where it can be broadcast to other clients. This is ideal for live video chat applications or other collaborative projects.

Both classes belong to the `flash.net` package. More detail is available from Adobe Community Help.

Using the stage

It is also possible to place and size a `Video` object on the stage using the Flash IDE rather than ActionScript. Simply right-click on the **Library** panel and select **New Video** from the context menu. From the **Video Properties** panel that appears, click on the **Video (ActionScript-controlled)** radio button before clicking on **OK**. A video clip will appear in the library, which you can drag to the stage and assign an instance name to.

See also

▸ *Saving to the camera roll*

▸ *Capturing with the default camera app*

Recording microphone audio

AIR provides an API that enables an application to connect to the built-in microphone. The microphone's raw data can be obtained, recorded for later use, processed as it is received, or routed to the device's speakers.

This recipe will show you how to use the `Microphone` and `ByteArray` classes to capture and record audio. You will need Flash Professional CS5.5 as microphone access for iOS is not supported by CS5 and AIR 2.0.

Getting ready

While all recent models from the iOS family contain a built-in microphone, previous generations of the iPod touch don't. The second and third-generation devices do, however, provide support for an external microphone, which can be used for this recipe.

From the book's accompanying code bundle, open `chapter10\recipe5\recipe.fla` into Flash Professional CS5.5.

Sitting on the stage you will find a dynamic text field with an instance name of `output` and three movie clips. Two of the movie clips represent buttons and are named `recordBtn` and `stopBtn` respectively. The `stopBtn` clip is positioned directly behind the `recordBtn` clip but sits on its own timeline layer for easy access. The third movie clip is named `micStatus` and covers the entire background. It is used to indicate when recording is taking place.

The library symbols for `recordBtn` and `stopBtn` are linked to a base class named `Button`. This class was introduced in the *Handling user interaction* recipe from *Chapter 4*.

We will add ActionScript to start recording data from the microphone when the user taps the `recordBtn` movie clip. Audio capture will end when `stopBtn` is pressed. To give feedback to the user that recording is taking place, we will move the `micStatus` movie clip's `playhead` to frame 2. The text field will be used to output confirmation that audio was successfully recorded.

This recipe will concentrate on the recording of microphone audio. We will cover playback of the audio in the next recipe.

How to do it...

Now let us write the ActionScript for this. Follow these steps:

1. Create a document class and name it `Main`.

2. Import the various classes required for this recipe and create two member variables—one to reference the device's microphone and another to store data captured from it:

```
package {

    import flash.display.MovieClip;
    import flash.events.MouseEvent;
    import flash.events.SampleDataEvent;
    import flash.media.Microphone;
    import flash.utils.ByteArray;

    public class Main extends MovieClip {

        private var mic:Microphone;
        private var soundData:ByteArray;

        public function Main() {
            // constructor code
        }
    }
}
```

3. Within the constructor, set up the movie clips and create a connection to the device's microphone:

```
public function Main() {
    micStatus.gotoAndStop(1);
    recordBtn.visible = true;
    stopBtn.visible = false;
    recordBtn.addEventListener(MouseEvent.MOUSE_UP,
        pressedRecordBtn);
    stopBtn.addEventListener(MouseEvent.MOUSE_UP,
        pressedStopBtn);

    mic = Microphone.getMicrophone();
    if(!Microphone.isSupported || mic == null)
    {
        recordBtn.visible = false;
    }
}
```

4. Add a handler for each button being pressed:

```
private function pressedRecordBtn(e:MouseEvent):void {
  startRecording();
}

private function pressedStopBtn(e:MouseEvent):void {
  stopRecording();
}
```

5. Next add a method that sets up the microphone and starts listening for live audio data. We will also instantiate a `ByteArray` object named `soundData`, which will be used to store the captured data:

```
private function startRecording():void {
  micStatus.gotoAndStop(2);
  recordBtn.visible = false;
  stopBtn.visible = true;

  soundData = new ByteArray();
  mic.gain = 100;
  mic.rate = 44;
  mic.addEventListener(SampleDataEvent.SAMPLE_DATA,
    sampleData);
}
```

6. Add an event handler that gets called every time audio data is available from the microphone. We will write a maximum of 2 MB of this audio data to our `ByteArray` object for later use:

```
private function sampleData(e:SampleDataEvent):void {
  while(e.data.bytesAvailable)
  {
    var sample:Number = e.data.readFloat();
    soundData.writeFloat(sample);
  }

  if(soundData.length > 2097152)
  {
    stopRecording();
  }
}
```

7. Finally add a method that stops listening for live audio data from the microphone. The total number of bytes recorded will be written to the `output` text field:

```
private function stopRecording():void {
  micStatus.gotoAndStop(1);
  stopBtn.visible = false;
  mic.removeEventListener(SampleDataEvent.SAMPLE_DATA,
    sampleData);
  output.text = (soundData.length + " bytes recorded");
}
```

8. Save the class and name its file `Main.as`.

9. Move back to your FLA and save it.

10. Publish the FLA and deploy the resultant `.ipa` file to your device.

11. Launch the app, tap the **RECORD** button and start speaking into the microphone. When you are finished, tap the **STOP** button.

The amount of audio data (in bytes) that was recorded will be written to the screen.

How it works...

Microphone support is provided by the `flash.media.Microphone` class. To connect to the device's microphone, make a call to the static `Microphone.getMicrophone()` method, which will return a new `Microphone` instance. If a microphone can't be found, then `null` will be returned instead.

The following code snippet is the call being made from within our document class' constructor:

```
mic = Microphone.getMicrophone();
```

Once you have a `Microphone` object, you can adjust the audio data that will be received. We did this within the `startRecording()` method by setting the `Microphone` object's gain and sample rate.

The gain is used to boost the microphone's signal and is set using the `gain` property. A value of `100` was used to maximize its loudness.

The sample rate dictates the quality of the audio that is captured and is specified by the `rate` property. Higher sample rates produce clearer audio but demand more from the CPU and require increased space to store. We set the `rate` property to `44`, specifying an actual sample frequency of 44 kHz. In other words, we will capture sound from the microphone 44,100 times per second! This is the highest permitted sample rate and records the clearest sound.

To actually start capturing audio from the microphone, add a `SampleDataEvent.SAMPLE_DATA` listener to the `Microphone` object. The `SAMPLE_DATA` event is continually dispatched as the microphone's audio buffer fills. We added the `SAMPLE_DATA` event listener within the `startRecording()` method immediately after setting the gain and sample rate:

```
mic.gain = 100;
mic.rate = 44;
mic.addEventListener(SampleDataEvent.SAMPLE_DATA, sampleData);
```

Each `SampleDataEvent` object has a `data` property, which is a `ByteArray` containing the current audio sampled from the microphone. Recording the audio is a simple case of copying this temporary data into a more permanent `ByteArray` object. You can see the code for this within the `SampleData()` event handler, where a loop is used to extract the sampled data and write it to the `soundData` member variable:

```
while(e.data.bytesAvailable)
{
  var sample:Number = e.data.readFloat();
  soundData.writeFloat(sample);
}
```

Each sample is represented by a floating point value. The loop, therefore, reads a float from the audio buffer and writes it to the `soundData` member variable. This process continues until the data stored within the `SampleDataEvent` object is empty.

To prevent the app from completely exhausting the device's memory, the `sampleData()` handler checks the size of the `soundData` member variable. If it exceeds 2 MB (2,097,152 bytes) in size, then recording is stopped and the number of recorded bytes is written to the `output` text field.

Audio capture is stopped by removing the `SAMPLE_DATA` event listener from the `Microphone` object. Take a look at the `stopRecording()` method to see this.

For more information regarding audio capture, perform a search for `flash.media.Microphone`, `flash.events.SampleDataEvent`, and `flash.utils.ByteArray` within Adobe Community Help.

There's more...

Following are some additional options open to you when recording from the microphone.

Microphone activity

You can determine the amount of sound that the microphone is detecting by querying the `Microphone` object's `activityLevel` property. This will return a value ranging from 0 to 100, with 0 being returned when no sound is detected.

It is also possible using the `setSilenceLevel()` method to specify an activity level threshold that must be met before audio is accepted by the microphone. The higher the activity level that is passed as a parameter, the louder an audio source must be before it is detected. This method also accepts an optional second parameter, which specifies the number of milliseconds of inactivity that must pass before sound is considered to have stopped.

As an example, add the following to your `startRecording()` method:

```
mic.setSilenceLevel(50, 2000);
mic.addEventListener(ActivityEvent.ACTIVITY, activityChanged);
```

Now add the following event handler:

```
private function activityChanged(e:ActivityEvent):void {
  output.text = "activating: " + e.activating + ", " +
    "activity level: " + mic.activityLevel;
  if(e.activating == false)
  {
    stopRecording();
  }
}
```

Finally, add the following import statement:

```
import flash.events.ActivityEvent;
```

Test these changes on your device. Your app won't dispatch SAMPLE_DATA events until the microphone's silence level is exceeded. Also, once activated, the microphone will deactivate again if silence occurs for more than two seconds.

Live streaming

The microphone's audio data was simply used locally in this recipe. However, it is possible, using the `NetConnection` and `NetStream` classes, to transmit the data to a Flash Media Server for broadcast to other clients. Additional detail can be found on Adobe Community Help by searching for both classes, which belong to the `flash.net` package.

See also

▸ *Playing recorded audio*

Playing recorded audio

After capturing the microphone's raw audio data, you will need a means of playing it back. This recipe will show you how to send the data to your device's speaker.

Getting ready

If you have completed the *Recording microphone audio* recipe, then you can work from the code you wrote for it. Alternatively, from the book's accompanying code bundle, open `chapter10\recipe6\recipe.fla` and use it as a starting point.

Currently the FLA will record audio from the microphone and store it within a member variable of type `ByteArray` named `soundData`. We will add code that plays back the audio once the user has finished recording it.

How to do it...

The following changes are required to read and playback the recorded audio:

1. Open `Main.as`.

2. Import the following three classes:

```
import flash.display.MovieClip;
import flash.events.Event;
import flash.events.MouseEvent;
import flash.events.SampleDataEvent;
import flash.media.Microphone;
import flash.media.Sound;
import flash.media.SoundChannel;
import flash.utils.ByteArray;
```

3. Also add a `Sound` and `SoundChannel` member variable:

```
private var mic:Microphone;
private var soundData:ByteArray;
private var sound:Sound;
private var channel:SoundChannel;
```

4. The `stopRecording()` method will need to make an additional call to initiate playback of the recorded audio. Add the following line at the end of the method:

```
private function stopRecording():void {
  micStatus.gotoAndStop(1);
  stopBtn.visible = false;
  mic.removeEventListener(SampleDataEvent.SAMPLE_DATA,
    sampleData);
  playRecording();
}
```

5. Now write the `playRecording()` method, which will initiate playback of the audio:

```
private function playRecording():void {
  soundData.position = 0;

  sound = new Sound();
  sound.addEventListener(SampleDataEvent.SAMPLE_DATA,
    playSampleData);

  channel = sound.play();
  channel.addEventListener(Event.SOUND_COMPLETE,
    playbackComplete);
}
```

6. Add a method that periodically pulls data from the `soundData` object for playback:

```
private function playSampleData(e:SampleDataEvent):void {
  for(var i:int=0; i<8192 && soundData.bytesAvailable>0; i++)
  {
    var sample:Number = soundData.readFloat();
    e.data.writeFloat(sample);
    e.data.writeFloat(sample);
  }
}
```

7. Finally, reset the button movie clips once audio playback is complete:

```
private function playbackComplete(e:Event):void {
  recordBtn.visible = true;
  stopBtn.visible = false;
}
```

8. Save your changes to the class.

9. Publish the FLA and test it on your device.

10. Start recording some audio and when you are finished, tap the **STOP** button.

The recorded audio will be played back through your device's speaker. If you don't hear anything then increase your speaker's volume and try again.

How it works...

Both the `Sound` and `SoundChannel` classes are used for audio playback.

We create a `Sound` object and add a `SAMPLE_DATA` event listener to it. This event is dispatched when there is no more audio data for the `Sound` object to play:

```
sound = new Sound();
sound.addEventListener(SampleDataEvent.SAMPLE_DATA,
  playSampleData);
```

A call is also made to the object's `play()` method, which returns a `SoundChannel` instance allowing playback to be monitored. We listen for the `SoundChannel` object dispatching `SOUND_COMPLETE` to determine when audio playback has ended:

```
channel = sound.play();
channel.addEventListener(Event.SOUND_COMPLETE,
    playbackComplete);
```

Initially the `Sound` object doesn't contain any audio data. The data from the entire recording is instead held by the `soundData` member variable, which is a `ByteArray`. As the `Sound` object has no audio data to play, it immediately dispatches a `SAMPLE_DATA` event, which is captured by the `playSampleData()` handler.

Within `playSampleData()`, we extract some audio data from the `soundData` member variable and feed it to the `Sound` object. This provides the `Sound` object with enough data to start playing audio. Each time its buffer runs low, it will dispatch another `SAMPLE_DATA` event and we will feed it more data. This process continues until the entire recording has been played.

The following is the code from the `playSampleData()` handler that is responsible for writing data to the `Sound` object's buffer:

```
for(var i:int=0; i<8192 && soundData.bytesAvailable>0; i++)
{
    var sample:Number = soundData.readFloat();
    e.data.writeFloat(sample);
    e.data.writeFloat(sample);
}
```

The `Sound` object's buffer is accessed through the `SampleDataEvent` parameter's `data` property. We, therefore, take a sample from the `soundData` member variable and write it to the `data` property's `ByteArray`. The `readFloat()` method is used to read a sample from `soundData`, while `writeFloat()` is used to write the same sample into the `Sound` object's buffer—each sample is represented by a floating point value.

However, we don't just write a single sample to the buffer—it would instantly empty again. Instead, we take the opportunity to write 8192 stereo samples, providing the object with 64 KB of audio data. Typically you can write between 2048 and 8192 stereo samples at a time. However, a runtime exception will be thrown if you attempt to write more than 64 KB of data to the buffer.

To create a stereo sample, we write each recorded sample to the `Sound` object twice:

```
e.data.writeFloat(sample);
e.data.writeFloat(sample);
```

While the microphone records monophonic data, your device is capable of stereo output. Therefore, when writing audio data to a `Sound` object, you need to write the sample to both the left and right channels. The first call to `writeFloat()` sends the sample to the left channel, while the second call sends it to the right.

For more information, perform a search for `flash.media.Sound` and `flash.media.SoundChannel` within Adobe Community Help.

There's more...

There are a few final pieces of information related to microphone audio playback.

Working with lower sample rates

The `Sound` class uses a sample rate of 44 kHz. If audio from the microphone was captured at an alternative frequency, then you will need to upscale it from the lower rate to 44 kHz before feeding it to the `Sound` object.

For example, if the `Microphone` object's `rate` property was set to a frequency of 22 kHz when recording, you would need to adjust the playback loop within `playSampleData()` to the following:

```
for(var i:int=0; i<4096 && soundData.bytesAvailable>0; i++)
{
   var sample:Number = soundData.readFloat();
   e.data.writeFloat(sample);
   e.data.writeFloat(sample);
   e.data.writeFloat(sample);
   e.data.writeFloat(sample);
}
```

Essentially the same sample is written to each channel twice, which up-scales the 22 kHz recording to 44 kHz. Notice that 4096 iterations of the loop are performed compared to 8192 previously. This is to ensure that no more than 64 KB of audio data is written to the `Sound` object's buffer, which is its upper limit.

The example provided here is somewhat simplistic and not recommended for the majority of the sample rates. A more thorough approach is to generate the missing data by interpolating between existing samples. In most cases, it is likely that you will want to avoid re-sampling your audio in realtime as doing so can be computationally expensive.

Additional detail regarding sample rate conversion can be found on Wikipedia: `http://en.wikipedia.org/wiki/Sample_rate_conversion`. Also, take a look at the SoundTouch AS3 library, which allows real time audio processing using ActionScript 3.0: `https://github.com/also/soundtouch-as3`.

Saving captured data

This and the previous recipe have simply held the recorded audio data in memory. Your application, however, may require recordings to be persistent. Using the classes provided in the `flash.filesystem` package, you can write binary data to your device and read it back later.

The following code snippet saves our recorded audio to the device:

```
var stream:FileStream = new FileStream();
var file:File =
  File.documentsDirectory.resolvePath("audio.dat");
stream.open(file, FileMode.WRITE);
stream.writeBytes(soundData);
stream.close();
```

Retrieving the data is just as easy:

```
soundData = new ByteArray();
var stream:FileStream = new FileStream();
var file:File =
  File.documentsDirectory.resolvePath("audio.dat");
stream.open(file, FileMode.READ);
stream.readBytes(soundData);
```

Data written to the file system can only be accessed by the app that placed it there. When the app is uninstalled, any data belonging to it is deleted.

Exporting as WAV or MP3

For this and the previous recipe, we have simply worked with the raw PCM data captured from the microphone. However, you may want to save your data in common audio formats such as MP3 and WAV. Unfortunately, AIR does not provide APIs for exporting in either of these formats. Instead, you will need to rely on third-party libraries.

WAV encoding is provided by the `WAVWriter` class, which is available at: `http://code.google.com/p/ghostcat/source/browse/trunk/ghostcatfp10/src/ghostcat/media/WAVWriter.as?spec=svn424&r=424`.

MP3 encoding can be achieved using the Shine library: `https://github.com/kikko/Shine-MP3-Encoder-on-AS3-Alchemy`.

See also

▸ *Recording microphone audio*

▸ *Controlling audio playback, Chapter 12*

▸ *Referencing an app's common directories, Chapter 13*

▸ *Writing files, Chapter 13*

11
Rendering Web Pages

In this chapter, we will cover:

- ▸ Opening a web page within Safari
- ▸ Rendering a web page within an app
- ▸ Navigating the browsing history
- ▸ Rendering a local web page
- ▸ Dynamically generating a local web page
- ▸ Capturing a snapshot of a web page

Introduction

The web has become such an integral part of our lives that even iOS apps regularly use web browser technology to perform certain tasks. This chapter will explore the HTML capabilities of AIR for iOS; from simply launching a web page within Safari, to more integrated experiences where web content is rendered directly within the app itself.

We will primarily focus on the `StageWebView` class introduced in AIR 2.6. However, those using Flash Professional CS5 and AIR 2.0 will find the *Opening a web page within Safari* recipe of use.

Opening a web page within Safari

AIR for iOS makes it possible to display web pages to the user. For many situations, the simplest solution is to launch Safari (the device's native web browser) from your app. Many applications take this approach and once the user is finished with the page, they can move back to their app using the app switcher.

Let us see how to load a web page into Safari from an AIR for iOS app.

Getting ready

From the book's accompanying code bundle, open `chapter11\recipe1\recipe.fla` into Flash Professional and use it as a starting point.

Sitting on the stage is a movie clip with an instance name of `twitterBtn`. The movie clip's library symbol is linked to a class named `Button`, which was introduced in the *Handling user interaction* recipe from *Chapter 4*.

Let us write some ActionScript to load `www.twitter.com` into Safari when the button is pressed.

How to do it...

We will utilize the package-level `navigateToURL()` function to launch Safari. Carry out the following steps:

1. Create a new document class and name it `Main`.

2. Add the following three import statements to the class:
   ```
   import flash.events.MouseEvent;
   import flash.net.navigateToURL;
   import flash.net.URLRequest;
   ```

3. Within the constructor, listen for the `twitterBtn` movie clip being pressed:
   ```
   public function Main() {
       twitterBtn.addEventListener(MouseEvent.MOUSE_UP,
         pressed);
   }
   ```

4. Now add an event listener, which launches Safari and loads Twitter's website into it:
   ```
   private function pressed(e:MouseEvent):void {
       var url:URLRequest = new URLRequest(
         "http://www.twitter.com");
       navigateToURL(url);
   }
   ```

5. Save the class and name the file `Main.as` when prompted.

6. Move back to the FLA and save it too.

7. Publish the FLA and test it on your device. Tapping the **twitter** button will launch and load `www.twitter.com` into Safari. If you are using iOS 4 or above, then use the app switcher to find and move back to your app.

How it works...

The `flash.net` package contains a package-level function named `navigateToURL()` that can be used to open a website directly within the Safari browser.

It accepts as an argument, a `URLRequest` representing the URL to be loaded:

```
var url:URLRequest = new URLRequest("http://www.twitter.com");
```

Once the request has been created, Safari can be launched and the requested URL loaded:

```
navigateToURL(url);
```

The `http` URI scheme within the requested URL is important. The `navigateToURL()` function can be used to launch many external iOS applications, with Safari being just one of them. By prefixing the URL with `http://`, AIR knows to launch Safari.

In addition, being a package-level function, `navigateToURL()` must be explicitly added to your class' list of import statements:

```
import flash.net.navigateToURL;
```

Your application will be suspended and moved to the background when Safari is launched from a device running iOS 4 or above. When the user is finished with the web page, it will be their responsibility to resume your app by selecting it from the home screen or app switcher. Launching Safari from an iOS 3 device, however, will close your app rather than suspend it— multitasking was not introduced until iOS 4. If you plan to support iOS 3, then save your app's state before launching Safari.

For more information, perform a search for `flash.net.navigateToURL` and `flash.net.URLRequest` within Adobe Community Help.

See also

- ▶ *Rendering a web page within an app*
- ▶ *Handling multitasking, Chapter 3*
- ▶ *Exiting gracefully from an app, Chapter 3*
- ▶ *Saving application state, Chapter 4*
- ▶ *Launching system applications, Chapter 13*

Rendering a web page within an app

Since AIR 2.6, it has been possible to load and display HTML content directly within an AIR for iOS app. This is convenient as it prevents the user from having to leave the app to view web pages. It also provides other benefits such as tighter OAuth (Open Authorization) integration, and the ability to include HTML banner ads.

This recipe will show you how to load a remote web page directly into your app.

Getting ready

The steps covered here are only applicable to those using Flash Professional CS5.5 and AIR 2.6 or above. The AIR 2.0 SDK does not provide an API for loading HTML within an app.

From the book's accompanying code bundle, open `chapter11\recipe2\recipe.fla` into Flash Professional CS5.5. The FLA's stage is empty but its AIR for iOS settings have already been applied, saving you the effort when it comes to publishing it.

How to do it...

We will be taking advantage of the `StageWebView` class to render a web page.

1. Create a document class and name it `Main`.

2. Add the following two import statements:

   ```
   import flash.geom.Rectangle;
   import flash.media.StageWebView;
   ```

3. Declare a `StageWebView` member variable:

   ```
   private var webView:StageWebView;
   ```

4. Within the constructor, use a `StageWebView` instance to load a web page:

   ```
   public function Main() {
     webView = new StageWebView();
     webView.stage = stage;
     webView.viewPort = new Rectangle(
       0, 0, stage.stageWidth, stage.stageHeight);
     webView.loadURL("http://www.yeahbutisitflash.com");
   }
   ```

5. Save the class and name the file `Main.as` when prompted.

6. Now publish the FLA and deploy the `.ipa` file to your device.

7. When launched, the `www.yeahbutisitflash.com` website will be loaded and displayed within your app. You will also be able to interact with the page. Try it!

How it works...

The `StageWebView` class allows both local and remote HTML content to be displayed within your app using iOS's native WebKit rendering engine.

`StageWebView` is not actually a normal display object and, therefore, cannot be added to Flash's display list. Instead it is a window that is drawn on top of your application, with items underneath being hidden from view. Unfortunately, this means you can't place display objects on top of a region being used by a `StageWebView` object.

When creating a `StageWebView` object, you must attach it directly to the stage and specify a viewport for its HTML content to be rendered within. To achieve this, set its `stage` and `viewPort` properties respectively. A `Rectangle` object is used to define the size and location of the viewport.

Once the `StageWebView` object is instantiated and set up, you can load a web page by passing a URL to its `loadURL()` method. Use a String to define the URL and prefix it with the relevant URI scheme, which for most cases will be `http://`. Omitting the URI scheme will prevent the page from loading.

You can hide a `StageWebView` object from view by setting its `stage` property to `null`. When you are finished with a `StageWebView` object, call its `dispose()` method. Doing so will help the garbage collector reclaim the memory sooner.

For more information, perform a search for `flash.media.StageWebView` within Adobe Community Help.

There's more...

The following information provides additional detail.

Page load events

You can determine the success or failure of a page load request by listening for the following two events from a `StageWebView` object:

- ▶ `Event.COMPLETE`: The requested page and its contents have loaded
- ▶ `ErrorEvent.ERROR`: An error occurred while attempting to load the page

A load error can occur for a number of reasons, one of which is the omission of the URI scheme from the URL. Details regarding a load error can be obtained from the `ErrorEvent` object's `errorID` and `text` properties.

Multiple instances

Multiple `StageWebView` objects can be created and used simultaneously; however, you only have limited control over their depth ordering. While it is not possible to dynamically change depths, the one most recently instantiated will sit above other `StageWebView` instances. However, Adobe recommends that you avoid overlapping instances.

Checking for support

The static `StageWebView.isSupported` property can be used to determine whether the `StageWebView` class is supported. Although this property returns `true` for all iOS devices, you should query it when writing cross-platform code.

Retina web pages within a standard screen resolution

On a Retina display device, a `StageWebView` object will exploit the device's higher resolution even if the AIR for iOS app itself is set to use the standard non-Retina resolution.

Including banner ads

Many developers include HTML banner ads directly within their applications. This allows the developer to distribute an app free of charge to the user, and generate revenue from the advertisements shown within the app instead.

The `StageWebView` class makes it possible to display banner ads provided by services such as AdMob. Take a look at the AdMob website for more information: `www.admob.com`.

OAuth support

Third parties such as Twitter and Google permit developers access to their server-side APIs. However, many of these APIs provide access to protected data and require the use of usernames and passwords. Many of these third parties now use the OAuth protocol, which gives users access to data while protecting their account credentials.

For example, if you intend to create an app that allows a user to sign in to Twitter, then OAuth will be required. To make the process as secure as possible, the user will actually sign in from a web page hosted by Twitter, meaning you will need to use a `StageWebView` object as part of your client implementation.

A two-part video tutorial by Adobe Developer Evangelist, Piotr Walczyszyn is available from Adobe TV demonstrating how to use OAuth within Adobe AIR applications: `http://tv.adobe.com/watch/adc-presents/introduction-to-oauth-for-secure-user-and-application-authorization`. For a more specific mobile example of OAuth using `StageWebView`, take a look at this video by Adobe Platform Evangelist, Mark Doherty: `www.flashmobileblog.com/2010/07/17/air2-5-stagewebview-demo-oauth-support`.

An OAuth ActionScript 3.0 library is available at: `http://code.google.com/p/oauth-as3`.

- ▸ *Navigating the browsing history*
- ▸ *Dynamically generating a local web page*
- ▸ *Opening a web page within Safari*
- ▸ *Capturing a snapshot of a web page*

Navigating the browsing history

As a user browses, visited pages are stored in the browsing history stack. The `StageWebView` class makes it possible to move through the browsing history and also detect when location changes take place.

This recipe will take you through the necessary steps to create a simple app that allows a user to navigate their page history as they browse.

Getting ready

You will need Flash Professional CS5.5 for this recipe.

An FLA has been provided as a starting point. From the book's accompanying code bundle, open `chapter11\recipe3\recipe.fla` into Flash Professional CS5.5.

Sitting on the stage are two movie clips that represent navigation buttons. We will use these to move backwards and forwards through the user's history stack. The first has an instance name of `backBtn`, while the second is named `forwardBtn`.

Both movie clips are linked to a base class named `Button`. This class was introduced in the *Handling user interaction* recipe from *Chapter 4*.

How to do it...

Let us make use of various methods and events related to the `StageWebView` class by performing the following steps:

1. Create a document class and name it `Main`.

2. Add the following import statements:

```
import flash.events.MouseEvent;
import flash.events.LocationChangeEvent;
import flash.geom.Rectangle;
import flash.media.StageWebView;
```

3. Declare a `StageWebView` member variable:

```
private var webView:StageWebView;
```

4. Within the constructor, set up the button movie clips and the `StageWebView` object:

```
public function Main() {
  backBtn.addEventListener(MouseEvent.MOUSE_UP, prevPage);
  forwardBtn.addEventListener(MouseEvent.MOUSE_UP, nextPage);
  backBtn.visible = false;
  forwardBtn.visible = false;

  webView = new StageWebView();
  webView.stage = stage;
  webView.viewPort = new Rectangle(
    0, 62, stage.stageWidth, stage.stageHeight-62);
  webView.addEventListener(
    LocationChangeEvent.LOCATION_CHANGE,
    locationChanged);
  webView.loadURL("http://www.yeahbutisitflash.com");
}
```

The `StageWebView` object's viewport has been positioned below the buttons, and a listener has been added for any changes to its URL. The navigation buttons have been made invisible as the user's history stack will initially be empty.

5. Now add a `locationChanged()` method that handles a change to the `StageWebView` object's URL:

```
private function locationChanged(e:LocationChangeEvent):void {
  backBtn.visible = webView.isHistoryBackEnabled;
  forwardBtn.visible = webView.isHistoryForwardEnabled;
}
```

This method sets the visibility of each button depending on the user's position within the history stack. If they can't navigate further back, then `backBtn` will be hidden. If they can't move forward, then `forwardBtn` will be hidden.

6. Finally add methods that handle each of the buttons being pressed:

```
private function prevPage(e:MouseEvent):void {
  webView.historyBack();
  backBtn.visible = webView.isHistoryBackEnabled;
}

private function nextPage(e:MouseEvent):void {
  webView.historyForward();
  forwardBtn.visible = webView.isHistoryForwardEnabled;
}
```

These two methods move the user either back or forward a page within the browsing history depending on the button that was pressed. Similar to the `locationChanged()` method, each button's visibility is also managed by its respective handler.

7. Save the class and name it `Main.as`.

8. Now publish the FLA and deploy the app to your device.

9. Launch the app and select any of the hyperlinks within the website. After visiting several pages, navigate through your history by pressing the navigation buttons.

How it works...

As you browse, pages you visit are stored in the browsing history stack. This includes pages you navigate to through hyperlinks or those loaded programmatically using `loadURL()`.

The `StageWebView` class provides methods for navigating the browsing history. Call the `historyBack()` method to move to the previously visited page, or `historyForward()` to move to the next page in the stack. Before making either of these calls, you need to determine if there is actually a web page to move to. The `isHistoryBackEnabled` property returns `true` if you are able to move back, while `isHistoryForwardEnabled` returns `true` if you can move forward.

Both `historyBack()` and `historyForward()` were called in response to the navigation buttons being pressed by the user.

We also listened for `LocationChangeEvent.LOCATION_CHANGE`, which is dispatched by a `StageWebView` object when its URL has changed. Within this event's handler, both `isHistoryBackEnabled` and `isHistoryForwardEnabled` were queried, with the value of each used to set the visibility of `backBtn` and `forwardBtn`.

For more information regarding managing the browsing history, perform a search for `flash.media.StageWebView` and `flash.events.LocationChangeEvent` within Adobe Community Help.

There's more...

Now let us talk about some other options when dealing with the browsing history.

Obtaining the current location

You can determine the URL of the current page by querying a `StageWebView` object's read-only `location` property. The URL will be returned as a string.

Stopping and reloading pages

The `StageWebView` class provides limited control over the loading of a page. A `stop()` method is provided for halting the current page load, while the page can be reloaded by calling `reload()`.

Detecting when the URL is about to change

In addition to `LOCATION_CHANGE`, there is also `LOCATION_CHANGING`, which indicates that a page's URL is about to change. The `LOCATION_CHANGING` event is dispatched when a hyperlink is selected or script running within the page changes the URL. This event is convenient as you can stop the new URL from loading by calling the `LocationChangeEvent` object's `preventDefault()` method.

To see this in action, first add the following event listener within your constructor:

```
webView.addEventListener(
    LocationChangeEvent.LOCATION_CHANGING, locationChanging);
```

Now add a handler for the event:

```
private function locationChanging(e:LocationChangeEvent):void
{
    e.preventDefault();
}
```

Publish and test the app. Your code changes will effectively block any hyperlinks that you select.

The `LOCATION_CHANGING` event does not fire after calls to `loadURL()`, `loadString()`, `historyBack()`, `historyForward()`, or `reload()`.

See also

▶ *Rendering a web page within an app*

Rendering a local web page

In addition to remote web pages, it is also possible to load and display local HTML files using the `StageWebView` class.

Let us bundle a web page with your application and load it at runtime.

Getting ready

This recipe requires Flash Professional CS5.5 and AIR 2.6 or above.

From the book's accompanying code bundle, open `chapter11\recipe4\recipe.fla` and use it as a starting point.

Sitting in the same location as the FLA is a folder named `html`, which contains the HTML page that has to be loaded by your app. Using Windows Explorer or Finder, take a look at the folder's contents. Also in the `index.html` file, you will find a PNG image and a style sheet, which are both used by the HTML.

How to do it...

We will split this recipe into two parts. First we will use the AIR for iOS Settings panel to bundle the local HTML with the app. Then we will write the ActionScript required to load and render it.

Bundling the HTML

Let us start by bundling the HTML content with your FLA.

1. Move to the AIR for iOS Settings panel by selecting **File | AIR for iOS Settings** from Flash's drop-down menu.

2. If it isn't already selected, click on the panel's **General** tab.

3. At the bottom of the panel is the **Included files** list. Click on the folder icon above the list; browse to and select `chapter11\recipe4\html`. You will now see **html** listed within the **Included files** list.

4. Now click on **OK** to close the **AIR for iOS Settings** panel.

Loading the bundled HTML

With the HTML now included with your FLA, we can focus on writing ActionScript.

1. Create a new document class and name it `Main`.

2. Add the following three additional import statements to the class:

   ```
   import flash.geom.Rectangle;
   import flash.media.StageWebView;
   import flash.filesystem.File;
   ```

3. Declare a `StageWebView` member variable:

   ```
   private var webView:StageWebView;
   ```

4. Finally, within the constructor, set up and load the local web page:

```
public function Main() {
    var url:String = File.applicationDirectory.resolvePath(
      "html/index.html").nativePath;

    webView = new StageWebView();
    webView.stage = stage;
    webView.viewPort = new Rectangle(
      0, 0, stage.stageWidth, stage.stageHeight);
    webView.loadURL(url);
}
```

5. Save the class and when prompted, name the file Main.as.

6. Move back to your FLA and save it too.

7. Now publish the FLA and test it on your device. The HTML page will load from your device's file system.

How it works...

Loading a web page stored locally on your device isn't too dissimilar to loading a remote page. The only extra step required is to first obtain the native path of the local HTML file that you wish to load. Passing a relative path to StageWebView.loadURL() will result in ErrorEvent.ERROR being dispatched.

All iOS apps are stored in their own home directory, and the app itself can read from and write to various sub-folders that exist within it. One such sub-folder is the Application directory, which is used to store the application and any files bundled with it. This is where you will find index.html and the other files associated with it.

The AIR SDK provides the flash.filesystem.File class, which lets you reference commonly used directories including the Application directory. It is then possible to refine the path using the File class' resolvePath() method. The following line of code obtains a reference to our index.html file stored within the Application directory:

```
File.applicationDirectory.resolvePath("html/index.html")
```

The resolvePath() method returns a File object. By calling its nativePath property, we can obtain a string that can be passed to the StageWebView object's loadURL() method. The following is the complete line of code:

```
var url:String = File.applicationDirectory.resolvePath(
    "html/index.html").nativePath;
```

As with any content you wish to bundle locally with your app, it is important that any file you include is sitting somewhere within the FLA's root folder.

For more information, perform a search for flash.filesystem.File and flash.media. StageWebView within Adobe Community Help.

There's more...

Web pages rendered within a `StageWebView` instance don't have to live in perfect isolation from your app.

Bi-directional ActionScript/JavaScript communication

Although limited, it is possible to perform bi-directional ActionScript/JavaScript communication using the `StageWebView` class. Doing so allows data to be passed between your app and an HTML page rendered within a `StageWebView` instance.

Documentation outlining the process involved can be found on the personal blog of Adobe developer, Sean Voisen: `http://sean.voisen.org/blog/2010/10/making-the-most-of-stagewebview`.

See also

▶ *Rendering a web page within an app*

▶ *Dynamically generating a local web page*

▶ *Referencing an app's common directories, Chapter 13*

Dynamically generating a local web page

We have covered how to display both remote and local web pages using the `StageWebView` class. It is also possible to generate HTML on the fly and render it directly within your iOS app.

Let us see how this is done by dynamically creating a web page that makes use of a PNG image and a style sheet.

Getting ready

The steps covered here are only applicable to those using Flash Professional CS5.5 and at least version 2.6 of the AIR SDK. AIR 2.0 does not support the `StageWebView` class.

We will require the use of the **as3corelib** API. It is a library of invaluable ActionScript 3.0 classes and utilities for all kinds of things including hashing, image encoding, and string manipulation. For this recipe, we will use the library's PNG encoder.

The as3corelib API is available from GitHub at: `http://github.com/mikechambers/as3corelib`. Click on the page's **Downloads** link and select **as3corelib-.93.zip** from the **Download Packages** section. Extract the `.zip` file to your Documents folder at: `packt\flash-ios-cookbook\`.

If you are using Windows, then the location of your Documents folder depends on the version of Windows you are running. For Windows Vista and Windows 7 it can be found at: `C:\Users\<username>\Documents\`. If you are using Windows XP, then it is at: `C:\Documents and Settings\<username>\My Documents\`.

Now open `chapter11\recipe5\recipe.fla` from the book's accompanying code bundle into Flash Professional CS5.5. Sitting within the Library panel is a PNG image that has a linkage name of `Image` assigned to it. We will include this image within our web page. For the remainder of this recipe, we will work from this FLA.

How to do it...

This recipe is broken into two main steps. We will start by linking the as3corelib API to our FLA. Once that is done, we will make use of the API to write the ActionScript that generates the page.

Linking to the as3corelib API

The as3corelib API comes in the form of a `.swc` file that must be statically linked to your FLA.

1. Select **File | ActionScript Settings** from Flash Professional's drop-down menu. This will open the **Advanced ActionScript 3.0 Settings** panel where you can add the SWC.

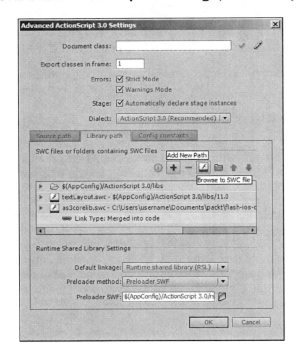

2. Select the **Library path** tab, then click on the **Add New Path** icon, which is represented by a **+** symbol.

3. Now click on the **Browse to SWC file** icon and select the following file from your Documents folder: `packt\flash-ios-cookbook\as3corelib-.93\as3corelib-.93\lib\as3corelib.swc`. It will be added to a list of SWC files to be included with your app when published. Expand its entry by clicking on the icon to the left of its path and ensure that its **Link Type** is set to **Merged into code**.

4. Close the **Advanced ActionScript 3.0 Settings** panel by clicking on the **OK** button at the bottom.

Generating the HTML

With the SWC linked to your FLA, you can now use the API it provides. Let us write some ActionScript to generate an HTML file and display it.

1. Start by creating a document class and naming it `Main`.

2. Add the following import statements, including as3corelib's PNG encoder class:

```
import flash.display.BitmapData;
import flash.filesystem.File;
import flash.filesystem.FileStream;
import flash.filesystem.FileMode;
import flash.geom.Rectangle;
import flash.media.StageWebView;
import flash.utils.ByteArray;
import com.adobe.images.PNGEncoder;
```

3. Declare a `StageWebView` member variable:

```
private var webView:StageWebView;
```

4. Within the class' constructor, call methods that will create the HTML page and load it into a `StageWebView` object:

```
public function Main() {
   createHtml();
   loadHtml();
}
```

5. Now add the method which creates the HTML page, including the style sheet and PNG image that is used by it:

```
private function createHtml():void {
   var cssString:String = "body" +
     "{ padding:0px; border:0px; margin:0px; " +
     "background-color:#cdc0af }";

   var htmlString:String = "<!DOCTYPE HTML>" +
```

```
        "<html>" +
          "<head>" +
            "<link rel='stylesheet' type='text/css' " +
            "href='styles.css' />" +
            "<meta name='viewport' " +
            "content='width=device-width; " +
            "height=device-height; initial-scale=1.0; " +
            "maximum-scale=1.0; user-scalable=0;' />" +
          "</head>" +
          "<body>" +
            "<img src='image.png' />" +
          "</body>" +
        "</html>";

    var image:BitmapData = new Image();

    writeFile(htmlString, "index.html");
    writeFile(cssString, "styles.css");
    writePng(image, "image.png");
}
```

6. The `createHtml()` method calls two support methods—`writeFile()` and `writePng()`. Add both to the class:

```
private function writeFile(text:String, name:String):void {
  var file:File = File.documentsDirectory.resolvePath(name);
  var stream:FileStream = new FileStream();
  stream.open(file, FileMode.WRITE);
  stream.writeUTFBytes(text);
  stream.close();
}

private function writePng(bd:BitmapData, name:String):void {
  var pngBytes:ByteArray = PNGEncoder.encode(bd);

  var file:File = File.documentsDirectory.resolvePath(name);
  var stream:FileStream = new FileStream();
  stream.open(file, FileMode.WRITE);
  stream.writeBytes(pngBytes);
  stream.close();
}
```

7. Finally, add the method which loads and displays the generated HTML page:

```
private function loadHtml():void {
  var url:String = File.documentsDirectory.resolvePath(
    "index.html").nativePath;
```

```
        webView = new StageWebView();
        webView.stage = stage;
        webView.viewPort = new Rectangle(
            0, 0, stage.stageWidth, stage.stageHeight);
        webView.loadURL(url);
    }
```

8. Save the class and, when prompted, name the file `Main.as`.

9. Move back to your FLA and save it too.

10. Now publish the FLA and test it on your device. The app will dynamically generate the HTML page and display it on the screen.

How it works...

This recipe has made heavy use of Flash's `File` and `FileStream` classes. When creating an HTML page on the fly, the generated HTML must first be written to the device's file system before being loaded by a `StageWebView` instance. Any local resources used by the HTML, such as style sheets and images, must also be written to the file system and match the relative paths used by the HTML.

Within the `createHtml()` method, we declared and initialized a string that contained our HTML. The following is the generated HTML:

```
<html>
  <head>
    <link rel='stylesheet' type='text/css'
      href='styles.css' />
    <meta name='viewport' content='width=device-width;
      height=device-height; initial-scale=1.0;
      maximum-scale=1.0; user-scalable=0;' />
  </head>
  <body>
    <img src='image.png' />
  </body>
</html>
```

Notice that it references a local style sheet named `styles.css` and an image named `image.png`. The image is the PNG from the FLA's library, while a string representing the style sheet is also generated within the `createHtml()` method.

All three—the HTML string, style sheet string, and PNG—are written to the same directory on the device's file system. This is done by our `writeFile()` and `writePng()` methods.

When an iOS app is installed, a few common directories are created within the app's home directory. One such directory is the Documents directory, which can be used to store application-specific data and temporary files. A reference to this directory can be obtained from the static `documentsDirectory` property of the `flash.filesystem.File` class. This is where we wrote our local web page to.

The `writeFile()` method creates a specified file within the Documents directory and writes a string of data to it. We call this method twice. First to write the HTML file and then again to write the style sheet. The file is created by using a `File` object to declare its location, then the object is passed to the `open()` method of a `FileStream` object:

```
var file:File = File.documentsDirectory.resolvePath(name);
var stream:FileStream = new FileStream();
stream.open(file, FileMode.WRITE);
```

Once the `FileStream` object has been opened, the actual file is written by calling `writeUTFBytes()` and passing the string to it. A call to `close()` is then made to end the process:

```
stream.writeUTFBytes(htmlString);
stream.close();
```

Writing the PNG file to the Documents directory is performed by the `writePng()` method and isn't too dissimilar to `writeHtml()`. First the bitmap data from the `Image` object is encoded in PNG format using the as3corelib library's `PNGEncoder` class:

```
var pngBytes:ByteArray = PNGEncoder.encode(bd);
```

A `FileStream` object is then used to write the PNG to the file system. The HTML and style sheet were both represented by a string. The PNG's data is stored within a `ByteArray` object. Therefore, rather than using `writeUTFBytes()`, a call to the `FileStream` object's `writeBytes()` method is made instead.

The final step is to create a `StageWebView` object and load `index.html` from the Documents directory into it. This is taken care of by the `loadHtml()` method.

More information regarding `flash.filesystem.File`, `flash.filesystem.FileStream`, and `flash.utils.ByteArray` can be obtained from Adobe Community Help.

There's more...

The following are a few more considerations when dynamically generating HTML content.

Cleaning-up

If you are using the app's Documents folder to store temporary files, then remember to delete them when finished. This can be done using either the `File` class' `deleteFile()` or `deleteFileAsync()` method.

Using loadString()

The `StageWebView` class has a `loadString()` method allowing a specified HTML string to be displayed. While this approach may seem easier than the steps outlined in this recipe, HTML content displayed using `loadString()` cannot load local resources, such as image files or style sheets.

See also

▶ *Rendering a web page within an app*

▶ *Rendering a local web page*

Capturing a snapshot of a web page

It is possible to copy the contents of a `StageWebView` object's viewport into a bitmap.

In this recipe, we will capture a snapshot of a web page and display a thumbnail of the bitmap below the page's viewport.

Getting ready

The steps covered in this recipe are only applicable to those using Flash Professional CS5.5 and AIR 2.6 or above. Flash Professional CS5 and AIR 2.0 do not provide support for the `StageWebView` class.

From the book's accompanying code bundle, open `chapter11\recipe6\recipe.fla` into Flash Professional CS5.5. The FLA's stage is empty but its AIR for iOS settings have already been applied.

How to do it...

In addition to `StageWebView`, we will make use of the `Bitmap` and `BitmapData` classes to store and display the snapshot.

1. Create a new document class and name it `Main`.

2. Add the following import statements and declare a `StageWebView` member variable:

```
package {

    import flash.display.Bitmap;
    import flash.display.BitmapData;
    import flash.display.MovieClip;
    import flash.events.Event;
    import flash.geom.Rectangle;
    import flash.media.StageWebView;

    public class Main extends MovieClip {

        private var webView:StageWebView;

        public function Main() {
            // constructor code
        }
    }
}
```

3. Within the constructor, set up the `StageWebView` object and listen for its web page successfully loading:

```
public function Main() {
    webView = new StageWebView();
    webView.stage = stage;
    webView.viewPort = new Rectangle(
        0, 0, stage.stageWidth, stage.stageWidth);
    webView.addEventListener(Event.COMPLETE, loaded);
    webView.loadURL("http://www.yeahbutisitflash.com");
}
```

4. Finally, add an event handler that grabs a bitmap of the loaded page and displays a thumbnail of it:

```
private function loaded(e:Event):void {
    var bd:BitmapData = new BitmapData(
        webView.viewPort.width, webView.viewPort.height);
    webView.drawViewPortToBitmapData(bd);

    var b:Bitmap = new Bitmap(bd);
    b.x = 0;
    b.y = 320;
    b.width = 160;
    b.height = 160;
    addChild(b);
}
```

5. Save the class and name its file `Main.as` when prompted.

6. Move back to your FLA and save it too.

7. Now publish the FLA and test it on your device. Once the web page loads, a snapshot of it will be captured and displayed as a thumbnail at the bottom-left corner of the screen.

How it works...

The `StageWebView` class provides `drawViewPortToBitmapData()`, which writes the pixel data from a `StageWebView` object's viewport into a `BitmapData` object.

First a `BitmapData` object needs to be instantiated:

```
var bd:BitmapData = new BitmapData(
  webView.viewPort.width, webView.viewPort.height);
```

Then the visible portion of the viewport can be drawn to the `BitmapData` object by calling `drawViewPortToBitmapData()`:

```
webView.drawViewPortToBitmapData(bd);
```

Care must be taken to ensure that the `BitmapData` object's dimensions match those of the viewport's. If not, then `drawViewPortToBitmapData()` will throw an `ArgumentError` exception. The `StageWebView.viewPort` property returns a `Rectangle`, which you can use to determine the viewport's width and height.

For additional information regarding the `flash.display.Bitmap` and `flash.display.BitmapData` classes, refer to Adobe Community Help.

There's more...

The following is one practical use for capturing a snapshot of a web page.

Overlaying display objects

Although the `StageWebView` object renders on top of Flash's display list, it is possible to sit display objects above your HTML content in situations where user interaction with the HTML isn't required. This is done by capturing a bitmap image of the `StageWebView`, and replacing it with the bitmap. You can then add display objects such as buttons, panels, and menus above the bitmap representation. To hide a `StageWebView` object from view, set its `stage` property to `null`.

See also

▶ *Rendering a web page within an app*

12
Working with Video and Audio

In this chapter, we will cover:

- ▸ Playing local FLV video
- ▸ Playing local H.264 video
- ▸ Controlling video
- ▸ Embedding audio
- ▸ Playing embedded audio
- ▸ Streaming audio
- ▸ Controlling audio playback

Introduction

With carriers able to support larger downloads and iOS hardware relentlessly marching forward, developers are able to build larger apps. Apple itself acknowledged this by doubling its over-the-air download limit, making it possible to include more bandwidth-heavy content such as video and high-quality audio.

On the web, the Flash platform has been a leader in both video and audio playback for many years. Adobe AIR brings many of these capabilities to iOS, enabling the creation of apps that will engage, inspire, and immerse the user.

This chapter will explore the many options for working with video and sound. It will start by guiding you through the steps required to include and play back video, before moving onto the handling of embedded and streaming audio.

Playing local FLV video

Key to the Flash platform's success over the years has been its FLV file format, which delivers Sorenson Spark or ON2 VP6 encoded video both locally and over the Internet.

In this recipe, we will see how to load FLV video that has been bundled with an AIR for iOS app.

Getting ready

Use `chapter12\recipe1\recipe.fla` from the book's accompanying code bundle as a starting point.

Also, an FLV video is available from `chapter12\resources\video.flv` and should be copied to `chapter12\recipe1\` before proceeding.

The video is intended to be viewed on a device held in a landscape orientation. To accommodate this requirement, the FLA's stage size has been set to 480x320 pixels rather than the default portrait orientation of 320x480.

How to do it...

This recipe is split into two main steps. First we will bundle the FLV video with the app, then we will write some ActionScript to play it back.

Bundling the FLV video

Perform the following steps to bundle the video with the app:

1. Open the AIR for iOS Settings panel by selecting **File | AIR for iOS Settings** from Flash's drop-down menu.
2. If it isn't already selected, click on the panel's **General** tab.
3. Set the **Rendering** field to **CPU**.
4. At the bottom of the panel is the **Included files** list. Click on the **+** symbol above the list and select `chapter12\recipe1\video.flv`. The video will now be bundled with your IPA file when the FLA is published.
5. Click on **OK** to close the AIR for iOS Settings panel.

Playing the FLV video

With the FLV now included within your FLA, we can turn our attention to the ActionScript required to play it.

1. Create a document class and name it `Main`.

2. Add the following import statements to the class:

```
import flash.desktop.NativeApplication;
import flash.desktop.SystemIdleMode;
import flash.display.MovieClip;
import flash.media.Video;
import flash.net.NetConnection;
import flash.net.NetStream;
```

3. Declare a constant to store the name of the FLV video:

```
static private const VIDEO_URL:String = "video.flv";
```

4. Create three member variables required to play back video:

```
private var netConnection:NetConnection;
private var netStream:NetStream;
private var video:Video;
```

5. Within the constructor, load and play back the FLV video:

```
public function Main() {
  NativeApplication.nativeApplication.systemIdleMode =
    SystemIdleMode.KEEP_AWAKE;

  netConnection = new NetConnection();
  netConnection.connect(null);

  netStream = new NetStream(netConnection);
  netStream.client = this;
  netStream.play(VIDEO_URL);

  video = new Video();
  video.attachNetStream(netStream);
  video.width = 480;
  video.height = 320;
  addChildAt(video, 0);
}
```

6. You will also need to provide callback methods that capture metadata and cue point events as the FLV plays. Add the following two empty methods to your document class:

```
public function onMetaData(dataObj:Object):void {
  ; // Do nothing.
}

public function onXMPData(dataObj:Object):void {
  ; // Do nothing.
}
```

7. Save both the class file and your FLA.

8. Publish the FLA and deploy the IPA to your device.

When launched, the app will load and play the FLV from the file system.

How it works...

Our code loads `video.flv` locally from the device and plays it back to the user. All files bundled with an app are copied to its Application directory during installation. This is the same folder where the app itself lives, and is where the FLV video is stored.

Loading and playing the video is a three-stage process that involves the `NetConnection`, `NetStream`, and `Video` classes.

First a `NetConnection` object is created and `null` is passed to its `connect()` method. This indicates that we won't be connecting to a Flash Media Server, and instead intend to either connect to a file that is stored locally on the device's file system or hosted on a web server. For this recipe, we used the local FLV that we bundled with the app:

```
netConnection = new NetConnection();
netConnection.connect(null);
```

Next a `NetStream` object is created and used to play the actual video. The `NetConnection` object is passed to the `NetStream` object's constructor, allowing it to stream the local video from the device:

```
netStream = new NetStream(netConnection);
netStream.client = this;
netStream.play(VIDEO_URL);
```

Finally the `NetStream` object is attached to a `Video` object, allowing the video to be displayed to the user:

```
video = new Video();
video.attachNetStream(netStream);
video.width = 480;
video.height = 320;
addChildAt(video, 0);
```

The `Video` class inherits from `flash.display.DisplayObject`, meaning it can be added to the display list and manipulated in an identical manner to all other display objects. Two `DisplayObject` properties that we use are `width` and `height` to set the video's size on screen. In order to maximize playback performance, ensure the dimensions match that of the FLV perfectly. Scaling an FLV video will degrade performance.

Notice that CPU rendering was selected for this recipe. Although the GPU can be used, the hardware video decoder isn't capable of decoding arbitrary resolutions, which can sometimes lead to the incorrect sizing of your `Video` object. Additionally, if you are using Flash Professional CS5 and AIR 2.0, then avoid GPU rendering of video altogether.

For more information, perform a search for `flash.net.NetConnection`, `flash.net.NetStream`, and `flash.media.Video` within Adobe Community Help.

There's more...

Now let us go back to the subject of metadata and cue points. We will also touch upon a few other considerations before moving on.

Metadata and cue point events

As a video plays, its `NetStream` object can be used to capture and process cue point and various metadata events including `onMetaData` and `onXMPData`.

While this recipe had no need for these events, we still had to write empty callback handlers for each. Failing to do so will result in a runtime exception being thrown when an event is triggered.

To handle these events, set the `NetStream` object's `client` property to an object that contains callback methods for each. The method names must match those of the events exactly. For this recipe, we simply set the `client` property to `this` and added the handlers to the document class.

Refer to `http://help.adobe.com/en_US/as3/dev/WSD30FA424-950E-43ba-96C8-99B926943FE7.html` for details regarding how to actually use the data from cue point and metadata events.

Playing remote FLV video

In addition to local playback, FLV video can be progressively streamed over HTTP from a remote location. Simply pass the video's URL to the `NetStream.play()` method to commence playback. You can also determine the status of the `NetStream` object's internal playback buffer by listening for it dispatching `NetStatusEvent.NET_STATUS`.

You can find more information about available `NetStream` events at `http://help.adobe.com/en_US/as3/dev/WS901d38e593cd1bac-3d11a09612fffaf8447-8000.html`.

Screen lock

When watching video, the screen will dim after a short period of inactivity from the user. Within this recipe's constructor, we prevent this from happening by setting `NativeApplication.systemIdleMode` to `SystemIdleMode.KEEP_AWAKE`.

While indefinitely preventing the screen from locking is acceptable for demonstration purposes, it is unlikely to be suitable for real-world applications. A better practice is to disable screen locking during playback of a video, and then re-enable it when the video is paused or stopped.

Maximizing playback performance

To maximize performance, minimize your display list and try not to overlay other graphical elements on top of the video during playback. Also attempt to limit the amount of ActionScript being executed during playback. This is especially true of older first and second generation hardware where FLV performance can struggle.

If you are using the AIR 3.0 SDK or above, then consider using hardware accelerated H.264 video above FLV as its playback performance and video quality is significantly better.

Bundling multiple videos

Files can be added individually to the **Included files** list, or you can specify a folder for inclusion. This is convenient when writing apps that have multiple videos as you can simply group the files within a single location. Every file within the folder will be bundled with your IPA.

See also

> ▸ *Playing local H.264 video*
> ▸ *Controlling video*
> ▸ *Preventing screen idle, Chapter 3*
> ▸ *Understanding GPU-Blend mode, Chapter 6*

Playing local H.264 video

AIR for iOS now provides support for the high-quality, low bit-rate H.264 video format, enabling best-in-class high-definition playback through the `StageVideo` class. By taking advantage of hardware acceleration, H.264 video reduces CPU usage and consumes less memory than comparable formats including FLV.

In this recipe, we will play back H.264 video that has been bundled locally with an app.

Getting ready

The steps covered here are applicable only to those using AIR 3.0 and above. If you are using Flash Professional CS5, then you will be unable to attempt this recipe.

From the chapter's accompanying code bundle, use `chapter12\recipe2\recipe.fla` as a starting point.

An H.264 encoded video is available from `chapter12\resources\video.mp4` and should be copied to `chapter12\recipe2\` before proceeding.

The video is intended to be viewed on a device held in a landscape orientation. To accommodate this requirement, the FLA's stage size has been set to 480x320 pixels rather than the default portrait orientation of 320x480.

How to do it...

This recipe is broken into two main steps. First we will bundle the H.264 video with the app, before writing some ActionScript to play it back.

Bundling the H.264 video

Perform the following steps to bundle the video with the app:

1. Open the AIR for iOS Settings panel by selecting **File | AIR for iOS Settings** from Flash's drop-down menu.
2. If it isn't already selected, click on the panel's **General** tab.
3. Set the **Rendering** field to **GPU**.
4. At the bottom of the panel is the **Included files** list. Click on the **+** symbol above the list and select `chapter12\recipe2\video.mp4`. The file will now be bundled with your IPA file when the FLA is published.
5. Click on **OK** to close the AIR for iOS Settings panel.

Playing the H.264 video

With the video now included within your FLA, we can turn our attention to the ActionScript required to play it.

1. Create a document class and name it `Main`.
2. Add the following import statements to the class:

```
import flash.desktop.NativeApplication;
import flash.desktop.SystemIdleMode;
import flash.display.MovieClip;
import flash.geom.Rectangle;
```

```
import flash.media.StageVideo;
import flash.net.NetConnection;
import flash.net.NetStream;
```

3. Declare a constant to store the name of the video:

```
static private const VIDEO_URL:String = "video.mp4";
```

4. Create three member variables required to play back video:

```
private var netConnection:NetConnection;
private var netStream:NetStream;
private var video:StageVideo;
```

5. Within the constructor, set-up and play back the video:

```
public function Main() {
  NativeApplication.nativeApplication.systemIdleMode =
    SystemIdleMode.KEEP_AWAKE;

  netConnection = new NetConnection();
  netConnection.connect(null);

  netStream = new NetStream(netConnection);
  netStream.client = this;

  video = stage.stageVideos[0];
  video.attachNetStream(netStream);
  video.viewPort = new Rectangle(0, 25, 480, 270);

  netStream.play(VIDEO_URL);
}
```

6. You will also need to provide a callback method that captures metadata events as the video plays. Add the following empty method to your document class:

```
public function onMetaData(dataObj:Object):void {
  ; // Do nothing.
}
```

7. Save both the class file and your FLA.

 The AIR Debug Launcher (ADL) does not currently support H.264 video playback. If you attempt to test this recipe using ADL, then you will receive a runtime error.

8. Publish the FLA and deploy the IPA to your device.

When launched, the app will load and play the H.264 video from the file system.

How it works...

Our code loads `video.mp4` locally from the device and plays it back to the user. All files bundled with an app are copied to its Application directory during installation. This is the same folder where the app itself lives and is where the H.264 video is stored.

Loading and playing the video is a four-step process that involves the `NetConnection`, `NetStream`, and `StageVideo` classes.

First a `NetConnection` object is created and `null` is passed to its `connect()` method. This indicates that we won't be connecting to a Flash Media Server, and instead intend to either connect to a file that is stored locally on the device's file system or hosted on a web server. For this recipe, we used the local FLV that we bundled with the app:

```
netConnection = new NetConnection();
netConnection.connect(null);
```

Next a `NetStream` object is created and will be used to play the actual video. The `NetConnection` object is passed to the `NetStream` object's constructor, allowing it to stream the local video from the device:

```
netStream = new NetStream(netConnection);
netStream.client = this;
```

The `NetStream` object needs to be attached to a `StageVideo` object in order for it to be displayed to the user. However, you don't explicitly create one yourself. Instead a `StageVideo` object is obtained from a vector array made available by the `Stage` object's `stageVideos` property. On iOS devices, this vector will contain a single `StageVideo` instance capable of rendering video:

```
video = stage.stageVideos[0];
video.attachNetStream(netStream);
```

The final step is to create a viewport for the video and begin playback. Video rendered by the `StageVideo` class is hardware-accelerated and not part of the display list. Instead, `StageVideo` instances are rendered behind the display list within a rectangular region, which specifies the absolute position and size of the video. Once the viewport has been defined, call the `NetStream` object's `play()` method:

```
video.viewPort = new Rectangle(0, 25, 480, 270);
netStream.play(VIDEO_URL);
```

The video used for this recipe is 400x224 pixels in size, but you may have noticed in the code above that the viewport has been assigned a rectangular region of 480x270. This scales the video to cover the screen's entire horizontal width while still maintaining the video's aspect ratio. Also, the viewport is shifted down by 25 pixels to ensure that it is vertically centered on screen.

GPU rendering was selected for this recipe. Decoding H.264 video is computationally expensive and requires hardware to ensure acceptable playback performance on iOS devices. Although the video is not part of the display list, it does sit behind it, meaning display objects such as UI components can be overlaid on top.

For more information, perform a search for `flash.net.NetConnection`, `flash.net.NetStream`, and `flash.media.StageVideo` within Adobe Community Help.

There's more...

Now let us go back to the subject of metadata. We will also touch upon a few other considerations before moving on.

Metadata and cue point events

As a video plays, its `NetStream` object can be used to capture and process cue point and various metadata events including `onMetaData`, `onCuePoint`, and `onXMPData`.

While this recipe had no need for the `onMetaData` event, we still had to write an empty callback handler for it. Failing to do so will result in a runtime exception being thrown when the event is triggered.

To handle this, and other events, set the `NetStream` object's `client` property to an object that contains callback methods for each. The method names must match those of the events exactly. For this recipe, we simply set the `client` property to `this` and added the handlers to the document class.

Refer to `http://help.adobe.com/en_US/as3/dev/WSD30FA424-950E-43ba-96C8-99B926943FE7.html` for details regarding how to actually use the data from cue point and metadata events.

Playing video captured by the default camera

Video successfully captured using the `CameraUI` class is stored temporarily on the device's file system. Using the `MediaEvent` object dispatched by `CameraUI`, it is possible to determine the video's URL in order to play it back. An example is given as follows:

```
private function captured(e:MediaEvent):void {
  var mediaPromise:MediaPromise = e.data;
  var videoUrl:String = mediaPromise.file.url;
  playVideo(videoUrl);
}
```

Once you have the URL, you can simply pass it to your `NetStream` object's `play()` method to initiate playback.

The `CameraUI` class is covered in the *Capturing with the default camera app* recipe from *Chapter 10*.

Determining the video's size

You can retrieve the width and height of the encoded video from a `StageVideo` object's `videoWidth` and `videoHeight` read-only properties. However, you first need to wait for this information to become available by listening for `StageVideoEvent.RENDER_STATE` being dispatched from your `StageVideo` instance.

Also, be careful when playing back video captured from the device's camera. On iOS, the camera captures video in landscape orientation. If your application uses a portrait aspect ratio, then you will need to swap the values of the `videoWidth` and `videoHeight` properties when specifying your viewport's dimensions.

For more information, perform a search for `flash.events.StageVideoEvent` within Adobe Community Help.

Playing remote H.264 video

In addition to local playback, H.264 video can be progressively streamed over HTTP from a remote location. Simply pass the video's URL to the `NetStream.play()` method to commence playback. You can also determine the status of the `NetStream` object's internal playback buffer by listening for it dispatching a `NetStatusEvent.NET_STATUS` event.

You can find more information about available `NetStream` events at `http://help.adobe.com/en_US/as3/dev/WS901d38e593cd1bac-3d11a09612fffaf8447-8000.html`.

Encoding H.264 video

H.264 video playback can be computationally expensive. With such a wide range of hardware configurations across the range of iOS devices, it is important that the correct encoding strategy is employed to guarantee playback on the lowest common denominator. Adobe provides some H.264 encoding recommendations at `www.adobe.com/devnet/devices/articles/mobile_video_encoding.html`.

You can encode video using the H.264 codec with Adobe Media Encoder, which comes with Flash Professional as an optional install. An introduction to Adobe Media Encoder can be found on the Adobe Developer Connection website at `www.adobe.com/devnet/flash/quickstart/video_encoder.html`.

Bundling multiple videos

Files can be added individually to the **Included files** list, or you can specify a folder for inclusion. This is convenient when writing apps that have multiple videos as you can simply group the files within a single location. Every file within the folder will be bundled with your IPA.

See also

▸ *Controlling video*

▸ *Preventing screen idle, Chapter 3*

▸ *Understanding GPU-Vector mode, Chapter 6*

Controlling video

As well as commencing playback, the `NetStream` class provides additional control of video. In this recipe, we will add the ability for the user to pause, resume, and restart either an FLV or H.264 video.

Getting ready

From the book's accompanying code bundle, open either `chapter12\recipe3-flv\recipe.fla` or `chapter12\recipe3-mp4\recipe.fla` and use it as a starting point. The first FLA's document class contains the code written for the *Playing local FLV video* recipe, while the second FLA contains the code from the *Playing local H.264 video* recipe.

Two movie clips have been added to the stage. The first has been given an instance name of `blocker`. The second has been named `controls` and sits in front of `blocker`. Both movie clips will sit in front of the FLV or H.264 video.

Within the `controls` movie clip are three buttons named `playBtn`, `restartBtn`, and `resumeBtn`. These will be used to play, restart, and un-pause the video respectively. Tapping anywhere on the screen during playback will pause the video.

The `blocker` movie clip has an alpha transparency of 60% and will be used to dim the video when it is currently being paused. During playback, `blocker` will be made invisible ensuring that the video isn't obscured. The following screenshot shows the video being dimmed by the `blocker` movie clip:

Before proceeding, you will also need to copy either an FLV or H.264 video to your FLA's root directory. If you are working with FLV video, then copy `chapter12\resources\video.flv` to `chapter12\recipe3-flv\`. For H.264 video, copy `chapter12\resources\video.mp4` to `chapter12\recipe3-mp4\`.

Okay, let us write the ActionScript required for this recipe.

How to do it...

Open the FLA's document class and make the following changes to it:

1. Add two new import statements:

```
import flash.events.MouseEvent;
import flash.events.NetStatusEvent;
```

2. Within the constructor, listen for the `NetStream` instance dispatching a `NetStatusEvent.NET_STATUS` event:

```
netStream = new NetStream(netConnection);
netStream.client = this;
netStream.addEventListener(NetStatusEvent.NET_STATUS,
    statusUpdated);
```

3. Also, remove the following line of code from the constructor:

```
netStream.play(VIDEO_URL);
```

 In the line above and throughout this recipe, `VIDEO_URL` is a constant containing the URL to the local video to be played. It will point to either `video.flv` or `video.mp4` depending on whether you are working with FLV or H.264 video.

We no longer want the video to start playing immediately. Instead we will wait for the user to tap the Play button.

4. Finally, at the end of the constructor, call a support method that will set up the playback controls:

```
setupControls();
```

5. Now add the actual `setupControls()` method. Add an event listener to each of the control buttons and make only the Play button visible initially—we will show the other buttons only when the video is paused.

```
private function setupControls():void {
  controls.playBtn.addEventListener(MouseEvent.MOUSE_UP,
    playVideo);
  controls.restartBtn.addEventListener(MouseEvent.MOUSE_UP,
    restartVideo);
```

```
controls.resumeBtn.addEventListener(MouseEvent.MOUSE_UP,
  resumeVideo);
stage.addEventListener(MouseEvent.MOUSE_UP, pauseVideo);

showBtns(["playBtn"]);
}
```

6. When the Play button is pressed, we will begin playback of the video and hide the controls from view. Add the following event handler to do this:

```
private function playVideo(e:MouseEvent):void {
  netStream.play(VIDEO_URL);
  hideBtns();
  e.stopPropagation();
}
```

7. The user will be able to pause the video by tapping anywhere on the screen during playback. When paused, the control panel's Restart and Resume buttons will be shown. Add an event handler for this and pause the NetStream object's video stream:

```
private function pauseVideo(e:MouseEvent):void {
  if(controls.visible == false)
  {
    netStream.pause();
    showBtns(["resumeBtn", "restartBtn"]);
  }
}
```

8. Now add an event handler for the Restart button. This handler will move back to the beginning of the NetStream object's video and also hide the controls from view:

```
private function restartVideo(e:MouseEvent):void {
  netStream.seek(0);
  netStream.resume();
  hideBtns();
  e.stopPropagation();
}
```

9. Write a similar handler for the Resume button, un-pausing the NetStream object's video stream:

```
private function resumeVideo(e:MouseEvent):void {
  netStream.resume();
  hideBtns();
  e.stopPropagation();
}
```

10. We also want to offer the user the chance to watch the video again once it has played to completion. Write a handler for the `NetStream` object's `NET_STATUS` event and show the Play button if the video has stopped:

```
private function statusUpdated(e:NetStatusEvent):void {
  if(e.info.code == "NetStream.Play.Stop")
  {
    showBtns(["playBtn"]);
  }
}
```

11. We are just about finished. Add the following two support methods to manage the visibility of the control buttons and the blocker:

```
private function hideBtns():void {
  controls.visible = false;
  blocker.visible = false;
}

private function showBtns(btns:Array):void {
  controls.visible = true;
  blocker.visible = true;
  for(var instName:String in controls)
  {
    if(btns.indexOf(instName) != -1)
    {
      controls[instName].visible = true;
    }
    else
    {
      controls[instName].visible = false;
    }
  }
}
```

12. Save your document class and move back to the FLA.

13. Publish and test the app on your device.

How it works...

The following three methods of the `NetStream` class were used to control video playback:

▶ `pause()`: Pauses the current video stream

▶ `resume()`: Resumes playback of the paused video stream

▶ `seek()`: Moves to a specific point in time within the video stream

The seek() method expects a time, measured in seconds, to move to. The time is actually an approximation as the NetStream object will move to the keyframe closest to it.

It should also be noted that the play() method should not be used to resume playback. It is used for commencing playback only. Instead call resume() to continue playback of a paused video.

The NetStream class does not provide a stop() method. Within our code example, the paused video was restarted from the beginning by seeking to the first keyframe, then resuming playback.

There's more...

Here are some last words before we leave video and move on to audio.

NetStream status

The NetStatusEvent object is dispatched in response to a plethora of useful status changes, errors, and warnings. Here are just a few strings that the info.code property can be queried for:

- NetStream.Play.Start: Playback has started
- NetStream.Play.Stop: Playback has stopped
- NetStream.Play.StreamNotFound: The video file cannot be found
- NetStream.Play.InsufficientBW: The client does not have sufficient bandwidth to play the video at its intended frame rate
- NetStream.Pause.Notify: The stream has paused
- NetStream.Unpause.Notify: The stream has un-paused
- NetStream.Buffer.Flush: Playback has ended and the buffer is now empty

You can determine the code's type by examining the info.level property, which will be set to one of the following strings: status, error, or warning. For a comprehensive list of supported strings, perform a search for flash.events.NetStatusEvent within Adobe Community Help.

The flash.net.NetConnection object also dispatches NetStatusEvent objects, which you can listen for.

Closing the video stream

When you are done with a video and you have no more need for it, call the `NetStream` object's `close()` method. This will stop the playback of the video and make the stream available for some other use.

Embedding audio

Sound is an important part of any application and when applied correctly can immerse the user within the interactive experience. In order to provide this experience, it is important that latency is minimized during playback. For example, there should be no delay when playing game sound effects or providing audio feedback from a user interface.

Flash allows sound files to be embedded directly within the library, providing the fastest playback path for your audio. Let us walk through the steps required to do this.

How to do it...

Perform the following steps to embed sound within an FLA's library:

1. From Flash Professional, create a new AIR for iOS document by selecting **File | New** (*Ctrl + N | Cmd + N*). From the **New Document** panel, select the **AIR for iOS** document type and click on the **OK** button.

    If you are a Flash Professional CS5 user, then it is known as an **iPhone OS** document rather than an **AIR for iOS** document.

2. Select **File | Import | Import to Library** from Flash's drop-down menu. A file browser window will appear.

3. From the browser window, navigate to and select `chapter12\resources\sound.mp3`. Click on the **Open** button. The sound file will be imported and listed within the Library panel as **sound.mp3**.

4. From the Library panel, right-click on **sound.mp3** and select **Properties** from the drop-down menu. The **Sound Properties** panel will open.

5. From the **Sound Properties** panel, select **ADPCM** from the **Compression** drop-down box. Ensure that the **Convert stereo to mono** checkbox is selected; set the **Sample rate** to **22kHz** and **ADPCM bits** to **4 bit**. If you are using Flash Professional CS5.5, then, as shown in the following screenshot, ensure that the panel's **Options** tab is selected first.

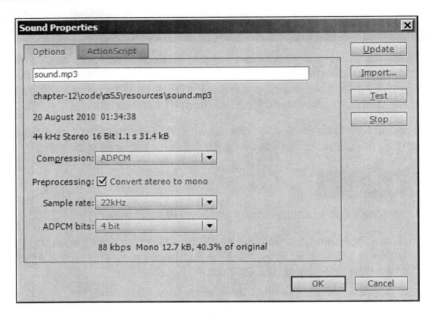

6. Now check the **Export for ActionScript** checkbox and change the text within the **Class** field to SoundEffect. If you are using Flash Professional CS5.5, then this should be performed from the panel's **ActionScript** tab.

7. Click on the **OK** button to close the panel.

8. Depending on your preference settings within Flash Professional, a warning panel may appear containing the following text:

   A definition for this class could not be found in the classpath, so one will be automatically generated in the SWF file upon export.

   This is expected. Click on the **OK** button to continue. The sound file has been assigned an ActionScript class name of SoundEffect.

9. Save your FLA.

How it works...

Embedding sound files within your library places them directly within the application's binary, making them immediately available for playback. However, adding sound files this way will increase your application's file size. The larger your application becomes, the longer it will take to load and the more memory it will consume. Before embedding a sound file, consider carefully whether or not you actually need immediate access to it.

It is also important that you select the appropriate audio codec for your embedded sound. Flash provides two types of codec: compressed and uncompressed. Compressed sound, such as MP3, consumes less space than an uncompressed sound, such as ADPCM. However, the device needs to decode the audio during playback which can be demanding especially if you are attempting to play several compressed sounds at once.

If you need to simultaneously play multiple sound files and with minimum latency, then use an uncompressed codec. Flash provides both ADPCM and RAW for this. Of course, using uncompressed audio will increase the memory consumed by your app.

If you are only playing a single sound at any one time, then opt for MP3. Doing so will reduce your app's memory footprint.

If you want to access your embedded audio using ActionScript, then you must assign a unique class name to each sound within the library. For this recipe, we assigned the class name `SoundEffect` to our embedded sound.

See also

- ► *Creating an AIR for iOS document, Chapter 2*
- ► *Playing embedded audio*

Playing embedded audio

ActionScript can be used to play back sound files embedded within an FLA's library. The sound must have a unique class name associated with it.

In this recipe, we will cover how to play such embedded sounds.

Getting ready

From the book's code bundle, open `chapter12\recipe5\recipe.fla` into Flash Professional and use it as a starting point.

The embedded sound from the *Embedding audio* recipe can be found in the FLA's library and has a class name of `SoundEffect` linked to it.

Also, sitting on the stage is a button named `playBtn`. We will play the embedded sound whenever this button is pressed.

How to do it...

Perform the following steps to play the sound associated with the `SoundEffect` class:

1. Create a document class and name it `Main`.

2. Import the `MouseEvent` class and listen for `playBtn` being pressed:

```
package {

    import flash.display.MovieClip;
    import flash.events.MouseEvent;

    public class Main extends MovieClip {

      public function Main() {
        playBtn.addEventListener(MouseEvent.MOUSE_UP,
          playSound);
      }
    }
}
```

3. Now add an event handler for the button and within it create an instance of the embedded sound's `SoundEffect` class:

```
private function playSound(e:MouseEvent):void {
  var soundEffect:SoundEffect = new SoundEffect();
}
```

4. Staying within the handler, call the `SoundEffect` object's `play()` method:

```
private function playSound(e:MouseEvent):void {
  var soundEffect:SoundEffect = new SoundEffect();
  soundEffect.play();
}
```

5. Save both your class file and the FLA.

6. Publish the app and test it on your device. Tap the button to initiate playback of the sound. Repeatedly tap the button to initiate several instances of it.

How it works...

Audio is played using a `flash.media.Sound` object. All embedded sounds that are linked for ActionScript usage will inherit from this class.

To use an embedded sound, simply instantiate it, then call its `play()` method. This is just one of many methods and properties that are provided by the `Sound` class.

In this recipe, we used an embedded sound file that had a class name of `SoundEffect` assigned to it. The following two lines of code were all that was needed to play it:

```
var soundEffect:SoundEffect = new SoundEffect();
soundEffect.play();
```

When `play()` is called, a `SoundChannel` object is created to play back the sound. Successive calls to `play()` creates new `SoundChannel` objects which independently play their own copy of the sound. You can hear this in action by repeatedly tapping the Play button within this recipe's example app.

Although we had no use for it in this recipe, the `play()` method returns a reference to a newly instantiated `SoundChannel` object, which can be used to control the sound's playback. This is covered in the *Controlling audio playback* recipe in this chapter.

There's more...

Let us look at a few more options available when playing sound.

Playback position

The `play()` method has a number of default parameters, the first of which starts playback from a specified position within the sound. The following example shows playback being commenced 500 milliseconds from the start:

```
soundEffect.play(500);
```

If omitted, the sound will be played from the beginning.

Looping

A sound can be looped by passing a value to the `play()` method's second parameter. In the following example, the sound plays at a point 200 milliseconds from the start, six times in succession:

```
soundEffect.play(200, 6);
```

If omitted, playback will occur only once.

See also

- ▶ *Embedding audio*
- ▶ *Controlling audio playback*

Streaming audio

When working with large sound files, you may want to keep them outside your application's binary in order to minimize its load time and memory consumption. The Sound class can stream an MP3 file from the web or locally from the device's file system, removing the need to embed the audio directly within your FLA.

In this recipe, we will bundle an MP3 file with an app and progressively play it back.

Getting ready

An `.mp3` file has been provided for this recipe. Using either Windows Explorer or Finder, copy `chapter12\resources\music.mp3` from the book's accompanying code bundle to `chapter12\recipe6\`.

Open `chapter12\recipe6\recipe.fla` within Flash Professional. Sitting in the center of the stage is a button named `playBtn`. We will write some ActionScript to stream `music.mp3` whenever this button is pressed.

How to do it...

This recipe will be split into two parts. First we will bundle an MP3 with the app, then we will write the ActionScript required to play it.

Bundling the MP3 file

Follow the steps to bundle the `.mp3` file with your app:

1. Open the AIR for iOS Settings panel by selecting **File | AIR for iOS Settings** from Flash's drop-down menu.

2. If it isn't already selected, click on the panel's **General** tab.

3. At the bottom of the panel is the **Included files** list. Click on the **+** symbol above the list and select `chapter12\recipe6\music.mp3`. The file will now be bundled with your IPA when the FLA is published.

4. Click on **OK** to close the AIR for iOS Settings panel.

Playing the MP3 file

With the MP3 now included within your FLA, let us turn our attention to the ActionScript required to stream it.

1. Create a document class and name it `Main`.

2. Add the following import statements to the class:

```
package {

    import flash.display.MovieClip;
    import flash.events.MouseEvent;
    import flash.media.Sound;
    import flash.net.URLRequest;

    public class Main extends MovieClip {

      public function Main() {
        // constructor code
      }
    }
}
```

3. Within the constructor, listen for `playBtn` being pressed:

```
public function Main() {
    playBtn.addEventListener(MouseEvent.MOUSE_UP, playSound);
}
```

4. Now let us add the button's event handler. Within it, create a `URLRequest` object for the local `music.mp3` file:

```
private function playSound(e:MouseEvent):void {
    var url:URLRequest = new URLRequest("music.mp3");
}
```

5. Finally, pass the request to a new `Sound` object and call its `play()` method:

```
private function playSound(e:MouseEvent):void {
    var url:URLRequest = new URLRequest("music.mp3");
    var sound:Sound = new Sound(url);
    sound.play();
}
```

6. Save both your class file and the FLA.

7. Publish the app and test it on your device. Tap the button to initiate streaming of the `.mp3` file. Repeatedly tap the button to initiate several instances of it.

How it works...

In addition to the playback of embedded audio, the `flash.media.Sound` class can stream external sound files. The technique employed is identical to progressive downloading used when playing FLV or H.264 video and can be used for sound files that are either bundled with the app or stored remotely on the web.

While Flash supports both compressed and uncompressed embedded audio, only `.mp3` files can be directly streamed using the `Sound` class. It is, therefore, advisable to keep the number of external files you simultaneously stream to a minimum as decoding the audio can be computationally expensive.

Playing an `.mp3` file using the `Sound` class is straightforward. First a `URLRequest` for the sound file needs to be created:

```
var url:URLRequest = new URLRequest("music.mp3");
```

Then the request is passed to a new `Sound` instance. The file starts to stream when the `Sound` object's `play()` method is called:

```
var sound:Sound = new Sound(url);
sound.play();
```

Once `play()` is called, the `Sound` object can't be used with another `.mp3` file. To stream a different file, create a new `Sound` object.

The following details are applicable to sound in general within Flash, but are of particular importance when dealing with MP3 files held either locally on the device's file system or on the web.

Increasing the buffer time

If the audio data is consumed faster than it is being loaded, then playback will be paused until the `Sound` object's internal buffer has filled again.

To help prevent buffer under run, you can increase the number of milliseconds of data that has gathered before playback begins. Use a `flash.media.SoundLoaderContext` object to specify the buffer time and pass it to the `Sound` object's constructor:

```
var context:SoundLoaderContext = new SoundLoaderContext(9000);
var sound:Sound = new Sound(request, context);
```

This example specifies that the buffer must contain 9000 milliseconds of audio data before playback is to continue. The default is 5000 milliseconds.

You can query the `Sound` object's `isBuffering` property to determine if the audio is currently paused while more data loads.

Monitoring load progress

When loading, a Sound object dispatches a number of events that can help you monitor its progress:

- ▸ Event.COMPLETE: The sound's data has been completely loaded
- ▸ ProgressEvent.PROGRESS: Dispatched periodically as data is received
- ▸ IOErrorEvent.IO_ERROR: The sound file could not be found

In addition, the ProgressEvent class provides the bytesLoaded and bytesTotal properties, which can be used to determine exactly how much of the file has loaded.

Sound length

The Sound class provides a length property, which can be used to determine the length of the current sound in milliseconds. When working with streaming sound, be careful as this property will return the length for only the data that has currently loaded. If you want to know the full sound file's duration, then wait for the Sound object to dispatch Event.COMPLETE first.

Sound metadata

MP3 audio can contain metadata in the form of ID3 tags, which contain information such as title, artist, album, and track number. If a file contains ID3 metadata, then Event.ID3 will be dispatched from its Sound object. You can listen for this event, and then use the Sound object's id3 property to read the tags.

The following code example shows the id3 property being enumerated in order to discover all tags embedded within the sound file:

```
private function ID3InfoReceived(e:Event):void {
  var id3:ID3Info = e.target.id3;
  for(var prop:String in id3)
  {
    trace(prop + ": " + id3[prop]);
  }
}
```

The ID3Info class can be found in the flash.media package.

Working with raw PCM sound data

Although the Sound class primarily allows for the loading and playback of external MP3 files, AIR 3.0 provides a new method for working with uncompressed PCM sound data. The loadPCMFromByteArray() method injects PCM 32-bit floating point sound data from a ByteArray object into a Sound object.

Playing audio in the background

From AIR 3.0 onwards, you can write multitasking applications that continue to play audio while in the background. This is achieved by inserting the `UIBackgroundModes` key into your application descriptor file:

```
<iPhone>
  <InfoAdditions>
    <![CDATA[<key>UIDeviceFamily</key>
            <array><string>1</string></array>
            <key>UIBackgroundModes</key>
            <array><string>audio</string></array>]]>
  </InfoAdditions>
```

Any audio that is currently playing when the app is closed will continue to do so.

See also

▶ *Embedding audio*

▶ *Controlling audio playback*

▶ *Editing the application descriptor file, Chapter 3*

Controlling audio playback

A `SoundChannel` object is created for each sound that is played. Using the class' API, you can control the playback of a sound.

In this recipe, we will learn how to pause and resume a sound.

Getting ready

An `.mp3` file and an FLA have been provided within the book's accompanying code bundle.

Open `chapter12\recipe7\recipe.fla` into Flash Professional. Sitting in the center of the stage is a button named `playBtn`. In the layer directly below is another button named `pauseBtn`. During this recipe, we will write ActionScript to toggle between the two, indicating whether or not the MP3 is currently playing.

The MP3 we will be using can be found at `chapter12\resources\music.mp3`. Before proceeding, copy it to the FLA's root folder at `chapter12\recipe7\`.

How to do it...

This recipe is covered in two main steps. First we will bundle the MP3 with the app, then we will write the ActionScript required to control its playback.

Bundling the MP3 file

Let us start by bundling the `.mp3` file with your app:

1. Open the AIR for iOS Settings panel by selecting **File | AIR for iOS Settings** from Flash's drop-down menu.

2. If it isn't already selected, click the panel's **General** tab.

3. At the bottom of the panel is the **Included files** list. Click on the **+** symbol above the list and select `chapter12\recipe7\music.mp3`. The file will now be bundled with your IPA file when the FLA is published.

4. Click on **OK** to close the AIR for iOS Settings panel.

Controlling playback

Now that the MP3 file has been included, let us focus on the ActionScript:

1. Create a document class and name it `Main`.

2. Import the classes required for this recipe:

```
import flash.display.MovieClip;
import flash.events.Event;
import flash.events.MouseEvent;
import flash.media.Sound;
import flash.media.SoundChannel;
import flash.net.URLRequest;
```

3. Declare the following member variables, which we will use to control the sound:

```
private var sound:Sound;
private var channel:SoundChannel;
private var pausePosition:int;
```

4. Within the constructor, add an event listener to each of the buttons and initially hide the Pause button from view:

```
public function Main() {
  pausePosition = 0;

  playBtn.addEventListener(MouseEvent.MOUSE_UP, playSound);
  pauseBtn.addEventListener(MouseEvent.MOUSE_UP, pauseSound);
  pauseBtn.visible = false;
}
```

Also notice that the `pausePosition` member variable has been initialized. Every time the MP3 is paused, we will update this variable with the time it was stopped at.

5. When the Play button is pressed, playback of the MP3 should either commence for the first time, or continue from where it was previously paused. We will also need to listen for the MP3 playing to completion. In addition, the Pause button should be shown, allowing the user to stop the MP3 at some point.

To manage all this, add the following event handler:

```
private function playSound(e:MouseEvent):void {
  if(sound == null)
  {
    var url:URLRequest = new URLRequest("music.mp3");
    sound = new Sound(url);
  }

  channel = sound.play(pausePosition);
  channel.addEventListener(Event.SOUND_COMPLETE, complete);
  toggleBtn();
}
```

6. When pausing playback of the MP3, the current point in time that was reached needs to be obtained and stored. Also, the Play button should be made available again, allowing the user to resume playback at their convenience. The following block of code handles this:

```
private function pauseSound(e:MouseEvent):void {
  pausePosition = channel.position;
  channel.stop();
  channel.removeEventListener(Event.SOUND_COMPLETE, complete);
  toggleBtn();
}
```

7. Add an event handler that is called when the MP3 plays to completion. This will reset the `pausePosition` member variable and also make the Play button visible again, allowing the user to restart playback of the MP3:

```
private function complete(e:Event):void {
  channel.removeEventListener(Event.SOUND_COMPLETE, complete);
  pausePosition = 0;
  toggleBtn();
}
```

8. Finally add the following support method, which is used to toggle between the Play and Pause button:

```
private function toggleBtn():void {
  playBtn.visible = !playBtn.visible;
  pauseBtn.visible = !pauseBtn.visible;
}
```

9. Now save both your class file and the FLA.

10. Publish the app and test it on your device. Toggle playback by pressing the Play and Pause buttons.

How it works...

When the Sound.play() method is called, a SoundChannel object is created and returned. A SoundChannel object is responsible for the playback of a single sound. Successive calls to Sound.play() will return additional SoundChannel objects, each playing their own copy of the Sound object's data.

While a call to play() will initially play the sound from start to finish, the SoundChannel class' API can be used to perform other operations. In this recipe, we utilized the class to provide pause and resume functionality to the user.

It is not possible to literally pause a sound during playback; the SoundChannel class only provides a method to stop playback. However, you can store the position in time that a sound was stopped at, and then replay the sound from that position later.

This was achieved by storing the position property before stopping the sound. The position property returns the sound's position in time, measured in milliseconds:

```
pausePosition = channel.position;
channel.stop();
```

Playback is resumed by passing the stored position to Sound.play(). Doing so plays the MP3 from the specified point in time and returns a new SoundChannel object representing it:

```
channel = sound.play(pausePosition);
```

Remember that the pausePosition member variable was initialized to 0 within the constructor. This guaranteed that the first time the Play button was pressed, playback of the MP3 would take place from the beginning.

When a sound has finished playing, its SoundChannel object will dispatch an Event. SOUND_COMPLETE event.

While we used an external MP3 for this recipe, playback of sound embedded within the library is also controlled in an identical manner.

For more information, perform a search within Adobe Community Help for `flash.media.Sound` and `flash.media.SoundChannel`.

Here is some final information regarding the control of sound.

Volume and panning

The volume and stereo panning of a sound can also be controlled. To do this, create a `flash.media.SoundTransform` object and either pass it to the `SoundChannel` object's `play()` method or the object's `soundTransform` property.

The `SoundTransform` object's constructor takes two parameters: the sound's volume and a value specifying its left-to-right panning. The volume ranges from `0` (silent) to `1` (full volume), while the panning ranges from `-1` (fully left) to `1` (fully right).

Following is an example where the sound is played at full volume and panned hard left:

```
soundTransform = new SoundTransform(1, -1);
soundChannel = sound.play(0, 1, soundTransform);
```

The sound's volume and panning can be adjusted at any point during playback. Simply make a change to your `SoundTransform` object and assign it to the `SoundChannel` object's `soundTransform` property:

```
soundTransform.pan = 0;
soundTransform.volume = 0.5;
soundChannel.soundTransform = soundTransfrom;
```

Note the use of the `SoundTransform` object's `pan` and `volume` properties to make the required alterations.

When testing stereo panning, be aware that you will need to use headphones as the loudspeaker found on iOS devices only delivers monophonic sound.

Global sound

As well as individual sounds, it is possible to control the volume and panning globally using the `flash.media.SoundMixer` class. It has its own `soundTransform` property, which when set affects all sound being played.

See also

► *Playing embedded audio*
► *Streaming audio*

13
Connectivity, Persistence, and URI Schemes

In this chapter, we will cover:

- ▸ Monitoring Internet connectivity
- ▸ Specifying a persistent Wi-Fi connection
- ▸ Referencing an app's common directories
- ▸ Writing files
- ▸ Reading files
- ▸ Launching system applications
- ▸ Launching the App Store
- ▸ Launching the Maps application
- ▸ Declaring device capabilities

Introduction

Significant ground has been covered during the course of the book but a few topics that we have touched upon deserve a little more attention. In this chapter, we will tie up those loose ends by exploring some additional uses for the application descriptor file, spending time understanding how to access the device's file system, and seeing how to open native iOS apps from Flash.

Monitoring Internet connectivity

It is a common occurrence for mobile applications to connect to the Internet at some point or another. For many, it will be for simple tasks, such as submitting a user's score or posting to a social network site. More sophisticated apps may attempt, for example, to aggregate data from various sources or even stream video from a Flash Media Server.

It is good practice to check that the device has an active Internet connection before trying to send or receive data. If an active connection cannot be found, then the app can adjust accordingly. For example, a game may hide its online leaderboards and remove any facilities for uploading scores.

This recipe will show you how to use AIR's `URLMonitor` class to check for the availability of an URL before calling it.

Getting ready

An FLA has been provided as a starting point.

From the book's accompanying code bundle, open `chapter13\recipe1\recipe.fla` into Flash Professional.

A dynamic text field named `output` covers the stage. We will write some ActionScript to check for Internet connectivity and display the results within the text field.

How to do it...

The `URLMonitor` class belongs to the `air.net` package and is not defined in the AIR runtime. Instead the class is included in the `aircore.swc` file, which must be statically linked to your FLA before it can be used.

Linking the SWC file

Let us link `aircore.swc` to the FLA before going on to write this recipe's ActionScript.

1. Select **File | ActionScript Settings** from Flash Professional's drop-down menu. This will open the ActionScript 3.0 Settings panel where you can add the SWC.

2. Select the **Library path** tab. Click on the **Add New Path** icon, which is represented by a **+** symbol.

3. Now click on the **Browse to SWC file** icon and select `aircore.swc` from your Flash installation folder. Its location depends on your version of Flash Professional. For CS5, browse to: `Adobe Flash CS5\AIK2.5\frameworks\libs\air\aircore.swc`. If you are using CS5.5, it is at: `Adobe Flash CS5.5\AIR2.6\frameworks\libs\air\aircore.swc`.

On Microsoft Windows, your installation of Flash Professional can be found at `C:\Program Files (x86)\Adobe`. On 32-bit versions of Windows, the path will be `C:\Program Files\Adobe`.

If you are using Mac OS X, then your Flash installation can be found at: `Macintosh HD/Applications`.

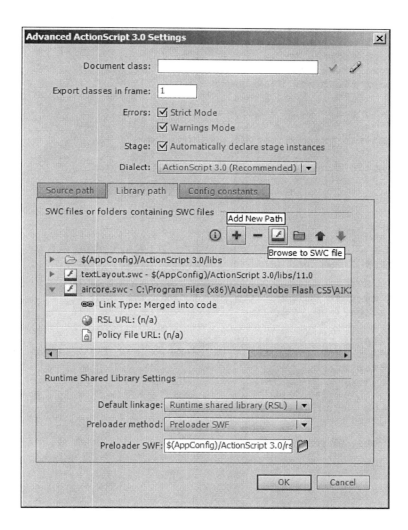

4. The SWC will be added to a list of libraries that will be used when publishing your app. Expand the SWC file's entry by clicking the icon to the left of its path, and ensure that its **Link Type** option is set to **Merged into code**.

5. Click on **OK** to close the panel.

Checking connectivity

With `aircore.swc` linked to your FLA, you can now use the API provided by the `URLMonitor` class. Okay, now let us write some ActionScript.

1. Create a document class and name it `Main`.

2. Add the following three import statements, and a `URLMonitor` member variable:

```
package {

    import air.net.URLMonitor;
    import flash.display.MovieClip;
    import flash.events.StatusEvent;
    import flash.net.URLRequest;

    public class Main extends MovieClip {

        private var monitor:URLMonitor;

        public function Main() {
            // constructor code
        }
    }
}
```

3. Create a `URLMonitor` instance that checks for the availability of a specific HTTP request, and listen for it dispatching `StatusEvent.STATUS`:

```
public function Main() {
    var request:URLRequest = new URLRequest(
        "http://www.yeahbutisitflash.com");

    monitor = new URLMonitor(request);
    monitor.addEventListener(StatusEvent.STATUS, statusUpdated);
    monitor.start();
}
```

4. Write a handler for the `URLMonitor` object's `STATUS` event:

```
private function statusUpdated(e:StatusEvent):void {
    if(monitor.available)
    {
        output.text = "Internet connection available.";
    }
    else
    {
        output.text = "Internet connection unavailable.";
    }
}
```

5. Save the class as `Main.as` and move back to your FLA.

6. Publish the FLA and test the app on your device. The following text should be output to the screen:

Internet connection available.

7. Try changing your document class to monitor a URL that doesn't exist. Republish and test your app. This time you will receive the following message:

Internet connection unavailable.

How it works...

The `URLMonitor` class monitors and detects changes in HTTP or HTTPS connectivity for a specified URL.

Its constructor accepts a `URLRequest` as a parameter, which contains the URL to probe. After creating the `URLMonitor` object, call its `start()` method to begin monitoring.

When the URL's availability is determined, the `URLMonitor` object dispatches `StatusEvent.STATUS`. You can query the `StatusEvent` object's `available` property to determine whether or not a connection to the URL can be made.

Monitoring continues until the `URLMonitor.stop()` method is called. It is also possible to determine if monitoring is currently taking place by checking the `URLMonitor.running` property.

For more information, perform a search for `air.net.URLMonitor` within Adobe Community Help.

There's more...

Here is some additional detail.

Monitoring sockets

The `air.net.SocketMonitor` class is similar to `URLMonitor` but detects connectivity changes for a host at a specified port. This is useful for applications, such as multiplayer games, where a socket server connection is required.

The `SocketMonitor` class' constructor expects the name of the host and its port to monitor:

```
monitor = new SocketMonitor("www.example.com", 6667);
```

Once instantiated, the `SocketMonitor` object is used in an identical manner to `URLMonitor`.

Polling interval

Both `URLMonitor` and `SocketMonitor` provide a `pollInterval` property that can be used to specify an interval, measured in milliseconds, for periodically polling the server.

By default, its value is `0`, meaning the server is polled immediately after `start()` is called, and thereafter only when the network status changes.

See also

▶ *Specifying a persistent Wi-Fi connection*

Specifying a persistent Wi-Fi connection

While many applications periodically connect to the Internet, there are some, such as chat clients and multiuser games that require a constant connection. These types of applications can be rendered useless if a persistent connection isn't available. By editing its application descriptor file, it is possible to stipulate that your app requires a persistent connection to a Wi-Fi network.

Let us see how to do this.

Getting ready

From the book's accompanying code bundle, open `chapter13\recipe2\recipe.fla` into Flash Professional and work from there. Its document class contains the code from the previous recipe, *Monitoring Internet connectivity*. Don't worry if you haven't attempted this recipe, as an understanding of it isn't required.

How to do it...

You can edit your application descriptor file from an external text editor or from Flash Professional. We will use Flash Professional.

1. Open the application descriptor file by selecting **File | Open** (*Ctrl + O* | *Cmd + O*) from Flash Professional's drop-down menu. From the file browser, select `recipe-app.xml`.

2. Scroll down the file until you find the following XML fragment:

```
<iPhone>
  <InfoAdditions>
    <![CDATA[<key>UIDeviceFamily</key>
            <array><string>1</string></array>]]>
  </InfoAdditions>
```

3. Within the CDATA node, add the following key-value pair to the XML:

```
<iPhone>
  <InfoAdditions>
    <![CDATA[<key>UIDeviceFamily</key>
            <array><string>1</string></array>
            <key>UIRequiresPersistentWiFi</key><true/>]]>
  </InfoAdditions>
```

4. Save the file.

5. Now publish the FLA, and install the resultant .ipa to your device.

6. Before launching the app, stop your device from automatically connecting to your Wi-Fi network. From your device's Settings, select **Wi-Fi** then tap on the icon to the far-right of your network's name. Doing so will take you to the settings page for that network. From here, press the **Forget this Network** button followed by **Forget**.

7. Now move back to the device's home screen and launch your app. iOS will notice that the app requires a persistent Wi-Fi connection and will display a native dialog box asking you to **Select a Wireless Network**. Select your network from the list and enter its password when prompted.

    Initially your app will report the following:

    Internet connection unavailable.

    But after a brief moment, it will detect your network connection and will update its status to the following:

    Internet connection available.

How it works...

Your FLA's application descriptor is an XML file that contains a list of iOS specific settings. Within the `<iPhone>` node is the `<infoAdditions>` node where you can set custom key-value pairs that can't be set within Flash. These are used to describe an app or used directly by it when launched.

For this recipe, we used the following key-value pair to alert the user when a persistent Wi-Fi connection could not be found:

```
<key>UIRequiresPersistentWiFi</key><true/>
```

When launched, the app detects the presence of this key and, therefore, checks to see if the device is connected to an active Wi-Fi network. If not, it will perform a search and display a network selection dialog containing a list of active Wi-Fi hot spots for the user to select from. Alternatively, if the device is in Airplane mode, then a dialog box is displayed informing the user of that fact.

Wi-Fi hardware can consume significant power. To preserve battery, iOS automatically switches off its Wi-Fi hardware after 30 minutes. If your app uses the `UIRequiresPersistentWiFi` key, then the Wi-Fi hardware will stay enabled for as long as the app remains active. If the device's screen locks, then the app is considered inactive and the Wi-Fi connection may be lost.

You can switch the `UIRequiresPersistentWiFi` key off by setting its value to `<false/>`. Alternatively, remove the entire entry from the application descriptor file.

See also

▶ *Editing the application descriptor file, Chapter 3*

Referencing an app's common directories

An iOS app resides within its own directory and has access to common sub-directories that are contained within it.

This recipe will show you how to reference each of these directories.

Getting ready

We will use `chapter13\recipe3\recipe.fla` from the book's accompanying code bundle as a starting point. Open it into Flash Professional.

A dynamic text field named `output` can be found on the stage. We will use this text field to display the native file path of each of the app's common directories.

How to do it...

Perform the following steps:

1. Create a new document class and name it `Main`.

2. Import the `File` class:
   ```
   import flash.display.MovieClip;
   import flash.filesystem.File;
   ```

3. Within the constructor, write each directory's native path to the `output` text field:
   ```
   public function Main(){
     output.text =
       "Application Directory:\n" +
       File.applicationDirectory.nativePath +
       "\n\nApplication Storage Directory:\n" +
       File.applicationStorageDirectory.nativePath +
       "\n\nDocuments Directory:\n" +
       File.documentsDirectory.nativePath +
       "\n\nUser Directory:\n" +
       File.userDirectory.nativePath;
   }
   ```

4. Save the class and when prompted, name the file `Main.as`.

5. Finally, publish the FLA and test it on your device. The paths for all four directories will be shown on screen.

How it works...

The directory that an app is stored within is known as **Application Home** and has a path similar to: `/var/mobile/Applications/97C9F144-E97A-40BB-A4CD-82FF31CA2A3C`. The string at the end of the path is an ID that uniquely identifies the application and is used to name the home directory during installation.

The `flash.filesystem.File` class makes several constants available that can be used to reference Application Home and its various sub-directories. These constants let you access the directories in a platform-independent manner, eliminating the need to remember lengthy native paths. They are:

- ▶ `File.userDirectory`: The Application Home directory
- ▶ `File.applicationDirectory`: A read-only directory that contains the application binary and any files bundled with it, such as the default launch screen
- ▶ `File.applicationStorageDirectory`: Any local shared object data is stored here
- ▶ `File.documentsDirectory`: Any application-specific data can be written to and retrieved from this directory

Of the four, `applicationDirectory` and `documentsDirectory` are perhaps the two that are used most often. Although you can't write to the Application directory, you can read from it and even copy files from it to other locations.

The Documents directory is useful for state management, allowing data files required by the application to be stored. These files can be anything, from simple preference files to images created by the user. This directory's contents are backed-up by iTunes.

If you wish to temporarily store files, then a `tmp` sub-directory is provided within Application Home. To reference folders that aren't provided as constants, use the `File` class' `resolvePath()` method to modify an existing `File` object. For example:

```
var tmpDir:File = File.userDirectory.resolvePath("tmp");
```

A `nativePath` property is also provided, allowing you to retrieve a directory's native path from a `File` object reference:

```
var nativePath:String = File.applicationDirectory.nativePath;
```

This is useful when using an API that expects a native path rather than a `File` object.

For more information, perform a search for `flash.filesystem.File` within Adobe Community Help.

Here are some more options when working with the `File` class and directories.

Creating directories

As well as referencing existing directories, the `File` class lets you create them using its `createDirectory()` method. The following two lines of code create a directory named `images` within the app's Documents directory:

```
var dir:File = File.documentsDirectory.resolvePath("images");
dir.createDirectory();
```

You can also delete a directory using either `deleteDirectory()` or `deleteDirectoryAsync()`. Listen for `Event.COMPLETE` when deleting a directory asynchronously.

- ▸ *Writing files*
- ▸ *Reading files*

Writing files

AIR provides a file system API that can be used to write files of any type to the device.

Let us see how to write a text file containing simple preferences data that might, for example, be used by a game.

An FLA has been provided as a starting point for this recipe.

From the book's accompanying support files, open `chapter13\recipe4\recipe.fla` into Flash Professional.

Sitting on the stage is a dynamic text field named `output`. We will write some preferences data to the device and use the text field to indicate when the data has been written.

How to do it...

The `flash.filesystem` package contains classes that provide file system access. Let us make use of some of those classes to write to the device.

1. Create a document class and name it `Main`.

2. Import the following classes:
```
import flash.display.MovieClip;
import flash.events.Event;
import flash.events.IOErrorEvent;
import flash.filesystem.File;
import flash.filesystem.FileMode;
import flash.filesystem.FileStream;
```

3. Add a `File` and `FileStream` member variable:
```
private var file:File;
private var stream:FileStream;
```

4. Create a method that writes the preferences data to the device, and call it from the constructor:
```
public function Main() {
  savePreferences();
}

private function savePreferences():void {
  file = File.documentsDirectory.resolvePath("prefs.txt");
  stream = new FileStream();
  stream.addEventListener(IOErrorEvent.IO_ERROR, ioError);
  stream.addEventListener(Event.CLOSE, fileSaved);
  stream.openAsync(file, FileMode.WRITE);
  stream.writeUTFBytes(
    "music_vol=0.5&sound_vol=0.7&difficulty=easy");
  stream.close();
}
```

5. Add a handler that gets called if an error occurs when writing the preferences data:
```
private function ioError(e:IOErrorEvent):void {
  output.appendText(e.errorID + ": " + e.text);
}
```

6. Add a second handler that gets called once the file has been successfully written to the device's file system:
```
private function fileSaved(e:Event):void {
  output.appendText("File Saved\n");
}
```

7. Save the class file and when prompted name it `Main.as`.

8. Publish the FLA and test it on your device. The preferences file will be written and the following text will be shown on screen:

   File Saved

How it works...

This recipe took advantage of the `flash.filesystem.File` and `flash.filesystem.FileStream` classes to write data to the device's file system. The data was represented by a series of name-value pairs that were written to the app's Documents directory as a text file.

When writing to a file, a reference representing it must first be obtained using the `File` class—this is true even for files that have yet to be created. As well as representing files, the `File` class can also be used to represent directories. A directory reference can also be refined by using `File.resolvePath()` to target a file or sub-folder relative to it.

The following line of code shows a `File` object being created for the preferences file:

```
file = File.documentsDirectory.resolvePath("prefs.txt");
```

The next step is to instantiate a `FileStream` object and use the `openAsync()` method to initialize it for writing:

```
stream = new FileStream();
stream.openAsync(file, FileMode.WRITE);
```

As you can see above, the `File` object is passed to `openAsync()`. As a second argument, the `FileMode.WRITE` constant is also passed, and indicates that data is to be written to the file. If the specified file doesn't exist, then `openAsync()` will create it. If it already exists, then its contents will be wiped.

The `FileStream` class dispatches various events when writing data. It dispatches `IOErrorEvent.IO_ERROR` if it can't create or find the file, and `Event.CLOSE` once it has finished writing data to it. Listeners for both events should be added:

```
stream = new FileStream();
stream.addEventListener(IOErrorEvent.IO_ERROR, ioError);
stream.addEventListener(Event.CLOSE, fileSaved);
stream.openAsync(file, FileMode.WRITE);
```

With the file opened for writing, `writeUTFBytes()` is called to actually write text to the file:

```
stream.writeUTFBytes(
  "music_vol=0.5&sound_vol=0.7&difficulty=easy");
```

The final step is to close the `FileStream` object, preventing any more data from being written:

```
stream.close();
```

It is important to understand that the file is not guaranteed to have been fully written by the time you call the `close()` method. When writing a significant amount of data to the device, it may take some time. If this is the case, then the `FileStream` object will delay closing the file until after all the data is written. Once it is finished, the `FileStream` object will dispatch `Event.CLOSE`.

While you can write files anywhere within the Application Home directory, due to sandbox restrictions, you can't write outside of it.

You can obtain more information regarding the `flash.filesystem.FileStream`, `flash.filesystem.File`, and `flash.filesystem.FileMode` classes from Adobe Community Help.

There's more...

Here is some more detail that should come in handy when writing to the device's local file system.

Working with data formats

The `FileStream` class provides many methods for writing data. Your choice of method depends on the data format you wish to use.

For example, when working with text, you have the `writeUTF()`, `writeUTFBytes()`, and `writeMultiByte()` methods available. If you opt to work with byte arrays, then there are `writeByte()` and `writeBytes()` methods. You can even write primitives using `writeBoolean()`, `writeDouble()`, `writeFloat()`, `writeInt()`, and `writeShort()`.

Writing synchronously

This recipe used `openAsync()`, meaning data could be written to the device asynchronously. Asynchronous operations take place in the background, allowing the execution of your ActionScript to continue rather than being blocked until the operation completes.

As an alternative to `openAsync()`, the `FileStream` class also provides `open()`, which allows data to be handled synchronously. Although execution will be blocked until the operation is complete, working synchronously is more straight forward as you aren't required to register for events. In the following code snippet, you can see an alternative version of `savePreferences()` method, which writes data synchronously:

```
private function savePreferences():void {
    file = File.documentsDirectory.resolvePath("prefs.txt");
    stream = new FileStream();
```

```
stream.open(file, FileMode.WRITE);
stream.writeUTFBytes(
  "music_vol=0.5&sound_vol=0.7&difficulty=easy");
stream.close();
output.appendText("File Saved\n");
}
```

 Examples throughout this book that write to the device's file system, do so synchronously to help maintain focus on the task at hand.

Monitoring progress

When asynchronously writing to a file, the `FileStream` object will periodically dispatch `OutputProgressEvent.OUTPUT_PROGRESS`. From this event object, you can monitor the progress of the write operation by checking its `bytesPending` and `bytesTotal` properties. The `bytesPending` property specifies the number of bytes that have still to be written, while `bytesTotal` represents the number of bytes that have been written so far.

Persistence

Writing to the file system allows you to save your application's state to the device. When the app is re-launched, it can use this saved data to start from where it previously left off.

As an alternative to AIR's file system API you can also use Flash's `SharedObject` class to manage state. In addition, small amounts of private data can be stored using the `EncryptedLocalStore` class introduced to iOS in AIR 3.0. Detail regarding encrypted local storage can be found within Adobe Community Help.

Another option is to store your data within a local SQLite database and use ActionScript to access it. Apple itself uses SQLite databases on iOS devices to store information, such as contacts.

Relational database theory and the SQLite API are outside the scope of this book. However, you can find more information on the subject from Adobe Community Help or by visiting the SQLite website at: `sqlite.org`.

See also

▸ *Saving application state, Chapter 4*

▸ *Referencing an app's common directories*

▸ *Reading files*

Reading files

AIR provides a file system API that can be used to read files of any type from the device.

In this recipe, we will see how to load a file previously written to the device.

Getting ready

If you haven't already done so, complete the *Writing files* recipe before proceeding.

You can continue to work with the code you wrote during that recipe. Alternatively, from the book's accompanying code bundle, open `chapter13\recipe5\recipe.fla` into Flash Professional and work from there.

How to do it...

Let us update the FLA's document class to load and display the preferences that were written to the device.

1. Open the document class.

2. Add a method that will load the preferences data:

```
private function loadPreferences():void {
   file = File.documentsDirectory.resolvePath("prefs.txt");
   stream = new FileStream();
   stream.addEventListener(IOErrorEvent.IO_ERROR, ioError);
   stream.addEventListener(Event.COMPLETE, fileLoaded);
   stream.openAsync(file, FileMode.READ);
}
```

3. Alter the class' `fileSaved()` handler, making it call the preceding method:

```
private function fileSaved(e:Event):void {
   output.appendText("File Saved\n");
   loadPreferences();
}
```

4. A COMPLETE event will be dispatched when the file has been loaded. Add a handler for it that parses and displays the file's preferences data:

```
private function fileLoaded(e:Event):void {
   var prefs:String = stream.readUTFBytes(stream.bytesAvailable);
   stream.close();

   var vars:URLVariables = new URLVariables(prefs);
```

```
    output.appendText(
      "File Loaded\n" +
      "music volume: " + vars.music_vol + "\n" +
      "sound volume: " + vars.sound_vol + "\n" +
      "difficulty: " + vars.difficulty + "\n"
    );
  }
```

5. The `fileLoaded()` handler makes use of Flash's `URLVariables` class to decode the preferences data. Add `URLVariables` to the document class' list of import statements:

```
import flash.net.URLVariables;
```

6. Save `Main.as`.

7. Publish the FLA and test it on your device.

The app will first write the preferences data to the file system before loading it back and displaying the preferences on screen.

How it works...

The steps required for reading data from the device's file system are almost identical to writing data.

First a `File` object is created that references the target file:

```
file = File.documentsDirectory.resolvePath("prefs.txt");
```

Then a `FileStream` object is instantiated and initialized using the `openAsync()` method. When a file is being read rather than written, `FileMode.READ` is passed as the method's second argument:

```
stream = new FileStream();
stream.openAsync(file, FileMode.READ);
```

And while `FileSystem.close()` is called immediately after `openAsync()` when writing a file, when reading, it shouldn't be called until the file's entire data has been obtained. This can be determined by listening for the `FileStream` object dispatching `Event.COMPLETE`.

To actually obtain the data, one of the `FileSystem` class' read methods is required. For this recipe, `readUTFBytes()` was used and the number of bytes to read from the file's buffer was passed to it:

```
var prefs:String = stream.readUTFBytes(stream.bytesAvailable);
stream.close();
```

The `FileStream` class' read-only `bytesAvailable` property was used when calling `readUTFBytes()`. This property states the size of the file once it is completely loaded. Also, notice that the file stream is closed after its data is read as there is no longer a need for it.

There's more...

You will find AIR's file system API invaluable for many of your iOS projects. Before we leave the subject, here are some final pieces of information to take with you.

Working with data formats

The `FileStream` class provides many methods for reading data from a file. Your choice of method depends on the format of the data you are reading.

For example, when working with text, the `readUTF()`, `readUTFBytes()`, and `readMultiBytes()` methods are available. If the file contains a byte array, then you can use the `readByte()` and `readBytes()` methods. Primitive types can be obtained using `readBoolean()`, `readDouble()`, `readFloat()`, `readInt()`, and `readShort()`.

Reading synchronously

As with the previous recipe, `openAsync()` was used, meaning the file was handled asynchronously. The following code uses the `open()` method instead to synchronously read this recipe's preferences file:

```
private function loadPreferences():void {
    file = File.documentsDirectory.resolvePath("prefs.txt");
    stream = new FileStream();
    stream.open(file, FileMode.READ);
    var prefs:String = stream.readUTFBytes(stream.bytesAvailable);
    stream.close();
}
```

> Examples throughout this book that read from the device's file system, do so synchronously to help maintain focus on the task at hand.

Monitoring progress

When asynchronously reading from a file, the `FileStream` object will periodically dispatch `ProgressEvent.PROGRESS`. From this event object, you can monitor the reading progress by checking its `bytesLoaded` and `bytesTotal` properties. The `bytesLoaded` property specifies the number of bytes that have been loaded, while `bytesTotal` represents the number of bytes that will be loaded if the file successfully loads.

Deleting files

You can delete a file using the `File` class' `deleteFile()` or `deleteFileAsync()` method. Listen for `Event.COMPLETE` when deleting asynchronously.

Other file modes

Two other file modes are available: `FileMode.APPEND` and `FileMode.UPDATE`.

The Append mode always writes to the end of the file, meaning that an existing file's data will be added to rather than destroyed.

Update mode lets you both read from and write to a file using a single file stream. To successfully manage this, the `FileStream` class provides the `position` property, which can be used to determine and set the current position within the file. The `position` property is incremented every time a byte is written or read. It is also possible to move to any point within a file by setting this property. When this is done, the next read or write operation will take place from that position.

See also

 ▸ *Referencing an app's common directories*
 ▸ *Writing files*

Launching system applications

On occasions you may want your app to provide functionality that is already available from iOS's system applications. To guarantee a consistent and familiar experience, it is possible to launch certain system apps rather than performing the task internally within your own. To enable this, iOS supports various URI schemes which can be used to launch a specific application.

In this recipe, you will learn how to use the `mailto` URI scheme to open and send e-mail from the Mail application.

Getting ready

From the book's accompanying code bundle, load `chapter13\recipe6\recipe.fla` into Flash Professional and use it as a starting point.

Sitting on its stage is a button with an instance name of `mailBtn`. When pressed, it will launch the device's Mail application and pre-populate an e-mail for the user to send.

Let us write the ActionScript required to make this happen.

How to do it...

We will make use of both Flash's `navigateToURL()` function and `URLRequest` class to launch the Mail application.

1. Create a document class and name it `Main`.

2. Import the following:

```
import flash.display.MovieClip;
import flash.events.MouseEvent;
import flash.net.navigateToURL;
import flash.net.URLRequest;
```

3. Within the constructor, listen for the button being pressed:

```
public function Main() {
   mailBtn.addEventListener(MouseEvent.MOUSE_UP, sendMail);
}
```

4. Create a method that will launch the Mail application and compose an e-mail. Within it, initialize strings that represent the recipient's e-mail address, the subject heading, and the e-mail's body:

```
private function sendMail(e:MouseEvent):void {
   var address:String = "someone@somewhere.com";
   var subject:String = "Flash iOS Apps Cookbook";
   var body:String = "Sent from the Mail application.";
}
```

In this code, replace someone@somewhere.com with the e-mail address you wish to target. For testing purposes, use your own.

5. Staying within the `sendMail()` method, construct a URL that uses the `mailto` URI scheme:

```
private function sendMail(e:MouseEvent):void {
   var address:String = "someone@somewhere.com";
   var subject:String = "Flash iOS Apps Cookbook";
   var body:String = "Sent from the Mail application.";
   var url:String = "mailto:" + address + "?subject=" +
     subject + "&body=" + body;
   var request:URLRequest = new URLRequest(url);
}
```

6. Finally, launch the Mail application by passing the URL to Flash's `navigateToURL()` function:

```
private function sendMail(e:MouseEvent):void {
   var address:String = "someone@somewhere.com";
   var subject:String = "Flash iOS Apps Cookbook";
   var body:String = "Sent from the Mail application.";
```

```
    var url:String = "mailto:" + address + "?subject=" +
      subject + "&body=" + body;
    var request:URLRequest = new URLRequest(url);
    navigateToURL(request);
}
```

7. Save the class file and when prompted name it `Main.as`.

8. Publish the FLA and test the app on your device. Tapping the button will open the Mail application, complete with a pre-populated e-mail.

How it works...

The `mailto` URI is used to launch the Mail application and compose an e-mail. The URI must be constructed and formatted correctly for the Mail application to understand it. Once constructed, pass the request to Flash's `navigateToURL()` package-level function to actually launch the app.

As a minimum, the recipient's e-mail address must be specified within the `mailto` URI:

```
mailto:someone@somewhere.com
```

You can also pre-fill fields within the e-mail by adding query string parameters to the URI. For example, the following pre-populates the e-mail's subject and body fields:

```
mailto:someone@somewhere.com?subject=Test&body=This is a test
```

The supported query string parameters are as follows:

▸ `subject`: The e-mail's Subject field

▸ `body`: The e-mail's body

▸ `to`: Allows the addition of more than one recipient within the To field

▸ `cc`: Allows recipients to be added to the carbon copy field

▸ `bcc`: Allows recipients to be added to the blind carbon copy field

When adding multiple recipients to a field, use a comma to separate each address.

The e-mail's body can be specified as plain text or HTML. Here is an example using HTML:

```
mailto:someone@somewhere.com?body=<a href='http://www.
yeahbutisitflash.com'>Yeah But Is It Flash?</a>
```

The `mailto` specification prohibits the selection of an e-mail account within the URI. When multiple accounts are associated with a device, the default account is always used. Attachments are also unsupported.

Launching a system application forces the current app into the background on iOS 4 or above. On pre-iOS 4 devices, the current app is closed completely. It is, therefore, advisable to store your app's state before opening a system application. When the user is finished using the system application, it will be their responsibility to re-launch your app from the device's home screen or from the fast app switcher.

There's more...

We have covered the `mailto` URI scheme, now let us look at a few other applications that can be opened by `navigateToURL()`.

Dialing a phone number

The `tel` URI scheme can be used to launch the iPhone's telephony application and dial a specified number. As the following example shows, the formatting of the `tel` URI is simple:

```
tel:1-408-555-5555
```

Most valid phone numbers are accepted, but to prevent malicious behavior, URIs containing the * or # characters aren't. When using the `tel` URI scheme, a phone number must always be specified within the URI.

Sending SMS messages

The iPhone's Messages application can be opened using the `sms` URI scheme. An optional phone number can be included, indicating that a new SMS message is to be created:

```
sms:1-408-555-1212
```

If the phone number is omitted, then the Messages application will open but won't create a message for the user to send.

It is not possible to pre-fill the message with text or specify more than one recipient.

Playing a YouTube video

The `navigateToURL()` function can be used to launch the native YouTube application. There is no specific URI scheme for this; instead a URL targeting the YouTube server is used.

Simply construct a URL containing the ID of a video you would like to play. The URL should take the following format: `http://www.youtube.com/watch?v=ID`. You can obtain a video's ID by visiting the YouTube website and extracting it from the browser's address bar.

Here is an example URL that can be passed to `navigateToURL()`:

```
http://www.youtube.com/watch?v=awNMSiGzuRk
```

URI schemes within HTML

URI schemes can also be embedded as links within HTML pages. This allows the user to launch system applications from within a `StageWebView` object. For example, the following HTML link will initiate a phone call:

```
<a href="tel:1-408-555-5555">Call us now!</a>
```

For more information regarding the `StageWebView` class, refer to *Chapter 11*.

See also

- ▸ *Exiting gracefully from an app, Chapter 3*
- ▸ *Opening a web page within Safari, Chapter 11*
- ▸ *Launching the App Store*
- ▸ *Launching the Maps application*

Launching the App Store

Publishers often promote their back catalogue within their latest releases, providing direct links to each of their products within the App Store. This not only makes the purchase process incredibly easy for the user, but also encourages impulse buying.

The App Store can be launched directly from your AIR for iOS app by passing a specific iTunes URL to Flash's `navigateToURL()` function. Let us see how to do this.

Getting ready

An FLA has been provided as a starting point for this recipe.

From the book's accompanying code bundle, open `chapter13\recipe7\recipe.fla` into Flash Professional. Sitting on its stage is a button named `storeBtn`.

Let us write some ActionScript to launch the App Store when this button is pressed.

How to do it...

We will open the App Store page for WeeWorld's WeeMee Avatar Creator app. First we will obtain a URL to the app's page, then we will write the actual code to link to it from our app.

Obtaining the app's URL

The URL format is complicated to construct. To simplify the process, Apple has created the online Link Maker tool.

1. Visit its web page at `http://itunes.apple.com/linkmaker`.

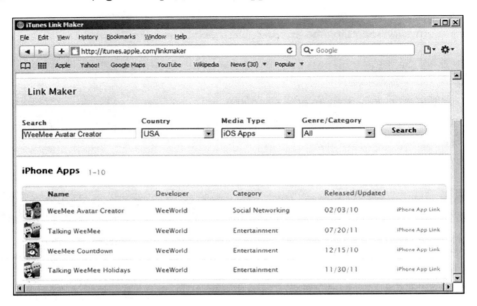

2. Define a search by filling in the page's fields. Enter **WeeMee Avatar Creator** into the **Search** field, set the country to **USA**, and select **iOS Apps** from the **Media Type** drop-down menu.

3. Click on the **Search** button on the right-hand side of the page to initiate a search. A list of matches will be generated and shown at the bottom of the page.

4. Look for **WeeMee Avatar Creator** listed within the **iPhone Apps** section and click on **iPhone App Link** on the right-hand side of its entry. A dialog box will appear containing details for the app.

5. Copy the **Direct Link** URL from the dialog box.

Linking to the app from ActionScript

Now let us write the ActionScript required to launch the App Store page.

1. Within Flash Professional, create a new document class and name it `Main`.

2. Add the required import statements and listen for `storeBtn` being pressed:

```
package {

    import flash.display.MovieClip;
    import flash.events.MouseEvent;
    import flash.net.navigateToURL;
    import flash.net.URLRequest;

    public class Main extends MovieClip {

      public function Main() {
        storeBtn.addEventListener(MouseEvent.MOUSE_UP,
          openAppStore);
      }
    }
}
```

3. Add an event handler for the button, and within it open the App Store using the URL obtained from the Link Maker tool:

```
private function openAppStore(e:MouseEvent):void {
    var url:String = "http://itunes.apple.com/us/app/weemee-avatar-
    creator/id352506978?mt=8&uo=4";
    var request:URLRequest = new URLRequest(url);
    navigateToURL(request);
}
```

4. Now save the document class' file, and when prompted name it `Main.as`.
5. Publish and test the app on your device. Tap the button to open the WeeMee Avatar Creator's entry within the App Store application.

How it works...

Passing an app's valid iTunes URL to Flash's `navigateToURL()` package-level function will open the App Store application for that app. The URL for a particular app can be retrieved from Apple's Link Maker online tool.

It is not just the App Store that can be opened from within your app. The Link Maker can create links to content on the iTunes Store and the iBookstore too. Simply perform a search for the content in question then obtain its URL.

The various stores can also be launched from an HTML link within a `StageWebView` object. The Link Maker provides the required HTML within the same dialog box as the **Direct Link** URL. You can copy it from the **HTML With Link** text box.

See also

- ▶ *Rendering a web page within an app, Chapter 11*
- ▶ *Launching system applications*
- ▶ *Launching the Maps application*

Launching the Maps application

Being location aware, mapping is an integral part of iOS. The native Maps application lets you find where you currently are, search for nearby points of interest, and obtain turn-by-turn directions. Many developers take advantage of Maps by opening it directly from their own app, providing the user with a consistent experience.

Let us see how to do this.

Getting ready

From the book's accompanying code bundle, open `chapter13\recipe8\recipe.fla` into Flash Professional.

Sitting on its stage is a button with an instance name of `mapBtn`. We will add code to show the location of Adobe's headquarters when this button is pressed.

How to do it...

We will use Flash's `URLRequest` class and `navigateToURL()` function to open the Maps application.

1. Create a document class and name it `Main`.

2. Import the classes required for this recipe and listen for the button being pressed:

```
package {

    import flash.display.MovieClip;
    import flash.events.MouseEvent;
    import flash.net.navigateToURL;
    import flash.net.URLRequest;

    public class Main extends MovieClip {

        public function Main() {
            mapBtn.addEventListener(MouseEvent.MOUSE_UP,
                openMaps);
        }
    }
}
```

3. Finally, add an event handler for the button and within it open the Maps application at Adobe's headquarters:

```
private function openMaps(e:MouseEvent):void {
    var addr:String = "Adobe Systems Inc, 345 Park Avenue, " +
        "San Jose, CA";
    var url:String = "http://maps.google.com/maps?q=" + addr;
    var request:URLRequest = new URLRequest(url);
    navigateToURL(request);
}
```

4. Save the class and when prompted name its file `Main.as`.

5. Publish and test the app on your device. Tap the button. The native Maps application will open and the location of Adobe's headquarters will be shown.

How it works...

If your app contains address or location information, you can forward that information to the Maps application. To do this, construct a URL and pass it to Flash's `navigateToURL()` package-level function. The URL should target the Google Maps server and contain one or more Google Maps parameters.

For this recipe, the Google Maps query parameter was used to map the location of Adobe's headquarters:

```
http://maps.google.com/maps?q=Adobe Systems Inc,
345 Park Avenue, San Jose, CA
```

The Maps application supports many of the Google Maps parameters but not all of them. Here is a list of those that are supported:

Parameter	Description
q	The query parameter. Its value is treated as if it had been typed into the query box on the Google Maps web page.
near	Can be used as the location part of a query.
ll	The latitude and longitude for the map's center point.
sll	The latitude and longitude from where a business search should take place.
spn	An approximate latitude and longitude span. The zoom level will be adjusted to fit.
sspn	A screen span. The zoom level will be adjusted to fit.
t	The type of map to display. Can select m for maps, k for satellite, or h for hybrid.
z	The map's zoom level ranging from 1 to 20.
saddr	The source address to use when generating directions.

Parameter	Description
daddr	The destination address to use when generating directions.
latlng	A custom ID format used by Google to identify businesses.
cid	Another custom ID format used by Google to identify businesses.

Launching the Maps application forces the current app into the background on iOS 4 or above. On pre-iOS 4 devices, the current app is closed completely. It is, therefore, advisable to store your app's state before opening Maps. When the user is finished with the Maps application, it will be their responsibility to re-launch your app from the device's home screen or from the fast app switcher.

Visit `http://mapki.com/wiki/Google_Map_Parameters` for a comprehensive description of each of the Google Maps parameters.

There's more...

Here are some other common uses for the Maps application.

Generating directions

You can instruct the Maps application to generate directions between two addresses. The following ActionScript snippet uses Google Maps' `saddr` and `daddr` parameters to produce driving directions between Adobe's and Apple's headquarters:

```
var saddr:String = "Adobe Systems, 345 Park Avenue, San Jose";
var daddr:String = "Apple, 1 Infinite Loop, Cupertino";
var url:String = "http://maps.google.com/maps?" +
  "saddr=" + saddr + "&daddr=" + daddr;
var request:URLRequest = new URLRequest(url);
navigateToURL(request);
```

Mapping your current location

You can also show the user their current location. This can be done by determining their approximate location using AIR's `Geolocation` class and passing that information to the Maps application.

The following ActionScript obtains the latitude and longitude from a `GeolocationEvent` object, and constructs a Google Maps URL:

```
private function geoUpdated(e:GeolocationEvent):void {
  var lat:Number = e.latitude;
  var lon:Number = e.longitude;
  var url:String = "http://maps.google.com/maps?" +
    "ll=" + lat + "," + lon;
  var request:URLRequest = new URLRequest(url);
  navigateToURL(request);
}
```

The `11` property is used when specifying a location's latitude and longitude. Both values are separated by a comma.

See also

▸ *Determining your current location, Chapter 9*

▸ *Launching system applications*

▸ *Launching the App Store*

Declaring device capabilities

The hardware and software capabilities of devices vary across the iOS family. For example, some feature a built-in camera, whereas others do not. It is important that your app can only be downloaded and installed on devices that are compatible with it. To enable this, the required capabilities can be explicitly set for your app.

You can't specify these capabilities directly from Flash Professional. Instead, you need to edit your FLA's application descriptor file. Let us see how to do this for an app that requires the presence of the native Messages application and an on-board GPS receiver.

Getting ready

From the book's accompanying code bundle, open `chapter13\recipe9\recipe.fla` and work from there. The FLA's stage is empty but its AIR for iOS settings have already been applied letting you easily publish once you are ready.

How to do it...

Let us edit your application descriptor file from within Flash Professional.

1. From Flash Professional, select **File | Open** and select `recipe-app.xml`.

2. Scroll down the file until you find the following XML fragment:

```
<iPhone>
  <InfoAdditions>
    <![CDATA[<key>UIDeviceFamily</key>
           <array><string>1</string></array>]]>
  </InfoAdditions>
```

3. Within the CDATA node, add the following key-value pair to the XML:

```
<iPhone>
  <InfoAdditions>
    <![CDATA[<key>UIDeviceFamily</key>
            <array><string>1</string></array>
            <key>UIRequiredDeviceCapabilities</key>
            <array>
              <string>sms</string>
              <string>gps</string>
            </array>]]>
  </InfoAdditions>
```

4. Save the file.

5. Publish the FLA. If you have an iOS device that lacks either the native Messages application or GPS, then try installing the .ipa file. You will receive an error message similar to the following one:

The app "c13 r9" was not installed because it is not compatible with this device.

How it works...

Your FLA's application descriptor is an XML file that contains a list of iOS specific settings. Within the <iPhone> node is the <infoAdditions> node where you can set custom key-value pairs that can't be set within Flash. These are used to describe an app or used directly by it when launched.

The UIRequiredDeviceCapabilities key is used to specify the capabilities required by your app. If the device lacks the capabilities, then the app won't be installed.

Each capability should be listed within an <array> node:

```
<key>UIRequiredDeviceCapabilities</key>
<array>
  <string>sms</string>
  <string>gps</string>
</array>
```

This example XML snippet shows the `sms` and `gps` capabilities being listed. The `sms` capability stipulates that your app requires the presence of the Messages application, while `gps` states that the device should include GPS hardware.

The following capabilities can be specified with the `UIRequiredDeviceCapabilities` key:

Capability	Description
telephony	The app requires the presence of the Phone application.
wifi	Networking features of the device will be accessed by the app.
sms	The app requires the presence of the Messages application.
still-camera	A camera is required to capture photos.
auto-focus-camera	A camera with auto-focus is required to capture photos.
front-facing-camera	The app requires a forward-facing camera.
camera-flash	A camera flash is required for taking photos or shooting video.
video-camera	A camera with video capabilities is required on the device.
accelerometer	Access to an accelerometer is required.
location-services	The app will attempt to retrieve the device's current location.
gps	The device should include GPS hardware for location tracking.
microphone	A built-in microphone is required by the app.

The capabilities listed within the application descriptor file are also used by the App Store to prevent users from downloading apps that they can't run.

Try to keep an eye on the official Apple documents as the list of device capabilities grows with each new release of iOS: `http://developer.apple.com/library/ios/#documentation/general/Reference/InfoPlistKeyReference/Articles/iPhoneOSKeys.html`.

Of course, whether you can take advantage of any new capabilities will also depend on future releases of AIR or any native extensions you decide to use.

There's more...

A final word regarding device capabilities.

Dropped support for ARMv6 devices

Apps published using AIR 2.6 and above do not support older ARMv6 iOS devices. AIR automatically includes the `armv7` and `opengles-2` capabilities in the application descriptor file in order to prevent owners of older iOS devices from downloading and installing these apps.

You do not need to explicitly add these two capabilities to the application descriptor file.

See also

> ▸ *Editing the application descriptor file, Chapter 3*

Index

Symbols

.ipa file 51
.swf file 90
 writeFile() method 318
 writePng()method 318

A

accelerationX property
 UPDATE 264
accelerationY property 264
accelerationZ property 264
accelerometer
 about 221, 247
 axes 265
 changes, responding to 261, 263
 device orientation, determining 265
 high-pass filter, applying 266
 low-pass filter, applying 265
 muted property 266
 orientation 265
 shake, detecting 267
 working 263, 264
Accelerometer class 263, 266
AccelerometerEvent.UPDATE event 263
Accelerometer.setRequestedUpdateInterval()
 method 263
accUpdated() event 270
accUpdated() handler 264
ActionScript
 bitmap animation, performing 187-189
 bitmaps, accessing 175
 image sizes, managing 178
 size restrictions 178
 working 177

addBitmapData() method 276
ad-hoc provisioning profile. *See* **test
 provisioning profile**
ADL 57
ADL (Ctrl + Enter | Cmd + Enter) 116
Adobe AIR 42
ADT 42, 58
**Advanced ActionScript 3.0 Settings panel
 119**
afterOrientation property 243
ahead-of-time compilation 58
AIR
 creating, for deployment settings 54-56
 creating, for general setting 50, 51
 creating, for iOS document 44, 46
AIR creation, for iOS document
 about 44
 frame rate 47
 requirements 44
 stage dimensions 46
 steps 44, 46
 working 46
AIR Debug Launcher. *See* **ADL
 ADL 8**
AIR Development Tool. *See* **ADT**
AIR for iOS
 about 42
 advantage 94
AIR, for iOS app
 web page, downloading within Safari 303
AIR, for iOS deployment setting
 about 54
 App ID, specifying 56
 deployment, types 56
 steps 54, 55

D

daddr parameter 382
Debug | End Debug Session (Alt + F12) 90
default aspect ratio
 auto aspect ratio 236
 FLA to landscape aspect ratio, locking 235
 setting 234
 working 235
default camera app
 about 282
 ActionScript, writing 283, 284
 captured data, reading 286
 captured image, displaying 285
 captured image, saving to camera roll 285
 errors, handling 285
 flash.media.CameraUI class, working 284,
  285
 starting with 282, 283
 video, capturing 286
Delete Anchor Point tool 112
deleteFileAsync() method 321, 373
deleteFile() method 373
Deployment tab 88
development certificate
 about 21
 CSR, approving 23
 distribution certificates 24
 obtaining 21, 22
 Team Admins 23
 Team Agent 23
 Team Member 23
 working 22
Development Provisioning Assistant 16
development provisioning profile
 about 35, 36
 additional types 38
 creating 36, 37
 distribution provisioning profile 38
 editing 37
 expiring 37
 multiple team members, working with 38
 testing, without device 37
 test provisioning profile 38
 working 37

device
 adding, in team environment 32
 limit, adding 32
 multiple devices, testing with 30, 31
 names, editing 32
 registering 29, 30
 UDID Sender 32
 working 31
device capabilities
 about 383
 ARMv6 devices 386
 declaring 383
 UIRequiredDeviceCapabilities key, working
  384, 385
device fonts
 advantages 195
 drawbacks 195
 enumerating 196, 197
 Fixed-width 196
 on iOS 196
 pixel density 197
 Sans-serif 196
 Serif 196
 TLF text 197
 using, with text fields 194, 195
 working 195, 196
device heading
 determining 253-256
 GPS receiver, simulating 257
 screen idle, preventing 257
 support, determining 256
deviceOrientation property 241
device shaking
 about 267
 accelerometer data, smoothing 271
 detecting 267, 269
 multiple axes, checking 270
 working 269
devices, iOS
 iPad 222
 iPhone 222
 iPod 222
device speed
 determining 253-256

Thank you for buying
Flash iOS Apps Cookbook

About Packt Publishing

Packt, pronounced 'packed', published its first book "*Mastering phpMyAdmin for Effective MySQL Management*" in April 2004 and subsequently continued to specialize in publishing highly focused books on specific technologies and solutions.

Our books and publications share the experiences of your fellow IT professionals in adapting and customizing today's systems, applications, and frameworks. Our solution based books give you the knowledge and power to customize the software and technologies you're using to get the job done. Packt books are more specific and less general than the IT books you have seen in the past. Our unique business model allows us to bring you more focused information, giving you more of what you need to know, and less of what you don't.

Packt is a modern, yet unique publishing company, which focuses on producing quality, cutting-edge books for communities of developers, administrators, and newbies alike. For more information, please visit our website: www.packtpub.com.

Writing for Packt

We welcome all inquiries from people who are interested in authoring. Book proposals should be sent to author@packtpub.com. If your book idea is still at an early stage and you would like to discuss it first before writing a formal book proposal, contact us; one of our commissioning editors will get in touch with you.

We're not just looking for published authors; if you have strong technical skills but no writing experience, our experienced editors can help you develop a writing career, or simply get some additional reward for your expertise.

Flash 10 Multiplayer Game Essentials

ISBN: 978-1-847196-60-6   Paperback: 336 pages

Create exciting real-time multiplayer games using Flash

1. A complete end-to-end guide for creating fully featured multiplayer games

2. The author's experience in the gaming industry enables him to share insights on multiplayer game development

3. Walk-though several real-time multiplayer game implementations

4. Packed with illustrations and code snippets with supporting explanations for ease of understanding

Flash Game Development by Example

ISBN: 978-1-849690-90-4   Paperback: 328 pages

Build 9 classic Flash games and learn game development along the way

1. Build 10 classic games in Flash. Learn the essential skills for Flash game development

2. Start developing games straight away. Build your first game in the first chapter

3. Fun and fast paced. Ideal for readers with no Flash or game programming experience

4. The most popular games in the world are built in Flash

Please check **www.PacktPub.com** for information on our titles

iPhone Applications Tune-Up

ISBN: 978-1-849690-34-8   Paperback: 312 pages

High performance tuning guide for real-world iOS projects

1. Tune up every aspect of your iOS application for greater levels of stability and performance

2. Improve the user's experience by boosting the performance of your app

3. Learn to use Xcode's powerful native features to increase productivity

4. Profile and measure every operation of your application for performance

5. Integrate powerful unit-testing directly into your development workflow

iPhone User Interface Cookbook

ISBN: 978-1-849691-14-7   Paperback: 500 pages

A concise dissection of Apple's iOS user interface design principles

1. Learn how to build an intuitive interface for your future iOS application

2. Avoid app rejection with detailed insight into how to best abide by Apple's interface guidelines

3. Written for designers new to iOS, who may be unfamiliar with Objective-C or coding an interface

4. Chapters cover a variety of subjects, from standard interface elements to optimizing custom game interfaces

Please check **www.PacktPub.com** for information on our titles

Lightning Source UK Ltd.
Milton Keynes UK
UKOW010305030212

186531UK00002B/113/P